Living Environment Core Curriculum Workbook
2nd Edition

The Authors:

Charmian Foster – Science Teacher and Science Chairperson – Retired

William Docekal – Science Teacher – Retired

About This Workbook:

The primary goal of this workbook is to provide students with the necessary information, strategies, vocabulary, and practice questions in order to pass the New York State Living Environment Regents. To this end, as a student, you must diligently work through all sections with complete comprehension. By doing so, your grades will improve cumulating with a passing grade on the Living Environment Regents.

Living Environment Core Curriculum Workbook
2nd Edition

The Introduction: Overview, Essential Information, and Additional Information
These sections will give you a comprehensive review of a specific topic in the New York State Living Environment curriculum. Carefully read all sections noting the italicized vocabulary words. Make sure you have a working knowledge of these words. In the Additional Information area are concepts/information related to the given topic and may appear on this year's Regents.

Diagrams:
These visual aids, along with the captions should enhance your understanding of specific concepts. First study the diagrams, then, read the given information.

Vocabulary:
We suggest reading the definitions, then matching them with the correct word or phase. Once you have completed this section, take time to memorize it. Look for help with the vocabulary by revisiting the Essential Information area.

Set 1: Questions and Answers
These questions will test your understanding of the topic. Do all questions in Set 1. Correct your work by going to the Answers for Set 1, which are located at the end of the topic section. The explanations will help you to understand any mistakes you have made.

Set 2: Questions
Correctly answering these questions will verify that you have mastered the subject topic. The answers to these questions are in a separate answer key.

Table of Contents

ECOLOGY AND HUMAN IMPACT

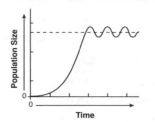

Overview:

Ecology is the scientific study of the relationships and interactions that living organisms have with respect to each other and their natural environment. Ecology involves an understanding of the components of nature and how these different components interact to create our environment. The study of ecology reveals many different ecosystems, each maintained by a delicate balance. In these different but connected ecosystems, individual species play a small but significant role in the working of the whole. Throughout the history of the Earth, the delicate balances found within ecosystems have been disrupted by natural and man-made influences. Given enough time, many ecosystems can adjust and regain their natural balance. Human actions, however, like creating air and water pollution, destroying habitats and depleting natural resources, etc., are seriously stressing many ecosystems and sending them out of balance. The saying "we are all connected" is so true. Our present and future actions will determine whether we leave a better planet for future generations.

Essential Information:

Ecological Relationships – The study of life on Earth is organized into levels that define living things and the environment in which they live. The *biosphere* includes all life on Earth. It is subdivided into various *ecosystems* that depend on climate and location. Within each ecosystem, there are *communities* made up of many different *populations* of living organisms that interact with their environment. There are both *abiotic* (non-living) and *biotic* (living) factors that influence life. Abiotic factors include sunlight, temperature, water, air, and soil, whereas, biotic factors include plants, animals, fungi, and bacteria. Within an ecosystem, organisms live in specific habitats – their surroundings. Within a habitat, each organism has a niche it fills or role that it fulfills within that habitat. Different species of organisms may appear to occupy the same habitat, but each has a different niche allowing it to survive in that habitat. Stable ecosystems have *producers*, known as *autotrophs*, that convert light energy from the Sun into chemical energy for use both for itself and other organisms. *Primary consumers*, also known as *heterotrophs*, feed on producers and transfer that energy as they too are consumed. This transfer of energy can be modeled in a *food web* or an *energy pyramid* (see page 3). Energy is passed up each level from producer to primary consumer to secondary consumer. At each level, some energy is lost as heat. Consumers that feed on plants are called *herbivores*, and those that feed on animals are known as *carnivores*. Also necessary in a stable ecosystem are *decomposers*, such as bacteria and fungi, which breakdown and recycle organic matter, dead or decaying organisms, into a usable form.

Ecosystems are constantly changing as energy moves through the system. Change occurs naturally to plant life in an ecosystem over time, and this is known as *succession*. In succession, as the composition and nutrient levels of the soil change, a progression of different plants will be established and replace others until the ecosystem reaches what is known as a *climax stage* – usually a mature forest. The ecosystem will remain stable at this stage until there is a major disruption, either natural (e.g. forest fire) or man-made (e.g. deforestation).

Populations within ecosystems are regulated or kept in check by various factors. Organisms are limited by the amount of *available resources* in an area. The population size that can be supported with resources in an area is known as the *carrying capacity*. When carrying capacity is reached, population growth will slow and level off. *Limiting resources*, such as necessary minerals or nutrients, can affect population growth. Without proper amounts of these nutrients, organisms will not survive. Disease and parasite activity regulate population numbers by keeping those numbers in check. In predator–prey relationships, biological interactions between two different species (like wolves and elk), have a direct effect on population numbers. For example, if the population number of one animal increases, it will impact the numbers of the other population. When conditions become crowded, diseases and parasites are spread more readily. Individuals already weakened by lack of resources may not survive, and therefore population numbers will decrease.

Human Impact – The increase in the world's human population has brought about many situations that have had *negative impacts* on ecosystems. Simply said, more people more problems. As the world population increases, there is a greater demand for resources and living space. Available resources can be either *renewable* (able to be replaced), like water, or *nonrenewable* (unable to be replaced), such as *fossil fuels*. Humans, needing space and housing, tend to destroy *habitats* such as forests and wetlands. More people require more food, so farm production must increase, requiring more chemicals to produce higher yields. Increased use of pesticides and chemicals in agriculture can increase soil and water pollution, ruining habitats and recreational areas.

Increased energy use has led to an increased burning of fossil fuels, creating air pollution, which leads to the formation of *acid rain*. This type of precipitation, having an acidic (low) pH, has adverse impacts on habitats, especially those that are located in the eastern parts of the United States. Burning fossil fuels produces *carbon dioxide*, a *greenhouse gas*, which, when released into the atmosphere, adds to *global warming*. Chemicals, such as *CFCs* from refrigerants, as well as other airborne chemicals, can also lead to the depletion of the *ozone layer*, allowing more harmful UV radiation to reach the Earth's surface, which increases the chance of skin cancer and cell mutations.

Humans have also introduced *non-native* species to ecosystems, either by accident or purposefully. These *invasive species* have no natural predators or population controls and outcompete native species, possibly leading to the extinction of those native species and, in some cases, the total disruption of an ecosystem.

Ecosystems are interconnected, and human action can alter the ecosystem's equilibrium. The result of this can cause an imbalance within the ecosystems. Loss of habitats has reduced populations of certain organisms resulting in loss of *biodiversity* or even extinction of many species. Unstable ecosystems could prevent the discovery of new medicine from plants. Through legislation, public awareness, educational programs, and conservation practices, humans can correct and reduce their negative impact on Earth.

Additional Information:

- Several invasive species introduced into New York State that have impacted ecosystems include: emerald ash borer, asian long horned beetle, and zebra mussels found in waterways, as well as purple loosestrife, which is a wetland plant, and hydrilla found in freshwater habitats.

- There are specific types of ecosystems found on Earth, each being defined by climate. The term, biome, is used to describe these large ecosystems types. Each biome has specific plants and animals that inhabit the area. Examples include: Tropical Rain Forests, Deserts, Temperate Deciduous Forests (NYS), and Arctic.

Diagrams:

1. **Ecosystem** – Shown here is a pond ecosystem illustrating how the biotic members of the ecosystem interact with one another as well as with the abiotic (non-living) environment. Within all ecosystems are specific habitats that support a number of niches. Each niche is filled by the activity of single species.

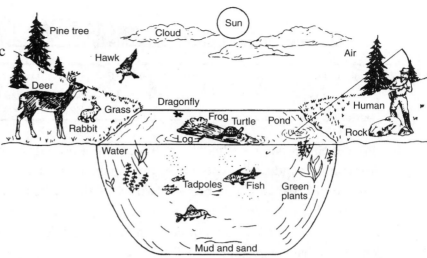

2. **Food Chain** – A food chain shows how living organisms get their food. It starts with a producer and ends with the largest consumer.

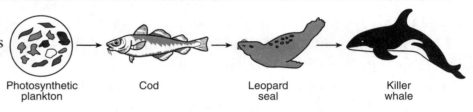

3. **Food Web** – A food web shows the flow of energy between organisms and the community as a whole. Energy, made by the producers, flows upward through the consumers, represented by the arrows. Food webs are much more stable than just simple food chains and have many more energy connections. Removal of an organism from a food web can impact those organisms above and below it within that web.

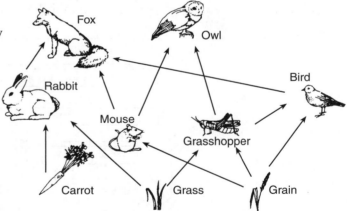

4. **Energy Pyramid** – In an energy pyramid, plants (producers) contain the most energy and are located at the bottom of the pyramid. Producers gain their energy from the Sun by photosynthesis. In the energy pyramid, organisms receive their energy from the level directly below them. As energy moves up it decreases, being lost to the environment as heat.

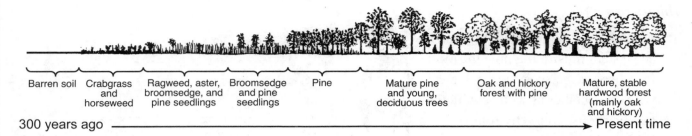

Barren soil | Crabgrass and horseweed | Ragweed, aster, broomsedge, and pine seedlings | Broomsedge and pine seedlings | Pine | Mature pine and young, deciduous trees | Oak and hickory forest with pine | Mature, stable hardwood forest (mainly oak and hickory)

300 years ago ⟶ Present time

5. **Ecological Succession** – This naturally occurring process takes place when vegetation changes as the environmental conditions evolve over time in an area. The beginning stages of this process involve the emergence of organisms that break down rocks that, when combined with organic material, form soil. Over time, the soil depth increases as larger grasses, shrubs and different trees take over the area. Eventually the area reaches a climax stage that is stable (hardwood forest) and remains until there is a disruption to that ecosystem.

6. **Acid Rain** – The full pH scale goes from 0 to 14, where 7 is neutral. Any pH value less than 7 is acidic. Rain is normally slightly acidic, having a pH around 5.5. When airborne pollutants, especially sulfuric or nitric compounds, are chemically joined with atmospheric moisture, acid rain results, lowering the pH of the precipitation. Acid rain is harmful to young aquatic life and their habitats.

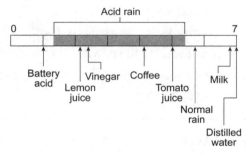

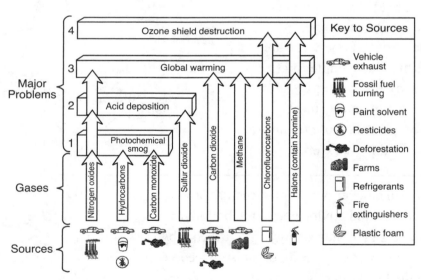

7. **Air Pollution Sources** – A large amount of air pollution is caused by the combustion of fossil fuels which releases large amounts of carbon dioxide, a greenhouse gas. Greenhouse gases have the ability to absorb much infrared radiation, resulting in an increase of atmospheric temperature. Chlorofluorocarbons or CFCs destroy ozone (O_3) molecules, causing the thinning of the ozone layer. The ozone layer traps much harmful ultraviolet (UV) radiation. UV radiation is linked to skin cancer, eye damage, and cell mutations. The reduction of the use of CFCs has had a positive impact on restoring the ozone within the upper atmosphere.

Ecology and Human Impact

Group A   *Directions* - Match the correct definition for the following terms:

1. _____ Biosphere

2. _____ Ecosystem

3. _____ Community

4. _____ Population

5. _____ Abiotic

6. _____ Biotic

7. _____ Biodiversity

8. _____ Energy pyramid

9. _____ Autotrophs

10. _____ Heterotrophs

11. _____ Food web

12. _____ Niche

13. _____ Herbivores

14. _____ Carnivores

15. _____ Nonrenewable resources

16. _____ Climax stage

A. A measure of the richness, with regard to species, that is found within an area. The more varied an ecosystem is, the more stable the ecosystem.

B. Organisms, known as producers, that synthesize their own food source (glucose) by using the process of photosynthesis.

C. All of the living populations that are found and interact within an ecosystem.

D. Complex interconnections that show the feeding relationships of organisms within an ecosystem. The more connections, the more stable the ecosystem.

E. The non-living factors that influence living organisms such as water, temperature, soil, and atmosphere.

F. An organism that feeds exclusively on plant material, example – a deer.

G. The living organisms found within an ecosystem.

H. The realized role that an organism fills within an ecosystem. It defines where it fits within a food web or energy pyramid.

I. All living organisms that encompass the Earth.

J. Organisms that must take in preformed nutrients (organic compounds). These consumers may ingest, absorb, or engulf their nutrients.

K. All living organisms of one species that live and interact within an ecosystem.

L. A model that shows the flow of energy in an ecosystem from producers to consumers. As energy flows up this model, it decreases being lost as heat.

M. The most biodiverse and stable stage of ecological succession.

N. Those resources that are unable to be replaced and, once used up, are gone. Fossil fuels are examples of this type of resource.

O. Organisms that feed exclusively on other animals, example – a fox.

P. The interactions of living organisms and non-living factors within a defined area.

1. _____ Succession

2. _____ Carrying capacity

3. _____ Predator-prey

4. _____ Invasive species

5. _____ Limiting resources

6. _____ Available resources

7. _____ Renewable resources

8. _____ Decomposers

9. _____ Fossil fuel

10. _____ Acid rain

11. _____ Greenhouse gases

12. _____ Global warming

13. _____ CFCs

14. _____ Ozone depletion

A. Atmospheric gases that absorb (trap) heat energy, increasing the temperature of the atmosphere. Carbon dioxide is an example of such a gas.

B. A predictable series of changes that occur to an area with respect to vegetation over time. In a forest ecosystem, once bare ground slowly develops into a forest setting.

C. A relationship between two animals where the population of one will feed on and influence the population of the other. For example – a fox population and a mouse population.

D. Those resources that can be replaced, recycled, or renewed, such as water, air, or trees.

E. The population that can be supported by the available nutrients and space within an ecosystem. This concept is usually shown by a graph.

F. The release of nitrogen, sulfur, and carbon compounds into the atmosphere that react with moisture producing precipitation with a pH of less than 7. This harmful precipitation can destroy habitats, especially in areas east of the release of the pollutants.

G. Organisms that break down and recycle organic material from decaying or dead organisms, examples: bacteria and fungi (mushrooms).

H. Those nutrients that support the growth of a population. When present, they allow the population to grow and maintain itself. When absent, they can limit the growth of the population.

I. Energy sources such as gas, coal, and oil that were formed from the decayed remains of ancient living organisms such as plants.

J. Chloroflourocarbons were once used in refrigerants like air conditioners and aerosol cans. They can lead to ozone depletion.

K. Non-native species that have been introduced into a new area. These species have no natural population checks so they outcompete and take over habitats of native species. An example is the plant Purple Loosestrife, found in NYS.

L. The break down of the ozone layer in the atmosphere by man-made chemicals such as CFCs, allowing harmful UV radiation to reach the Earth's surface.

M. Multiple complex conditions, such as increasing greenhouse gases and ozone depletion, that cause the Earth's atmosphere to heat up. This increased atmospheric temperature can lead to habitat destruction and eventually to extinction of certain species.

N. Items that an organism requires in order to survive including water, air, and nutrients.

1. Which ecological term includes everything represented in the illustration below?

   (1) ecosystem   (3) population
   (2) community   (4) species   1 _____

2. In an ecosystem, the presence of many different species is critical for the survival of some forms of life when

   (1) ecosystems remain stable over long periods of time
   (2) significant changes occur in the ecosystem
   (3) natural selection does not occur
   (4) the finite resources of Earth increase

   2 _____

3. Decomposers are important in the environment because they

   (1) convert large molecules into simpler molecules that can then be recycled
   (2) release heat from large molecules so that the heat can be recycled through the ecosystem
   (3) can take in carbon dioxide and convert it into oxygen
   (4) convert molecules of dead organisms into permanent biotic parts of an ecosystem   3 _____

4. Which statement best describes a situation where competition occurs in an ecosystem?

   (1) A deer outruns an attacking wolf.
   (2) A deer, during the winter, consumes tree bark.
   (3) A deer and a rabbit consume grass in a field.
   (4) A deer and a rabbit are both startled by a hawk flying overhead.   4 _____

5. In some areas, foresters plant one tree for every tree they cut. This activity is an example of

   (1) lack of management of nonrenewable natural resources
   (2) a good conservation practice for renewable natural resources
   (3) a good conservation practice for nonrenewable natural resources
   (4) lack of concern for renewable natural resources   5 _____

6. A food chain is illustrated below.

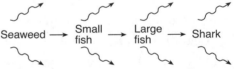

   The ⌇⌇➝ arrows represented most likely indicate

   (1) energy released into the environment as heat
   (2) oxygen produced by respiration
   (3) the absorption of energy that has been synthesized
   (4) the transport of glucose away from the organism   6 _____

7. An environment can support only as many organisms as the available energy, minerals, and oxygen will allow. Which term is best described by this statement?

(1) biological feedback
(2) carrying capacity
(3) homeostatic control
(4) biological diversity   7 _____

8. Communities have attempted to control the size of mosquito populations to prevent the spread of certain diseases such as malaria and encephalitis. Which control method is most likely to cause the least ecological damage?

(1) draining the swamps where mosquitoes breed
(2) spraying swamps with chemical pesticides to kill mosquitoes
(3) spraying oil over swamps to suffocate mosquito larvae
(4) increasing populations of native fish that feed on mosquito larvae in the swamps   8 _____

9. In an attempt to improve environmental quality, local officials in a county in New York State want to build a garbage-to-steam plant. At the plant, garbage would be burned to produce energy, but air pollution would also be produced. In order to decide whether or not to build this plant, the community must consider

(1) the trade-offs involved
(2) new genetic technology
(3) the natural process of succession
(4) energy flow between organisms   9 _____

10. In a forest community, a shelf fungus and a slug live on the side of a decaying tree trunk. The fungus digests and absorbs materials from the tree, while the slug eats algae growing on the outside of the trunk. These organisms do not compete with one another because they occupy

(1) the same habitat, but different niches
(2) the same niche, but different habitats
(3) the same niche and the same habitat
(4) different habitats and different niches
                                        10 _____

11. An earthworm lives and reproduces in the soil. It aerates the soil and adds organic material to it. The earthworm is a source of food for other organisms. All of these statements together best describe

(1) a habitat
(2) autotrophic nutrition
(3) an ecological niche
(4) competition   11 _____

12. The graph below shows the growth of two populations of paramecia grown in the same culture dish for 14 days.

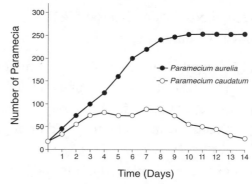

Which ecological concept is best represented by the graph?

(1) recycling   (3) competition
(2) equilibrium (4) decomposition 12 _____

13. Organisms from a particular ecosystem are shown below.

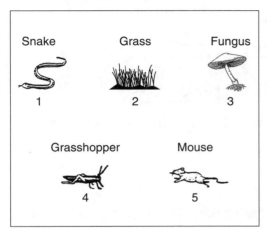

Snake   Grass   Fungus
  1   2   3

Grasshopper   Mouse
    4   5

Which statement concerning an organism in this ecosystem is correct?

(1) Organism 2 is heterotrophic.
(2) Organism 3 helps recycle materials.
(3) Organism 4 obtains all of its nutrients from an abiotic source.
(4) Organism 5 must obtain its energy from organism 1.   13 _____

14. If humans remove carnivorous predators such as wolves and coyotes from an ecosystem, what will probably be the first observable result?

(1) The natural prey will die off.
(2) Certain plant populations will increase.
(3) Certain herbivores will exceed carrying capacity.
(4) The decomposers will fill the predator niche.   14 _____

15. In an ecosystem, nutrients would be recycled if they were transferred directly from herbivores to carnivores to

(1) hosts   (3) decomposers
(2) prey   (4) autotrophs   15 _____

16. A population of chipmunks migrated to an environment where they had little competition. Their population quickly increased but eventually stabilized as shown in the graph.

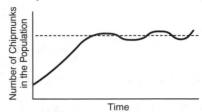

Which statement best explains why the population stabilized?

(1) Interbreeding between members of the population increased the mutation rate.
(2) The population size became limited due to factors such as availability of food.
(3) An increase in the chipmunk population caused an increase in the producer population.
(4) A predator species came to the area and occupied the same niche as the chipmunks.   16 _____

17. Imported animal species often disrupt an ecosystem because in their new environment, they will most likely

(1) eliminate the genetic variation of the autotrophs
(2) increase the number of mutations in the herbivores
(3) have no natural enemies
(4) be unable to produce offspring   17 _____

18. Competition for biotic resources can be illustrated by organisms fighting for a limited amount of

(1) air to breathe
(2) water to drink
(3) mates for breeding
(4) space for nesting   18 _____

19. Stage *D* in the diagram below is located on land that was once a bare field.

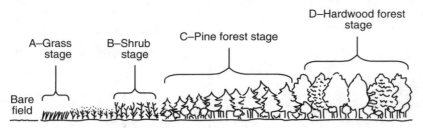

The sequence of stages leading from bare field to stage *D* best illustrates the process known as

(1) replication   (2) recycling   (3) feedback   (4) succession   19_____

Base your answer to question 20 on the food web and graph below. The graph represents the interaction of two different populations, *A* and *B*, in the food web.

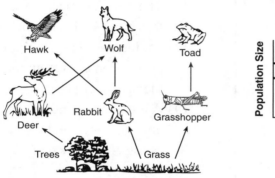 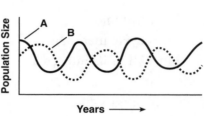

20. *a)* Population *A* is made up of living animals. The members of population *B* feed on these living animals. The members of population *B* are most likely

(1) scavengers   (2) autotrophs   (3) predators   (4) parasites   a_____

b) Which organism carries out autotrophic nutrition?

(1) hawk   (2) grasshopper   (3) grass   (4) deer   b_____

21. On which day did the population represented in the graph reach the carrying capacity of the ecosystem?

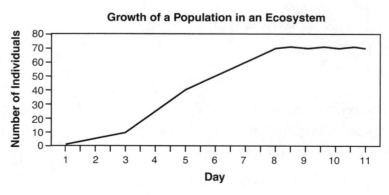

(1) day 11   (2) day 8   (3) day 3   (4) day 5   21_____

22. Human activities continue to place strains on the environment. One of these strains on the environment is the loss of biodiversity. Explain what this problem is and describe some ways humans are involved in both the problem and the possible solutions. In your answer be sure to:

a) state the meaning of the term biodiversity _____

_____

b) state one negative effect on humans if biodiversity continues to be lost

_____

c) suggest one practice that could be used to preserve biodiversity in New York State

_____

23. The graph represents the amount of available energy at successive nutrition levels in a particular food web.

The Xs in the diagram represents the amount of what?

_____

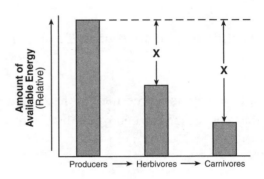

24. The diagram below represents some energy transfers in an ecosystem.

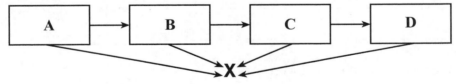

a) Which type of organism is most likely represented by letter X? _____

b) What happens to energy as it moves from A to D? _____

25. In the accompanying energy pyramid, identify one organism that would be found at level X.

_____

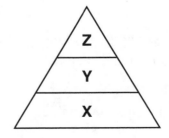

Base your answers to question 26 on the information below.

A student uses a covered aquarium to study the interactions of biotic and abiotic factors in an ecosystem. The aquarium contains sand, various water plants, algae, small fish, snails, and decomposers. The water contains dissolved oxygen and carbon dioxide, as well as tiny amounts of minerals and salts.

26. *a)* Describe one specific way the fish population changes the amount of one specific abiotic factor in this ecosystem.

_____

b) Identify one source of food for the decomposers in this ecosystem. _____

c) Describe one specific way the use of this food by the decomposers benefits the other organisms in the aquarium.

_____

d) Identify the primary source of energy for this aquarium ecosystem. _____

27. *a)* A food web is represented to the right. Give a statement that best describes energy in this food web.

_____

_____

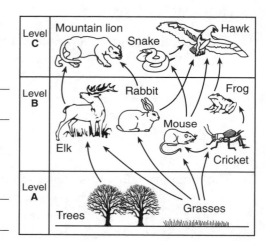

b) If the mountain lion was removed, how would this impact other populations?

_____

_____

c) Name a herbivore shown in this food web. _____

28. Explain why damage to the ozone shield is considered a threat to many organisms.

_____

29. The diagram represents an energy pyramid constructed from data collected from an aquatic ecosystem.

Why is the ecosystem most likely unstable?

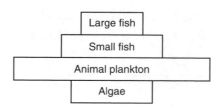

_____

Base your answers to question 30 on the accompanying diagram.

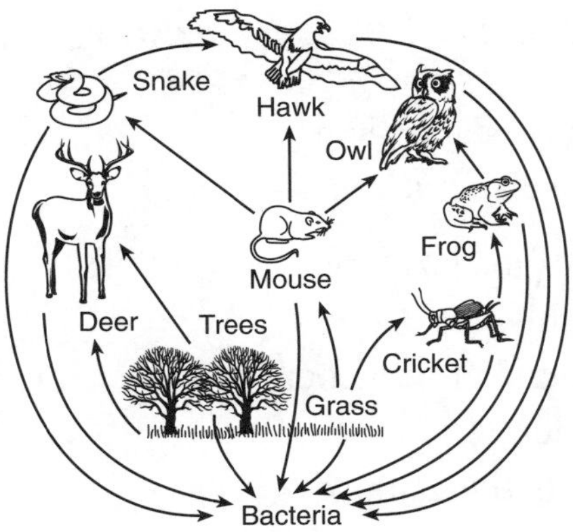

30. a) Which organism carries out autotrophic nutrition?

_____

b) State what would most likely happen to the cricket population if all of the grasses were removed.

_____

c) What is the role of bacteria within a food web? _____

31. State one reason why the amount of carbon dioxide in the atmosphere has increased in the last 100 years.

_____

Base your answers to question 32 on the passage below and on your knowledge of biology.

On April 20, 2010, an explosion occurred at an oil well in the Gulf of Mexico, causing millions of gallons of oil to escape into the water over the next few months. Large areas of the Gulf were covered by oil. As the oil washed ashore, many areas along the coastline that were breeding grounds for various bird species were contaminated. By November 2010, researchers along the coast and in the Gulf had collected 6104 dead birds, 609 dead turtles, and 100 dead mammals. Although the oil well had provided oil for energy for a large number of people, the oil spill had a great effect on the ecosystems in and around the Gulf of Mexico.

32. a) Explain how the original decision to drill for oil in the Gulf of Mexico could be considered a trade-off.

_____

b) State one benefit of drilling for oil in the Gulf of Mexico._____

c) State one possible reason why it will most likely take the bird populations more time to recover from this oil spill than it will mammal populations.

_____

33. Explain why an ecosystem requires a constant input of energy.

_____

34. What is meant by the carrying capacity of a particular population in an ecosystem?

_____

1. A food web is more stable than a food chain because a food web

   (1) transfers all of the producer energy to herbivores
   (2) reduces the number of niches in the ecosystem
   (3) includes alternative pathways for energy flow
   (4) includes more consumers than producers   1_____

2. The diagram below represents a model of a food pyramid.

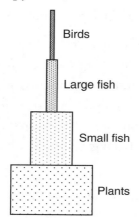

   Which statement best describes what happens in this food pyramid?

   (1) More organisms die at higher levels than at lower levels, resulting in less mass at higher levels.
   (2) Energy is lost to the environment at each level, so less mass can be supported at each higher level.
   (3) When organisms die at higher levels, their remains sink to lower levels, increasing the mass of lower levels.
   (4) Organisms decay at each level, and thus less mass can be supported at succeedingly higher levels.   2_____

3. Which ecosystem has a better chance of surviving when environmental conditions change over a long period of time?

   (1) one with a great deal of genetic diversity
   (2) one with plants and animals but no bacteria
   (3) one with animals and bacteria but no plants
   (4) one with little or no genetic diversity   3_____

4. The diagrams below show some changes in an environment over time.

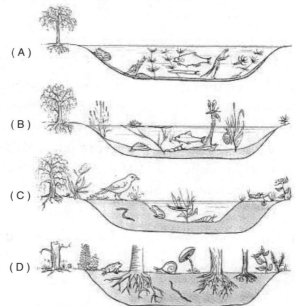

   Which phrase best describes this sequence of diagrams?

   (1) the path of energy through a food web in a natural community
   (2) the altering of an ecosystem by a natural disaster
   (3) natural communities replacing each other in an orderly sequence
   (4) similarities between an aquatic ecosystem and a terrestrial ecosystem   4_____

5. By causing atmospheric changes through activities such as polluting and careless harvesting, humans have

(1) caused the destruction of habitats
(2) affected global stability in a positive way
(3) established equilibrium in ecosystems
(4) replaced nonrenewable resources

5_____

6. The diagram below illustrates the relationships between organisms in an ecosystem.

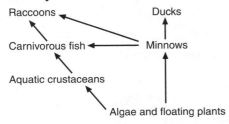

Which change would most likely reduce the population size of the carnivorous fish?

(1) an increase in the autotroph populations
(2) a decrease in the duck population
(3) an increase in the raccoon population
(4) a decrease in pathogens of carnivorous fish

6_____

7. In a stable, long-existing community, the establishment of a single species per niche is most directly the result of

(1) parasitism
(2) interbreeding
(3) competition
(4) overproduction

7_____

8. A stable pond ecosystem would not contain

(1) materials being cycled
(2) biotic factors
(3) decomposers
(4) more consumers than producers

8_____

Base your answers to question 9 on the diagram below.

9. a) Which organism carries out autotrophic nutrition?

(1) frog   (3) plant
(2) snake   (4) grasshopper   a_____

b) The base of an energy pyramid for this ecosystem would include a

(1) frog   (3) plant
(2) snake   (4) grasshopper   b_____

10. In an ecosystem, which component is not recycled?

(1) water   (3) oxygen
(2) energy   (4) carbon   10_____

11. Vultures, which are classified as scavengers, are an important part of an ecosystem because they

(1) hunt herbivores, limiting their populations in an ecosystem
(2) feed on dead animals, which aids in the recycling of environmental materials
(3) cause the decay of dead organisms, which releases usable energy to herbivores and carnivores
(4) are the first level in food webs and make energy available to all the other organisms in the web   11_____

12. "Natural ecosystems provide an array of basic processes that affect humans." Which statement does not support this quotation?

(1) Bacteria of decay help recycle materials.
(2) Trees add to the amount of atmospheric oxygen.
(3) Treated sewage is less damaging to the environment than untreated sewage.
(4) Lichens and mosses living on rocks help to break the rocks down, forming soil.

12_____

13. The carrying capacity of a given environment is least dependent upon

(1) recycling of materials
(2) the available energy
(3) the availability of food and water
(4) daily temperature fluctuations

13_____

14. Increased efforts to conserve areas such as rain forests are necessary in order to

(1) protect biodiversity
(2) promote extinction of species
(3) exploit finite resources
(4) increase industrialization

14_____

15. Changes in the chemical composition of the atmosphere that may produce acid rain are most closely associated with

(1) insects that excrete acids
(2) runoff from acidic soils
(3) industrial smoke stack emissions
(4) flocks of migrating birds

15_____

16. Which practice would most likely deplete a nonrenewable natural resource?

(1) harvesting trees on a tree farm
(2) burning coal to generate electricity in a power plant
(3) restricting water usage during a period of water shortage
(4) building a dam and a power plant to use water to generate electricity

16_____

17. Which statement concerning the producers in the ocean ecosystem shown below is correct?

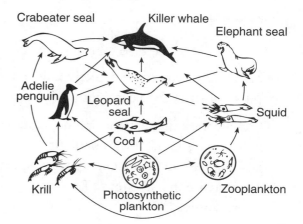

(1) An increase in the types of producers will most likely decrease the available energy for the squid.
(2) A producer in this ecosystem is the zooplankton.
(3) If all the producers in this ecosystem are destroyed, the number of heterotrophs will increase, but the ecosystem will reach a new equilibrium.
(4) Since there is only one group of producers, their numbers must be large enough to supply the energy for the rest of the food web.

17_____

18. In December 2004, a tsunami (giant wave) destroyed many of the marine organisms along the coast of the Indian Ocean. What can be expected to happen to the ecosystem that was most severely hit by the tsunami?

(1) The ecosystem will change until a new stable community is established.
(2) Succession will continue in the ecosystem until one species of marine organism is established.
(3) Ecological succession will no longer occur in this marine ecosystem.
(4) The organisms in the ecosystem will become extinct.   18_____

19. Which concept is represented in the graph below?

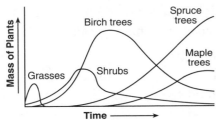

(1) ecological succession in a community
(2) cycling of carbon and nitrogen in a forest
(3) energy flow in a food chain over time
(4) negative human impact on the environment   19_____

20. An energy pyramid containing autotrophs and other organisms from a food chain is represented.

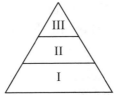

Carnivores would most likely be located in

(1) level I, only
(2) level I and level II
(3) level III, only
(4) level II and level III   20_____

21. Four environmental factors are listed below.

A. energy   C. oxygen
B. water   D. minerals

Which factors limit environmental carrying capacity in a land ecosystem?

(1) A, only
(2) A, C, and D, only
(3) B, C, and D, only
(4) A, B, C, and D   21_____

22. The relationship that exists when athlete's foot fungus grows on a human is an example of

(1) predator/prey
(2) producer/consumer
(3) parasite/host
(4) decomposer/autotroph   22_____

23. Which change is a cause of the other three?

(1) increased fossil fuel consumption
(2) destruction of the ozone shield
(3) increased industrialization
(4) destruction of natural habitats   23_____

24. The release of products of combustion into the air often causes the formation of ozone near the surface of Earth. This ground-level ozone damages plants and affects their ability to absorb carbon dioxide. The doubling of ground-level ozone since 1850 is most likely due to

(1) the chemical composition of the upper atmosphere
(2) emissions from vehicles and industrial processes
(3) the extinction of certain animal species
(4) a greater use of nuclear fuel   24_____

25. Which diagram best illustrates the relationship between humans (H) and ecosystems (E)?

H
E
(1)

E
H
(2)

H
E
(3)

H
E
(4)

25_____

26. A new island formed by volcanic action may eventually become populated with biotic communities as a result of

    (1) a decrease in the amount of organic material present
    (2) decreased levels of carbon dioxide in the area
    (3) the lack of abiotic factors in the area
    (4) the process of ecological succession   26_____

27. Decomposers are important in the environment because they

    (1) convert large molecules into simpler molecules that can then be recycled
    (2) release heat from large molecules so that the heat can be recycled through the ecosystem
    (3) can take in carbon dioxide and convert it into oxygen
    (4) convert molecules of dead organisms into permanent biotic parts of an ecosystem   27_____

28. What is the major environmental factor limiting the numbers of autotrophs at great depths in the ocean?

    (1) type of seafloor
    (2) amount of light
    (3) availability of minerals
    (4) absence of biotic factors   28_____

29. El Niño is a short-term climatic change that causes ocean waters to remain warm when they should normally be cool. The warmer temperatures disrupt food webs and alter weather patterns. Which occurrence would most likely result from these changes?

    (1) Some species would become extinct, and other species would evolve to take their place.
    (2) Some populations in affected areas would be reduced, while other populations would increase temporarily.
    (3) The flow of energy through the ecosystem would remain unchanged.
    (4) The genes of individual organisms would mutate to adapt to the new environmental conditions.   29_____

30. Which type of model provides the most complete representation of the feeding relationships within a community?

    (1) a material cycle
    (2) a predator-prey association
    (3) a food chain
    (4) a food web   30_____

31. Car exhaust has been blamed for increasing the amount of carbon dioxide in the air. Some scientists believe this additional carbon dioxide in the air may cause

    (1) global warming
    (2) increased biodiversity
    (3) habitat preservation
    (4) ozone destruction   31_____

32. Increased human population growth usually results in

    (1) a decrease in the need for farming
    (2) a need for stronger environmental protection laws
    (3) lower levels of air and water pollution
    (4) an increase in natural wildlife habitats   32_____

33. The accompanying diagram represents a pyramid of energy in an ecosystem.

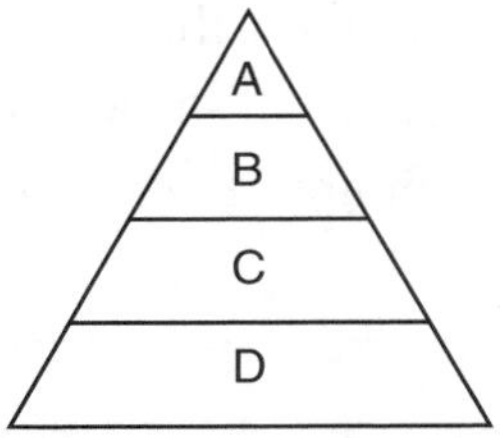

A
B
C
D

a) Which level in the pyramid would most likely contain members of the plant kingdom? _____

b) Which level in the pyramid would mostly likely contain a primary consumer? _____

c) What level would contain the least amount of available energy? _____

Base your answers to question 34 on the diagram of a food web.

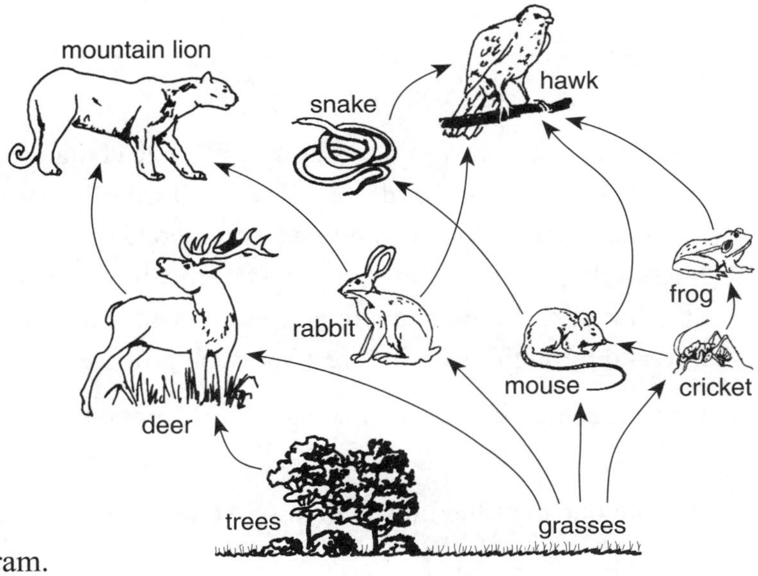

34. a) If the population of mice is reduced by disease, what change will most likely occur in the food web?

_____

_____

mountain lion

snake

hawk

frog

rabbit

mouse

cricket

deer

trees

grasses

b) What is the original source of energy for this food web? _____

c) Name a biotic factor shown in the diagram.

_____

d) Which organisms are not shown in this diagram but are essential to a balanced ecosystem? _____

e) State one example of a predator-prey relationship found in the food web. Indicate which organism is the predator and which is the prey.

_____

f) Identify a secondary consumer in this web. _____

35. Dissolved oxygen (DO) can be found in an aquatic ecosystem and is often one factor that affects the size of populations of aquatic organisms. Water temperature is very important in determining the amount of DO in a water supply. The colder the temperature of the water, the more DO the water can hold.

State one possible reason why the biodiversity of an aquatic ecosystem could decrease if the water temperature were to increase.

_____

_____

36. Identify one abiotic factor that would directly affect the survival of organism *A* shown in the accompanying diagram.

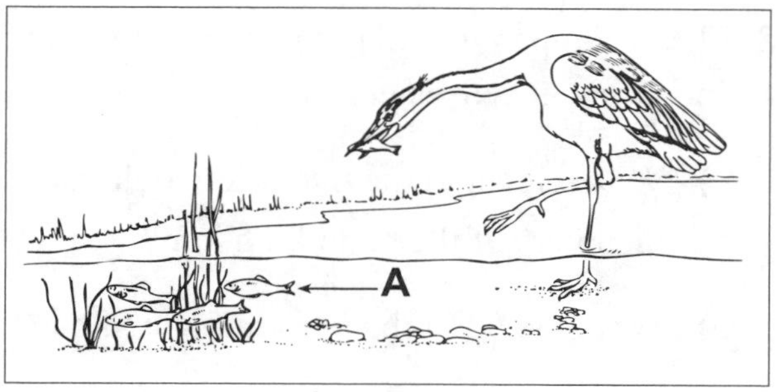

_____

37. Explain why most ecologists would agree with the statement "A forest ecosystem is more stable than a cornfield."

_____

38. A tropical rain forest in the country of Belize contains over 100 kinds of trees as well as thousands of species of mammals, birds, and insects. Dozens of species living there have not yet been classified and studied. The rain forest could be a commercial source of food as well as a source of medicinal and household products. However, most of this forested area is not accessible because of a lack of roads and therefore, little commercial use has been made of this region. The building of paved highways into and through this rain forest has been proposed.

Discuss some aspects of carrying out this proposal to build paved highways. In your answer be sure to:

a) state one possible impact on biodiversity and one reason for this impact

_____

b) state one possible reason for an increase in the number of some producers as a result of road building _____

c) identify one type of consumer whose population would most likely increase as a direct result of an increase in a producer population _____

d) state one possible action the road builders could take to minimize human impact on the ecology of this region _____

_____

e) To build this road, thousands of trees will be removed and burned. How would this potentially impact global warming?_____

_____

39. State one possible negative impact of importing a natural predator to control a pest.

_____

Base your answers to question 40 on the information below.

Thirty grams of hay (dried grasses) were boiled in 500 milliliters of water, placed in a culture dish, and allowed to stand. The next day, a small sample of pond water was added to the mixture of boiled hay and water. The dish was then covered and its contents observed regularly. Bacteria fed on the nutrients from the boiled hay. As the populations of bacteria increased rapidly, the clear mixture soon became cloudy. One week later, microscopic examination of samples from the culture showed various types of protozoa (single-celled organisms) eating the bacteria.

40. *a)* The protozoa that fed on the bacteria can best be described as _____

b) Label each level of the accompanying energy pyramid with an organism mentioned in the paragraph that belongs at that level.

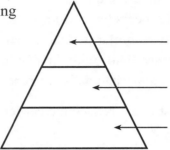

Base your answers to question 41 on the diagram below, which represents the changes in an ecosystem over a period of 100 years.

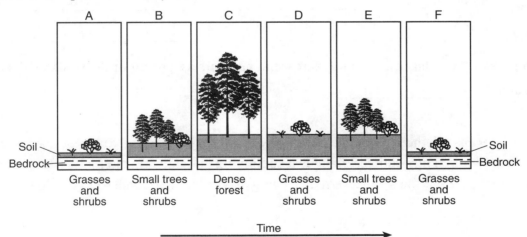

41. *a)* State one biological explanation for the changes in types of vegetation observed from *A* through *C*.

_____

b) Identify one human activity that could be responsible for the change from *C* to *D*.

_____

c) Which letter diagram would most likely have the greatest biodiversity?_____

42. The accompanying diagram represents a food web.

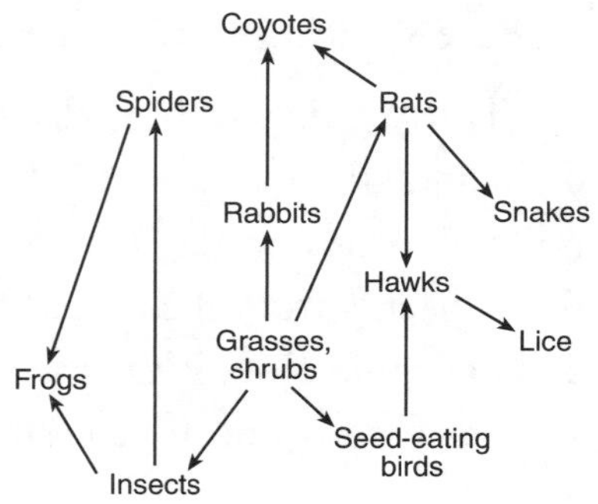

The arrows only point away from "Grasses, shrubs" and not toward them. State one biological reason that this is so.

_____

_____

Coyotes
Spiders   Rats
        Rabbits   Snakes
                Hawks
Frogs   Grasses,   Lice
        shrubs
            Seed-eating
Insects   birds

Base your answers to question 43 on the information below.

The ice fields off Canada's Hudson Bay are melting an average of three weeks earlier than 25 years ago. The polar bears are therefore unable to feed on the seals on these ice fields during the last three weeks in spring. Polar bears have lost an average of 10% of their weight and have 10% fewer cubs when compared to a similar population studied just 20 years ago. Scientists have associated the early melting of the ice fields with the fact that the average world temperature is about 0.6°C higher than it was a century ago and this trend is expected to continue.

43. *a)* What ecological problem most likely caused the earlier melting of the ice fields in the Hudson Bay area of Canada? _____

_____

b) State one specific long-term action that humans could take that might slow down or reduce the melting of the ice fields._____

_____

c) Which prey of the polar bears would increase in numbers as a result of the situation described in the reading? _____

44. Currently, Americans rely heavily on the burning of fossil fuels as sources of energy. As a result of increased demand for energy sources, there is a continuing effort to find alternatives to burning fossil fuels. Discuss fossil fuels and alternative energy sources. In your answer be sure to:

a) state one disadvantage of burning fossil fuels for energy

_____

b) identify one energy source that is an alternative to using fossil fuels _____

c) state one advantage of using this alternative energy source

_____

d) state one disadvantage of using this alternative energy source

_____

Base your answers to question 45 on the information and table below.

The variety of organisms known as plankton contributes to the unique nutritional relationships in an ocean ecosystem. Phytoplankton include algae and other floating organisms that perform photosynthesis. Plankton that cannot produce food are known as zooplankton. Some nutritional relationships involving these organisms and several others are shown in the table below.

Nutritional Relationships in a North Atlantic Ocean Community

Animals in Community	Food Eaten by Animals in Community				
	Codfish	Phytoplankton	Small Fish	Squid	Zooplankton
codfish			X		
sharks	X			X	
small fish		X			X
squid	X		X		
zooplankton		X			

45. *a*) Humans are currently overfishing codfish in the North Atlantic. Explain why this could endanger both the shark population and the squid population in this community.

_____

b) According to the table, which organism can be classified as both an herbivore and a carnivore?

_____

c) Complete the accompanying food web using the information from the above table.

d) If phytoplankton were removed, what would happen to this ocean ecosystem?

_____

_____

e) Identify an organism not shown that is needed to maintain a stable community?

_____

f) State what the arrows in the food chain represent.

_____

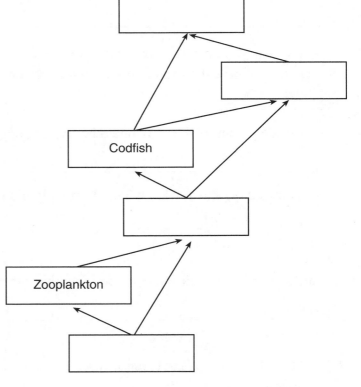

Codfish

Zooplankton

Base your answers to question 46 on the article below which was written in response to an article entitled "Let all predators become extinct."

Predators Contribute to a Stable Ecosystem

In nature, energy flows in only one direction. Transfer of energy must occur in an ecosystem because all life needs energy to live, and only certain organisms can change solar energy into chemical energy.

Producers are eaten by consumers that are, in turn, eaten by other consumers. Stable ecosystems must contain predators to help control the populations of consumers.

Since ecosystems contain many predators, exterminating predators would require a massive effort that would wipe out predatory species from barnacles to blue whales. Without the population control provided by predators, some organisms would soon over populate.

46. *a*) Draw an energy pyramid in the given space that illustrates the information underlined in the second paragraph. Include *three* different, specific organisms in the energy pyramid.

b) Explain the phrase "only certain organisms can change solar energy into chemical energy," in the underlined portion of the first paragraph. In your answer be sure to identify the type of nutrition carried out by these organisms

_____

c) Explain why an ecosystem with a variety of predator species might be more stable over a long period of time than an ecosystem with only one predator species.

_____

d) Beside predators, identify one other type of population control.

_____

e) Name an organism what would drastically increase if all predators within a large lake were removed._____

47. State one specific environmental problem that can result from burning coal to generate electricity.

_____

48. Explain why using a food chain is more limiting than using a food web to show relationships between organisms in an ecosystem.

_____

1. 1   The picture shows both the living (biotic) and non-living (abiotic) components of the environment, which make up an ecosystem. All other choices are only parts of an ecosystem.

2. 2   The presence of many different species within an ecosystem (biodiversity) allows for variation. This variation provides multiple food sources for consumers within a food web. If environmental changes were to remove one food source, others would still be available, allowing the consumer to survive.

3. 1   Decomposers, acting on living matter, convert larger molecules into simpler molecules, often through a digestive process. These simpler molecules can then be recycled through the ecosystem, primarily as nutrients within the food chain.

4. 3   Competition occurs when two organisms are utilizing the same resource. In the case of deer and rabbit, they are both eating the same food, grass, and there would be competition for that resource.

5. 2   Trees are a renewable resource, and for every tree that is cut down, at least one tree seedling should be planted. This good conservation practice is implemented by almost all industries that harvest trees, such as paper companies.

6. 1   In all food chains and webs, as one moves up the chain(s), energy is released as heat. This release of heat energy is a result of metabolic activity within that organism as it uses that food source.

7. 2   Carrying capacity can be defined as the population number that can be supported by all the resources within an ecosystem. Once the carrying capacity is reached, population growth will level off due to competition for available nutrients, energy sources, space, etc.

8. 4   Choice 4 would cause the least disruption to the ecosystem because the fish are already native to that area. The other choices will affect non-target species by harming or destroying habitats or killing species other than mosquitoes.

9. 1   In the decision to build this garbage-to-steam energy plant, the community must be informed of the positive and negative aspects of the project. This plant will provide useful energy in the form of steam, but the trade-offs will involve air pollution and an increase in truck traffic, along with other possible negative consequences.

10. 1   Since the slug and the shelf fungus live in or on the decaying tree, they share the same habitat. They use different types of nutrients and, therefore, occupy different niches within the ecosystem. The slug is an herbivore, feeding on algae (on the tree), whereas the shelf fungus is a decomposer, obtaining its nutrients from materials absorbed from the decaying tree.

11. 3   A niche is the role that an organism plays within its ecosystem. The earthworm acts as a decomposer by adding nutrients back into the soil and as a food (prey) for consumers (predators) in the food chain.

12. 3   Two different populations of Paramecium placed in the same environment, the culture dish, must compete for space and available nutrients. The group, Paramecium aurelia, appears to have outcompeted Paramecium caudatum because their population numbers increased, while Paramecium caudatum's numbers decreased.

13. 2   Fungus, a decomposer, perform an essential role in the food web by breaking down organic matter and recycling these nutrients back into the ecosystem. Grasses are autotrophic – organisms that can synthesize their own food. Heterotrophic organisms cannot synthesize their own food, so they must obtain organic material present in other organisms.

14. 3   Wolves and coyotes are secondary consumers or carnivores within a food chain/web. Their prey usually consists of plant-eating animals or herbivores. If there was no predation from wolves or coyotes, the herbivore population would be unchecked, and population growth would increase. This growth could exceed the carrying capacity of the population that can be supported in terms of nutrition or space within a particular ecosystem.

15. 3   When a carnivore dies, decomposers such as bacteria and worms will break down the organism into chemical nutrients like carbon and nitrogen, which are then released back in to the environment.

16. 2   Initially, with no competition, conditions would favor an increase in the population of the chipmunks. As the population became larger, several factors, such as availability of food and disease, may limit population growth. These factors would stabilize growth of the population (shown by the leveling off of the graph).

17. 3   An invasive species is a non-native species that has been introduced in a foreign area. These species have no natural population checks, so they outcompete and take over habitats of native species.

18. 3   A biotic resource must be a living factor within an ecosystem.

19. 4   The process indicated by the diagram is ecological succession. Succession is the progression of an ecosystem from a stage of no vegetation (bare rock or soil) to a stage of vegetation (climax forest) that will remain constant unless disrupted by man or a natural disaster. See diagram 5, page 4.

20. *a*) 3   The population represented by B is made up of predators. Predators feed on other living animals (prey) and their populations would reflect a shadow relationship. In this relationship a decrease in the prey population would cause a decrease in the predator population because less food would be available and as the prey population increases, so will the predator population increased.

    b) 3   Grass is the producer that carries out photosynthesis or autotrophic nutrition.

Copyright © 2017
Topical Review Book Company

21. 2 Day 8 represents the day when the carrying capacity was reached. Carrying capacity is defined as the population number that can be maintained by the available resources in that environment. At day 8, the population is no longer growing or increasing and has leveled off. This indicates that the carrying capacity has been reached, and the population has reached a level where the available resources can maintain but not increase the population.

22. *a*) Biodiversity defined: many different species living within a particular habitat
    or   variation in types of organisms living in a particular habitat

   b) Negative effects on humans from loss of biodiversity: disruption of the food chain
    or   loss of organisms that could supply medical cures   *or*   unstable ecosystems
    or   loss of available genes from development of new varieties of organisms

   c) Practices to preserve biodiversity: set aside lands for wilderness areas
    or   establish laws that regulate hunting and fishing or reduction in pollution
    or   set up laws to protect habitats (Other answers are possible.)

Explanation: Biodiversity is an important aspect for any ecosystem. The variation of many different species allows the ecosystem to be stable. In a healthy biodiverse system, the loss of one individual or species will not topple or disrupt the food chain/pyramid. With so many different organisms, there may be a plant or plants that may provide medical cures for present illnesses. Also, within the variety of organisms are different genes that could be used to develop a new trait/strain within other organisms for use perhaps in agriculture. To protect ecosystems from future loss of biodiversity, there must be awareness ranging from the government to the individual. Laws must be established that prevent further habitat destruction and over-hunting. Laws must also be set up that protect ecosystems from pollution by setting standards and establishing practices to reduce the threat of pollution.

23. Answer: X represents the amount of energy lost as heat to the environment.

Explanation: Energy that is not transferred through an energy pyramid is lost as heat (X) to the environment.

24. *a*) Answer: Letter **X** represents a decomposer.

   Explanation: The diagram represents the flow of energy in the form of a food chain. The first rectangle (**A**) represents producers, and the other rectangles represent consumers, all of which, in time, will be broken down by decomposers (**X**) into nutrients for recycling purposes.

   b) Answer: decrease

   Explanation: As food moves through a food chain or web, energy is released (lost) as heat. The release of heat is a result of the metabolic activity within that organism as it uses that food source.

25. Answer: grasses *or* trees *or* any producer

Explanation: Letter X represents producers within an energy pyramid. Producers are autotrophs that convert the Sun's energy into chemical energy using the process of photosynthesis. Both grasses and trees carry out photosynthesis and would be found at level X.

26. *a*) Answer: fish release CO_2 *or* fish release nitrogenous waste products *or* removes oxygen

Explanation: An abiotic factor is a nonliving component of an ecosystem. Within this ecosystem, the abiotic factors are water, sand, gases, minerals, and salts. Fish have the ability to directly affect several of these factors. Through respiration, fish add CO_2 to water, while removing O_2. Through excretion, fish can release nitrogenous wastes, such as ammonia into the water.

b) Acceptable answers include but are not limited to: dead animals *or* dead plants *or* organism waste See explanation for *c*).

c) Acceptable answers include but are not limited to: Decomposers return basic materials such as nitrates and CO_2 to the ecosystem for reuse by other organisms. *or* Decomposers recycle nutrients.

Explanation: Decomposers act as recyclers of organic materials within an ecosystem. They generally break down complex materials into simpler nutrient forms. In order to be a stable ecosystem, decomposers must be present to break down materials, otherwise the system would have a buildup of organic material and become toxic.

d) Answer: sunlight

Explanation: Producers take in energy from the Sun and convert that light energy into the chemical energy of glucose or sugar.

27. *a*) Acceptable answers include but are not limited to:
The energy, which is being lost as heat, decreases as it moves up through the different levels.
or The energy content of each level is transferred to a higher level.

Explanation: In a food web, organisms at Level *A* are autotrophs and receive their energy in the form of sunlight (an abiotic source). Energy moves up a food web from Level *A* to *B* to *C*. The greatest amount of energy is found at *A*, and energy decreases as one moves up through the levels.

b) Answer: The number of elks and rabbits would increase. *or* There would be no predators to control elk or rabbit populations. *or* Grass and tree populations would decrease.

Explanation: Elimination of mountain lions would lead to an overpopulation of elks and rabbits that were sources of food for mountain lions. This would result in overgrazing by these herbivores.

c) Answer: Any animal found in Level *B* except for the frog.

Explanation: A herbivore is any animal that feeds exclusively on plant material.

28. Answer: expose organisms to UV rays *or* increase the chance of mutations in cells *or* increase skin cancer *or* cause eye damage

Explanation: Ozone, located in the upper atmosphere, absorbs much of the harmful ultraviolet rays given off by the Sun. CFCs and other airborne chemicals can thin out this protected ozone layer causing more UV rays to reach the Earth's surface. When this occurs, these high-energy rays can do harm to living cells.

29. Acceptable answers include but are not limited to: There are not enough producers.
or The number of producers is not sufficient to support the number of consumers.

Explanation: This ecosystem is unstable because the number of producers (algae) is far less than the number of primary consumers (plankton). With fewer algae or producers present, less energy is available to be transferred up the energy pyramid, making this ecosystem unstable.

30. *a*) Answer: trees *or* grass

Explanation: Trees and grasses are producers that carry out photosynthesis or autotrophic nutrition.

b) Answer: The cricket population would decrease.

Explanation: Crickets feed on grass. If grass was removed, crickets would lose their food source and their population numbers would decrease.

c) Answer: to break down dead matter *or* recycle nutrients into the environment *or* They are decomposers.

Explanation: Decomposers, like bacteria or fungi, break down organic material. This action recycles nutrients back into the environment.

31. Answer: burning fossil fuels

Explanation: The burning of fossil fuels releases carbon dioxide, which is a greenhouse gas. Greenhouse gases trap (absorb) heat energy within the atmosphere, resulting in global warming.

32. *a*) Acceptable responses include, but are not limited to:
People could get oil to be used for energy, but they might damage the environment while doing it. *or* Oil companies provide many jobs for people, but there could be a negative effect on the environment.

Explanation: A trade-off involves both the positive and negative effects of an action being explored before a decision is made. The trade-off occurs when a decision is made with the hope that the positives or benefits outweigh the negative effects. In some cases, the negatives may be too dangerous to proceed.

b) Acceptable responses include, but are not limited to: create jobs *or* increased revenue for the state *or* increased supply of U.S. oil *or* decreased reliance on foreign oil

Explanation: Oil production brings jobs and money to the drilling region.

c) Answer: More birds were killed. *or* The breeding grounds were contaminated.

Explanation: Researchers collected 6,104 dead birds, while 100 mammals died. This large number of dead birds would severely affect the recovery time for this species. Some of the oil will stay in the birds' environment for years contaminating their breeding grounds.

33. Acceptable responses include, but are not limited to:
Energy is always lost as it is transferred through the ecosystem.
or Energy is continuously needed for metabolic processes.
or It is needed so that autotrophs can make food.

Explanation: Without energy, abiotic organisms would die. Energy is lost as it is transferred up through the food web or energy pyramid. This loss of energy, in the form of heat, needs to be constantly replenished.

34. Answer: See answer 7, page 25.

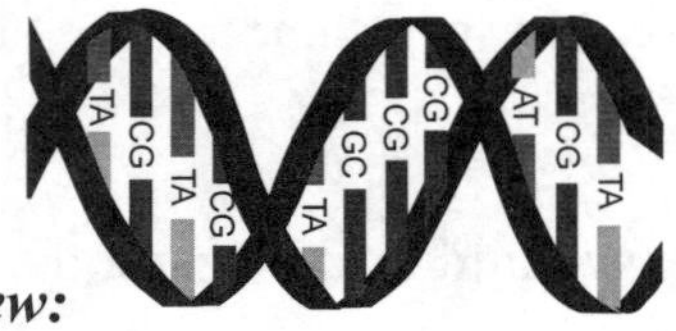

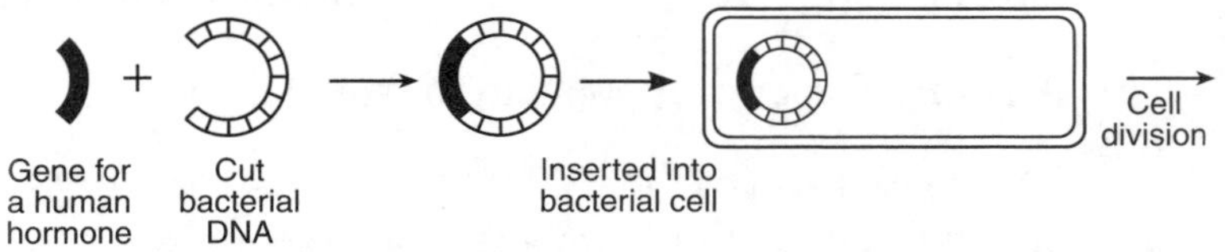

Overview:

Living organisms have a set of genetic instructions that determine the characteristics of their structures and functions. The genetic instructions are passed from parent to offspring through a process of reproduction. During inheritance of these traits, the genetic instructions can be changed leading to variation. Genetic instructions are found in the form of a code within DNA molecules. Each set of genetic codes or DNA is unique to each individual organism.

Humans have used artificial techniques to alter genetic information. Through breeding practices and biotechnology, humans are developing new combinations of genes and new varieties of organisms.

Organization Relationship: Cell → Nucleus → Chromosome → DNA → Gene → Molecular Bases (A,T,C,G)

Essential Information:

<u>DNA's Role</u> – In all living organisms, cells store coded genetic information in the form of *DNA*. DNA is composed of *nucleotides*, which consist of sugar, phosphate, and *molecular bases* that form genetic sequences. These molecular bases are represented by letters that are the beginning of their molecular names: A = Adenine, T = Thymine, C = Cytosine, G = Guanine. Molecular bases form complimentary pairs: A with T and C with G. These bases form sequences within DNA called genes, which code for specific proteins that determine an organism's traits or characteristics. Genetic material is organized in the cell for efficient replication practices as well as protein synthesis. DNA is coiled and packed into structures known as chromosomes. *Chromosomes* are located within a nucleus or genetic area within a cell.

DNA's *double helix* structure allows it to serve as a *template* for *DNA replication*. DNA "unzips" using enzymes, and new *nucleotides* attach to exposed strands forming two new identical DNA strands. This process allows for continuity of genetic material to be passed from parent to offspring. This process is an essential part of asexual as well as sexual reproduction. *Asexual reproduction* results in offspring that are identical to the parent, while *sexual reproduction* results in offspring that resemble but are not identical to the parent. The processes of mitosis and meiosis rely on the replication of DNA. *Mitosis* is the process of cell division that produces identical daughter cells for growth and repair, whereas *meiosis* is the process of cell division that produces sex cells or gametes. Each process uses DNA replication. DNA also serves to store the codes for the production of proteins, which are vital to the proper functioning of cells and all living things. Within the cell, *protein synthesis* occurs when coded genetic information is copied and transferred from the nucleus to *ribosomes*.

<u>RNA's Role</u> – The copy and transfer of genetic information involves a second nucleic acid, RNA. RNA is single stranded and uses a molecular base represented by U instead of T, making the complimentary pairs: A with U and C with G. In the ribosome, amino acids are assembled into chains forming a protein molecule. The sequence of the amino acids is determined by the sequence of molecular bases on the copied RNA strand. A sequence of three bases on RNA, known as a codon, codes for a particular amino acid. A universal chart allows geneticists and researchers to convert RNA code into an amino acid. The original code for every protein begins with DNA. Each protein has a specific shape that determines its function, all based on the sequence of those amino acids.

Expression of Genes – When gene sequences in DNA are accessed to make specific proteins, those genes are said to be expressed. The phrase "genes are turned on" may also be used to describe *gene expression*. Gene expression is regulated or controlled by several factors. There are internal controls that allow genes to be expressed when proteins are needed. The environment can also influence gene expression. Factors such as sunlight and temperature can determine whether genes may be expressed.

Mutations – Changes in genetic sequences are known as mutations. A gene sequence can be changed through *deletion* – where a portion of the genetic code is lost or missing; through *addition* – where a section of genetic code has been added to the existing sequence; or through *substitution* – a process where information from one chromosome is traded with another chromosome. During meiosis, closely aligned chromosomes may trade sections in a process known as *crossing over*. This results in a new genetic makeup in the chromosome. Some mutations may promote genetic variation, becoming either beneficial or detrimental to a population. There are many *mutagenic agents* that can cause mutations within DNA, including chemicals, UV rays, X–rays, and other types of radiation exposure. In order for a mutation to be passed from one generation to another, the DNA in a sex cell (egg or sperm) must be changed. Mutation to DNA in body cells will not result in a mutation being passed to the next generation.

Gene Manipulation – Humans have altered genetic information through *selective breeding* to create enhanced varieties of plants and animals. By choosing organisms with the most desired traits and breeding them, farmers and breeders have created many new varieties. With greater knowledge of DNA and genes, humans can now use *genetic engineering* to manipulate DNA to produce new traits within existing organisms. By using *restriction enzymes* that cut DNA, scientists can cut, copy, and move DNA segments from one individual organism to another. When the DNA segment is inserted into the DNA of another organism, such as bacteria, the altered DNA will then contain a foreign DNA segment and also express it. For example, the human hormone insulin is now genetically engineered using bacteria (see diagram 5). Researchers have also been able to *clone* organisms by inserting a whole set of genetic instructions for an organism into an egg cell. Cloned organisms will contain genetic information identical to the donor parent organism.

Using these techniques and their increasing knowledge of genetics, researchers have been able to locate disease-causing genes and develop preventative measures to help fight those diseases. Researchers have also genetically engineered hormones and enzymes that could provide economical advantages and produce fewer side effects when used in medicines. Other genetic techniques such as gel electrophoresis (see diagram 6) are used to identify individuals as well as determine paternity, based on the genetic information available. The use of genetic engineering so far has led to advances in agriculture and medicine that have benefited mankind.

Additional Information:
- Many genetic disorders are a result of a change in the genetic sequence of a gene. This change may lead to a disruption in the synthesis of necessary proteins. Several genetic disorders include cystic fibrosis, hemophilia, and sickle cell anemia.

- Identical twins are genetically identical, having the same DNA, and are always the same sex. But different environmental influences throughout their lives affect which genes are switched on or off. Thus, the twins will show different characteristics based on that environmental effect on gene expression.

- RNA has several forms. mRNA is utilized to transcribe or copy the genetic code and bring it to the ribosome. tRNA brings amino acids to the ribosome to be assembled into proteins based on genetic code.

- Sometimes chromosomes fail to separate during the process of meiosis, resulting in gametes that have either an additional chromosome or a missing chromosome. This is known as non-disjunction. When these gametes are joined during fertilization, the resulting offspring will have one extra or one less chromosome from the normal species chromosome number. A person who has an extra chromosome (number 21) has Down syndrome, a disorder that exhibits some health abnormalities.

- Many environmental disruptions that have been caused by man can lead to genetic mutation. This is especially true in places that have had serious nuclear disasters, like the Chernobyl nuclear power plant, located in Russia and the Fukushima Daiichi nuclear power plant, located in Japan.

- Because DNA is unique to each individual, it has become useful in many biotechnological procedures as well as in forensic investigation.

- Scientist have successfully mapped the human genetic code. This mapping called The Humane Genome Project and can provide valuable information to researchers and geneticists.

Diagrams:

1. **Organization of Genetic Material** – This diagram shows the organization of genetic material found within a chromosome. This double helix of DNA is wound and tightly coiled within the structure of a chromosome. Chromosomes are found within a nucleus of a cell.

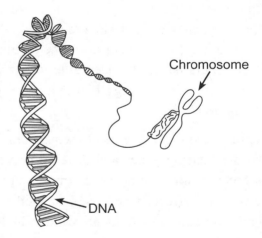

2. **DNA Double Helix Structure** – The DNA double helix structure acts to store genetic information and serves as a template for DNA replication. Shown are molecular base sequences, which are paired with complimentary bases (A – T and C – G). Sequences of these molecular bases represent genes that can code for a particular protein and genetic trait.

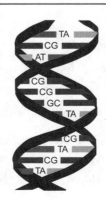

3. **Human Gene** – The accompanying diagram represents the gene pattern for human chromosome 11. Some of the genes are identified and labeled as causing certain illnesses or diseases. Research into the arrangement and location of specific genes on chromosomes has led to many discoveries for correcting genetic defects.

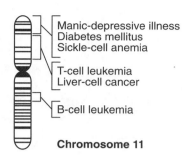

Manic-depressive illness
Diabetes mellitus
Sickle-cell anemia

T-cell leukemia
Liver-cell cancer

B-cell leukemia

Chromosome 11

4. **Protein Synthesis** – DNA, which is found in the nucleus of the cell, stores genetic information that can be copied and transferred from the nucleus to the ribosomes of a cell. At the ribosomes, the coded instructions will be converted into a protein. This process is known as protein synthesis and takes place in every cell.

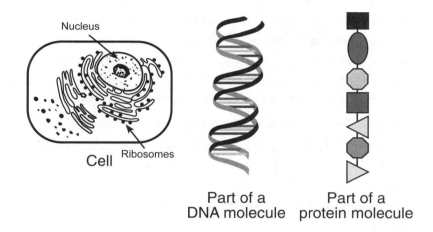

Nucleus

Cell   Ribosomes

Part of a
DNA molecule

Part of a
protein molecule

5. **Protein Synthesis in a Ribosome** – This diagram illustrates the process of protein synthesis as it occurs within the ribosome, Structure X. The newly formed molecules are amino acids that are aligned together in sequence to create proteins based on the code from mRNA. Notice the complimentary pairs in RNA, *A* with *U* and *C* with *G*.

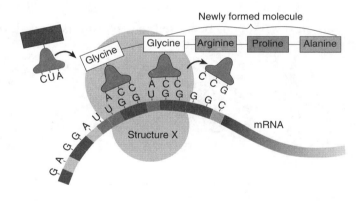

Newly formed molecule

Glycine   Glycine   Arginine   Proline   Alanine

Structure X   mRNA

6. **Gel Electrophoresis** – This diagram represents the results of gel electrophoresis, a process where DNA fragments are separated and moved by electric current to identify or look for relationships between living organisms. DNA molecules are cut into fragments of various lengths by enzymes and then loaded into a gel. Electric currents cause these fragments to migrate through the gel at varying distances and speeds. Smaller pieces move farther than larger ones. The patterns that develop as a result of this process can be used in crime investigations and evolutionary determinations.

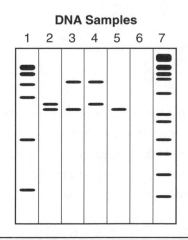

DNA Samples

1   2   3   4   5   6   7

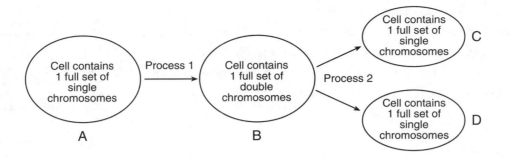

7. **Mitotic Cell Division in Asexual Reproduction** – In this diagram, a single cell organism, such as paramecium, is undergoing asexual reproduction. Process 1 is replication in which the DNA structure is being copied. In process 2, the cell divides producing two identical cells, each with a full set of single chromosomes. Process 1 and 2 are directly involved in mitotic cell division. This results in the genetic content of *C* and *D* being identical to parent cell *A*.

8. **Genetic Information in Asexual Reproduction** – This ameba is undergoing asexual reproduction. Daughter cells *B* and *C* will contain the same genetic information as cell *A*. In asexual reproduction, resulting offspring are identical to the parent.

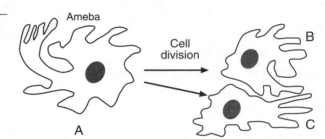

The offspring of these organisms will also have the same genetic information as the parent. No genetic variation will occur because the offspring is a result of the asexual process of budding.

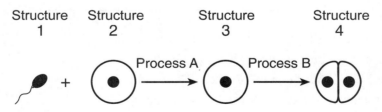

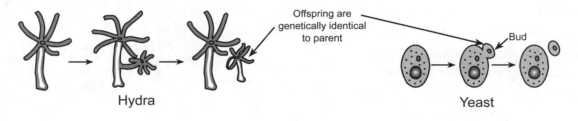

9. **Meiosis and Genetic Information** – During the process of meiosis, sperm (Structure 1) and egg cell (Structure 2) are produced with half the genetic information of the parent cells. During fertilization (Process *A*), genetic information from sperm and egg combine and provide a full set of genetic instructions in the resulting cell (Structure 3). This cell undergoes mitosis (Process *B*) in order to grow and develop into a complete organism.

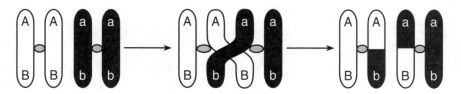

10. **Chromosome Crossing Over** – The diagram represents the process of crossing over, which occurs during meiosis. Genetic material is exchanged between chromosomes, and new genetic combinations are created resulting in genetic variation within the offspring.

11. **Uncontrolled Cell Growth** – The diagram above shows the effect of genetic mutations that occur in skin cells when mitotic division proceeds uncontrollably. These cells may result in a tumor or form of cancer.

12. **Mutation** – This diagram shows a normal gene sequence and three mutated sequences of a segment of DNA. Mutation *A* is *deletion* where the first *A* in the normal sequence has been deleted. Mutation *B* is *substitution* where *G* has taken the place for *C*. Mutation *C* is *addition* where a *G* has been inserted between the two *T*'s.

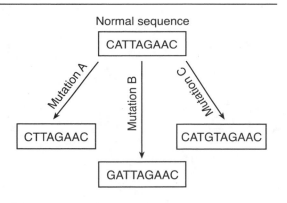

13. **Genetic Engineering** – The process of genetic engineering is represented by this diagram. Enzymes are used to cut open a ring of bacterial DNA as well as to cut out an insulin gene from human DNA. The human insulin gene is then inserted into the bacterial DNA, resulting in a new genetic combination. This newly combined bacterial DNA will now produce human insulin.

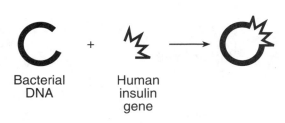

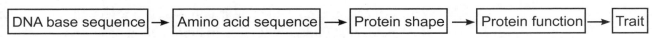

14. **DNA and the Expression of Genetic Traits** – The sequence in this diagram represents the relationship between DNA and the expression of a genetic trait. DNA code provides the template that determines the order of linked amino acids. Specific sequences of amino acids build proteins that have specific shapes and functions that are expressed as a trait.

Vocabulary Refresher

Group A   *Directions* - Match the correct definition for the following terms:

1. _____DNA

2. _____ Chromosome

3. _____Gene

4. _____Protein

5. _____Trait

6. _____Molecular bases

7. _____Double helix

8. _____Template

9. _____DNA replication

10. _____Nucleotide

11. _____Protein synthesis

12. _____Deletion

13. _____Crossing over

14. _____Gene expression

A. Four molecules (represented by A, T, C, and G) that provide the codes for amino acids and ultimately, proteins within living organisms. These molecules are complimentary to each other with A binding to T and C binding with G.

B. Building block of DNA consisting of a sugar, a phosphate group, and a molecular base (A, C, T, or G).

C. A process where a genetic code found in DNA is copied and converted into a chain of amino acids.

D. A pattern that provides the basis for an identical copy to be made.

E. A sequence of molecular bases within a DNA molecule that code for a particular protein.

F. A tightly packed coil of DNA that is found in the nucleus of a cell.

G. A process where the genetic information found within DNA is changed into a functional product like a protein. This protein may take the form of a physical feature or a functional chemical.

H. A characteristic (structure or function) that an organism exhibits as a result of the genetic code within its DNA.

I. A twisted ladder-like structure with a backbone of sugar and phosphate and internal rungs made of complimentary molecular bases.

J. The process where chromosomes overlap and sections of these chromosomes are exchanged during meiosis resulting in genetics variations.

K. A process where two identical DNA molecules are synthesized from an original DNA molecule.

L. An organic molecule that contains a unique genetic code within the sequences of its molecular bases for each living organism.

M. An organic molecule that is composed of a sequence of amino acids that plays a vital role in the function of all living organisms. An example is an enzyme.

N. A mutation where part of the genetic code is missing or incomplete.

Genetics

Group B *Directions* - Match the correct definition for the following terms:

1. _____Asexual reproduction

2. _____Sexual reproduction

3. _____Mitosis

4. _____Meiosis

5. _____Ribosome

6. _____Amino acid

7. _____Mutation

8. _____Mutagenic agent

9. _____Selective breeding

10. _____Restriction enzyme

11. _____Genetic engineering

12. _____Clone

13. _____RNA

A. Molecules that when arranged in specific sequences act as the building blocks of proteins. There are 20 different types of these.

B. A form of cell division that takes place within the sex organs of organisms and results in the formation of gametes (sex cells), having one-half the original chromosomes of the parent cell.

C. Any factor such as chemicals or radiation, that leads to a change in the genetic code.

D. A process where a parent organism divides into two new genetically identical offspring. Examples include budding and binary fission.

E. A sudden change in the genetic code or sequence of molecular bases within DNA.

F. An enzyme that locates a particular gene sequence on DNA and "cuts" the DNA at that site, creating DNA fragments of various sizes. These enzymes are used in many biotech processes.

G. An exact genetic copy. The process can be applied to a cell or to a whole organism.

H. A form of cell division where two daughter cells are produced from a parent cell that are genetically identical to the parent cell.

I. A single stranded nucleic acid which contains the molecular bases, A, U, C and G. This molecule plays a vital role in the synthesis of proteins.

J. A process involving two parent organisms that produce offspring, which may resemble but are genetically different from the parent organism.

K. A process where organisms with desirable traits are bred to enhance or maintain a trait, or increase variety.

L. A cell organelle that serves as the site for protein synthesis.

M. A process where a gene from one organism is inserted into the DNA of another organism. The new recombinant DNA will express that inserted gene.

1. The instructions for the traits of an organism are coded in the arrangement of

    (1) glucose units in carbohydrate molecules
    (2) bases in DNA in the nucleus
    (3) fat molecules in the cell membrane
    (4) energy-rich bonds in starch molecules

    1_____

2. Scientific studies show that identical twins who were separated at birth and raised in different homes may vary in height, weight, and intelligence. The most probable explanation for these differences is that

    (1) original genes of each twin increased in number as they developed
    (2) one twin received genes only from the mother while the other twin received genes only from the father
    (3) environments in which they were raised were different enough to affect the expression of their genes
    (4) environments in which they were raised were different enough to change the genetic makeup of both individuals

    2_____

3. For centuries, certain animals have been crossed to produce offspring that have desirable qualities. Dogs have been mated to produce Labradors, beagles, and poodles. All of these dogs look and behave very differently from one another. This technique of producing organisms with specific qualities is known as

    (1) gene replication
    (2) natural selection
    (3) random mutation
    (4) selective breeding

    3_____

4. Which process will increase variations that could be inherited?

    (1) mitotic cell division
    (2) active transport
    (3) recombination of base subunit sequences
    (4) synthesis of proteins

    4_____

5. The diagram below shows a process that can occur during meiosis.

    The most likely result of this process is

    (1) a new combination of inheritable traits that can appear in the offspring
    (2) an inability to pass either of these chromosomes on to offspring
    (3) a loss of genetic information that will produce a genetic disorder in the offspring
    (4) an increase in the chromosome number of the organism in which this process occurs

    5_____

6. Which statement best describes human insulin that is produced by genetically engineered bacteria?

    (1) This insulin will not function normally in humans because it is produced by bacteria.
    (2) This insulin is produced as a result of human insulin being inserted into bacteria cells.
    (3) This insulin is produced as a result of exposing bacteria cells to radiation, which produces a mutation.
    (4) This insulin may have fewer side effects than the insulin previously extracted from the pancreas of other animals.

    6_____

7. Individual cells can be isolated from a mature plant and grown with special mixtures of growth hormones to produce a number of genetically identical plants. This process is known as

(1) cloning
(2) meiotic division
(3) recombinant DNA technology
(4) selective breeding   7_____

8. Which statements best describe the relationship between the terms chromosomes, genes, and nuclei?

(1) Chromosomes are found on genes. Genes are found in nuclei.
(2) Chromosomes are found in nuclei. Nuclei are found in genes.
(3) Genes are found on chromosomes. Chromosomes are found in nuclei.
(4) Genes are found in nuclei. Nuclei are found in chromosomes.   8_____

9. The diagram below represents a section of a molecule that carries genetic information.

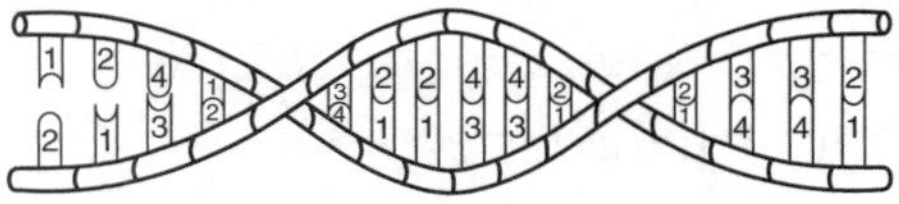

The pattern of numbers represents

(1) a sequence of paired bases
(2) the order of proteins in a gene
(3) folds of an amino acid
(4) positions of gene mutations   9_____

10. Asexually reproducing organisms pass on hereditary information as

(1) sequences of A, T, C, and G
(2) chains of complex amino acids
(3) folded protein molecules
(4) simple inorganic sugars   10_____

11. In sexually reproducing species, the number of chromosomes in each body cell remains the same from one generation to the next as a direct result of

(1) meiosis and fertilization
(2) mitosis and mutation
(3) differentiation and aging
(4) homeostasis and dynamic equilibrium   11_____

12. Enzymes are used in moving sections of DNA that code for insulin from the pancreas cells of humans into a certain type of bacterial cell. This bacterial cell will reproduce, giving rise to offspring that are able to form

(1) human insulin
(2) antibodies against insulin
(3) enzymes that digest insulin
(4) a new type of insulin   12_____

13. A change in the base subunit sequence during DNA replication can result in

(1) variation resulting from changes within the genetic code
(2) rapid evolution of an organism
(3) synthesis of antigens to protect the cell
(4) recombination of genes within the cell   13_____

14. Plants inherit genes that enable them to produce chlorophyll, but this pigment is not produced unless the plants are exposed to light. This is an example of how the environment can

(1) cause mutations to occur
(2) influence the expression of a genetic trait
(3) result in the appearance of a new species
(4) affect one plant species, but not another   14_____

15. If the ribosomes of a cell were destroyed, what effect would this most likely have on the cell?

(1) It would stimulate mitotic cell division.
(2) The cell would be unable to synthesize proteins.
(3) Development of abnormal hereditary features would occur in the cell.
(4) Increased protein absorption would occur through the cell membrane. 15_____

16. Which statement describes asexual reproduction?

(1) Adaptive traits are usually passed from parent to offspring without genetic modification.
(2) Mutations are not passed from generation to generation.
(3) It always enables organisms to survive in changing environmental conditions.
(4) It is responsible for many new variations in offspring. 16_____

17. A change in the order of DNA bases that code for a respiratory protein will most likely cause

(1) the production of a starch that has a similar function
(2) the digestion of the altered gene by enzymes
(3) a change in the sequence of amino acids determined by the gene
(4) the release of antibodies by certain cells to correct the error 17_____

18. In sexually reproducing organisms, mutations can be inherited if they occur in

(1) the egg, only
(2) the sperm, only
(3) any body cell of either the mother or the father
(4) either the egg or the sperm 18_____

19. A product of genetic engineering technology is represented.

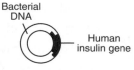

Which substance was needed to join the insulin gene to the bacterial DNA as shown?

(1) a specific carbohydrate
(2) a specific enzyme
(3) hormones
(4) antibodies 19_____

20. DNA samples were collected from four children. The diagram below represents the results of a procedure that separated the DNA in each sample.

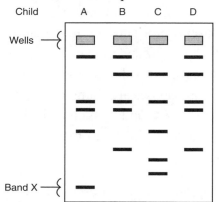

Band X represents the
(1) largest fragment of DNA that traveled the fastest
(2) smallest fragment of DNA that traveled the fastest
(3) largest fragment of DNA that traveled the slowest
(4) smallest fragment of DNA that traveled the slowest 20_____

21. Which process can produce new inheritable characteristics within a multicellular species?

(1) cloning of the skin cells
(2) mitosis in muscle cells
(3) gene alterations in gametes
(4) differentiation in nerve cells 21_____

22. Offspring that result from meiosis and fertilization each have

    (1) twice as many chromosomes as their parents

    (2) one-half as many chromosomes as their parents

    (3) gene combinations different from those of either parent

    (4) gene combinations identical to those of each parent   22_____

23. Which statement concerning the reproductive cells in the diagram is correct?

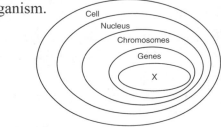

    (1) The cells are produced by mitosis and contain all the genetic information of the father.

    (2) If one of these cells fertilizes an egg, the offspring will be identical to the father.

    (3) Each of these cells contains only half the genetic information necessary for the formation of an offspring.

    (4) An egg fertilized by one of these cells will develop into a female with the same characteristics as the mother.   23_____

24. A mutation that can be inherited by offspring would result from

    (1) random breakage of chromosomes in the nucleus of liver cells

    (2) a base substitution in gametes during meiosis

    (3) abnormal lung cells produced by toxins in smoke

    (4) ultraviolet radiation damage to skin cells   24_____

25. The diagram below represents single-celled organism A dividing by mitosis to form cells B and C. Cells A, B, and C all produced protein X. What can best be inferred from this observation?

    (1) Protein X is found in all organisms.

    (2) The gene for protein X is found in single-celled organisms, only.

    (3) Cells A, B, and C ingested food containing the gene to produce protein X.

    (4) The gene to produce protein X was passed from cell A to cells B and C.   25_____

26. The diagram below represents levels of organization within a cell of a multicellular organism.

The level represented by X is composed of

    (1) four types of base subunits

    (2) folded chains of glucose molecules

    (3) twenty different kinds of amino acids

    (4) complex, energy-rich inorganic molecules   26_____

27. A chemical known as 5-bromouracil causes a mutation that results in the mismatching of molecular bases in DNA. The offspring of organisms exposed to 5-bromouracil can have mismatched DNA if the mutation occurs in

    (1) the skin cells of the mother

    (2) the gametes of either parent

    (3) all the body cells of both parents

    (4) only the nerve cells of the father   27_____

28. Sexually produced offspring often resemble, but are not identical to, either of their parents. Explain why they resemble their parents but are not identical to either parent.

_____

_____

29. If 20% of a DNA sample is made up of cytosine, C, what percentage of the sample is made up of adenine, A? _____ %

30. Arrange the following structures from largest to smallest.

a chromosome   **a nucleus**   **a gene**

Largest _____

↓   _____

Smallest _____

Base your answers to question 31 on the information and chart below.

Amino Acid	Abbreviation	DNA Code
Phenylalanine	Phe	AAA, AAG
Tryptophan	Try	ACC
Serine	Ser	AGA, AGG, AGT, AGC, TCA, TCG
Valine	Val	CAA, CAG, CAT, CAC
Proline	Pro	GGA, GGG, GGT, GGC
Glutamine	Glu	GTT, GTC
Threonine	Thr	TGA, TGG, TGT, TGC
Asparagine	Asp	TTA, TTG

In DNA, a sequence of three bases is a code for the placement of a certain amino acid in a protein chain. The table above shows some amino acids with their abbreviations and DNA codes.

31. *a*) Which amino acid chain would be produced by the DNA base sequence below?

C-A-A-G-T-T-A-A-A-T-T-A-T-T-G-T-G-A

(1) Val—Glu—Phe—Asp—Thr—Asp   (3) Val—Glu—Phe—Asp—Asp—Thr

(2) Val—Pro—Phe—Asp—Asp—Thr   (4) Val—Glu—Phe—Thr—Asp—Asp   a _____

b) Identify one environmental factor that could cause a base sequence in DNA to be changed to a

different base sequence. _____

c) Describe how a protein would be changed if a base sequence mutates from GGA to TGA.

_____

Base your answers to question 32 on the information below.

Scientists are increasingly concerned about the possible effects of damage to the ozone layer.

32. Damage to the ozone layer has resulted in mutations in skin cells that lead to cancer. Will the mutations that caused the skin cancers be passed on to offspring? Support your answer.

Answer:_____ Supporting statement:_____

_____

33. A child is born with a genetic disorder to parents who show no symptoms of the disorder. Explain the type of information a genetic counselor might provide to these parents. In your answer, be sure to:

a) explain why the child exhibits symptoms of the genetic disorder even though the parents do not

_____

b) identify one technique that can be used to detect a genetic disorder

_____

c) identify one genetic disorder _____

34. Scientists have successfully cloned sheep and cattle for several years. A farmer is considering the advantages and disadvantages of having a flock of sheep cloned from a single individual. Discuss the issues the farmer should take into account before making a decision. Your response should include:

a) how a cloned flock would be different from a noncloned flock

_____

b) one advantage of having a cloned flock

_____

c) one disadvantage of having a cloned flock

_____

d) one reason that the farmer could not mate these cloned sheep with each other to increase the size of his flock

_____

e) one reason that the offspring resulting from breeding these sheep with an unrelated sheep would not all be the same

_____

35. Identical twins have the same genetic material, but they may develop slightly different characteristics. State one reason that would cause this.

_____

Base your answers to question 36 on the information and diagram.

The four wells represented in the diagram were each injected with fragments that were prepared from DNA samples using identical techniques.

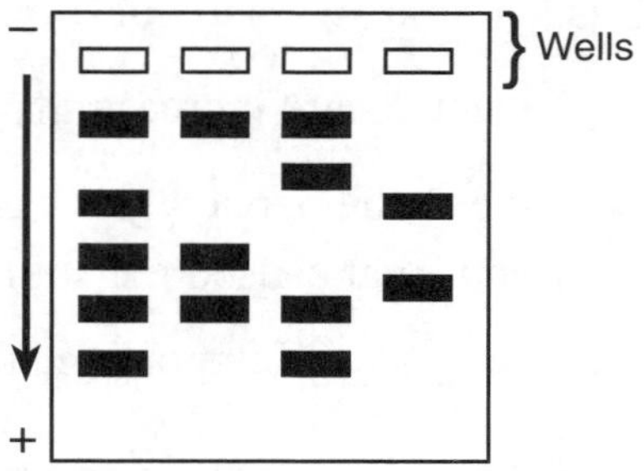

36. *a)* This laboratory procedure is known as

_____ .

b) The arrow represents the direction of the movement of the DNA fragments. What is responsible for the movement of the DNA in this process?

_____

c) The four samples of DNA were taken from four different individuals. Explain how this is evident from the results shown in the diagram.

_____

d) Identify the substance that was used to treat the DNA to produce the fragments that were put into the wells. _____

37. Rabbits eat plants and in turn are eaten by predators such as foxes and wolves. A population of rabbits is found in which a few have a genetic trait that gives them much better than average leg strength.

a) Predict how the frequency of the trait for above average leg strength would be expected to change in the population over time. Explain your prediction.

Frequency: _____

Explanation: _____

b) State what is likely to happen to the rabbits in the population that do not have the trait for above average leg strength.

_____

38. The segments of DNA below were extracted from two different species of plants. The segments represent the same region of DNA that codes for a particular pigment (color) in these species.

Plant Species *A*: A C C G C A G G G A T T C G C
Plant Species *B*: A C C G G A G C G A T T C G C

A restriction enzyme is used to cut the DNA from species *A* and *B*. The enzyme binds to the sequence G G G A T T and cuts between *G* and *A*. State how many cuts will be made in the DNA sequences of each species when this enzyme is used.

Plant species *A* cuts: _____   Plant species *B* cuts: _____

39. The table shows the number of individual molecules obtained when a DNA molecule from a bacterial species is broken down.

| Molecules from Bacterial DNA ||
Molecule	Number
sugar	4.6 million
phosphate	4.6 million
adenine (A)	1.75 million
cytosine (C)	0.55 million
guanine (G)	0.55 million
thymine (T)	1.75 million

a) What data in the data table indicate that adenine pairs with thymine in a DNA molecule?

_____

_____

b) Explain how the data table would differ if the molecular data reflected bacterial RNA instead of DNA.

_____

_____

40. The work of a cell is carried out by the many different types of molecules it assembles. Most of these molecules are proteins. Explain how the cell is able to make the many different proteins it needs. Your response should include:

a) identify where in the cell the information necessary to construct a particular protein is located and the specific molecule that contains this information

Where: _____ Specific molecule: _____

b) identify *both* the cellular structure that assembles these proteins and the kinds of molecules that are used as the building blocks of the proteins

Cellular structure: _____

Molecules: _____

41. Discuss the process used by scientists to insert a gene from one organism into the DNA of another. Your response should include:

a) identify the scientific technique used to insert a gene from one organism into another.

_____

b) describe the function of a gene

_____

c) identify the type of molecule used to cut the gene from the DNA of an organism

_____

d) state *one* benefit of this technique to humans

_____

1. Meiosis and fertilization are important processes because they may most immediately result in

   (1) many body cells
   (2) immune responses
   (3) genetic variation
   (4) natural selection   1 _____

2. In the diagram below, strands I and II represent portions of a DNA molecule.

   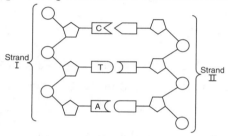

   Strand II would normally include

   (1) AGC   (3) TAC
   (2) TCG   (4) GAT   2 _____

3. The letters in the diagram represent genes on a particular chromosome. Gene *B* contains the code for an enzyme that cannot be synthesized unless gene *A* is also active. Which statement best explains why this can occur?

   (1) A hereditary trait can be determined by more than one gene.
   (2) Genes are made up of double-stranded segments of DNA.
   (3) All the genes on a chromosome act to produce a single trait.
   (4) The first gene on each chromosome controls all the other genes on the chromosome.   3 _____

4. In Siamese cats, the fur on the ears, paws, tail, and face is usually black or brown, while the rest of the body fur is almost white. If a Siamese cat is kept indoors where it is warm, it may grow fur that is almost white on the ears, paws, tail, and face, while a Siamese cat that stays outside where it is cold, will grow fur that is quite dark on these areas. The best explanation for these changes in fur color is that

   (1) the gene for fur color is modified by interactions with the environment
   (2) the location of pigment-producing cells determines the DNA code of the genes
   (3) skin cells that produce pigments have a higher mutation rate than other cells
   (4) an environmental factor influences the expression of this inherited trait   4 _____

5. Which statement best describes a chromosome?

   (1) It is a gene that has thousands of different forms.
   (2) It has genetic information contained in DNA.
   (3) It is a reproductive cell that influences more than one trait.
   (4) It contains hundreds of genetically identical DNA molecules   5 _____

6. Which statement is true of both mitosis and meiosis?

   (1) Both are involved in asexual reproduction.
   (2) Both occur only in reproductive cells.
   (3) The number of chromosomes is reduced by half.
   (4) DNA replication occurs before the division of the nucleus   6 _____

7. What determines the kind of genes an organism possesses?

   (1) type of amino acids in the cells of the organism

   (2) sequence of the subunits A, T, C, and G in the DNA of the organism

   (3) size of simple sugar molecules in the organs of the organism

   (4) shape of the protein molecules in the organelles of the organism   7 _____

8. If a set of instructions that determines all of the characteristics of an organism is compared to a book, and a chromosome is compared to a chapter in the book, then what might be compared to a paragraph in the book?

   (1) a starch molecule

   (2) an egg

   (3) an amino acid

   (4) a DNA molecule   8 _____

9. People with cystic fibrosis inherit defective genetic information and cannot produce normal CFTR proteins. Scientists have used gene therapy to insert normal DNA segments that code for the missing CFTR protein into the lung cells of people with cystic fibrosis. Which statement does not describe a result of this therapy?

   (1) Altered lung cells can produce the normal CFTR protein.

   (2) Altered lung cells can divide to produce other lung cells with the normal CFTR gene.

   (3) The normal CFTR gene may be expressed in altered lung cells.

   (4) Offspring of someone with altered lung cells will inherit the normal CFTR gene.   9 _____

10. The diagrams below represent some steps in a procedure used in biotechnology.

Letters X and Y represent

   (1) hormones that stimulate the replication of bacterial DNA

   (2) biochemical catalysts involved in the insertion of genes into other organisms

   (3) hormones that trigger rapid mutation of genetic information

   (4) gases needed to produce the energy required for gene manipulation   10 _____

11. Plants in species A cannot fight most fungal infections. Plants in species B make a protein that kills many fungi. One possible way for humans to produce species A plants with the ability to synthesize this protein would be to

   (1) mutate fungal DNA and introduce the mutated DNA into species B using a virus

   (2) add DNA from species B into the soil around species A

   (3) insert the gene for the protein from species B into a chromosome in species A

   (4) cross species A and a fungus to stimulate the synthesis of this protein   11 _____

12. A small amount of DNA was taken from a fossil of a mammoth found frozen in glacial ice. Genetic technology can be used to produce a large quantity of identical DNA from this mammoth's DNA. In this technology, the original DNA sample is used to

   (1) stimulate differentiation in other mammoth cells

   (2) provide fragments to replace certain human body chemicals

   (3) act as a template for repeated replication

   (4) trigger mitosis to obtain new base sequences   12 _____

13. The diagram below represents a protein molecule present in some living things.

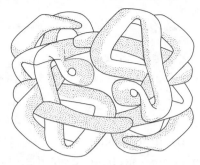

This type of molecule is composed of a sequence of

(1) amino acids arranged in a specific order
(2) simple sugars alternating with starches arranged in a folded pattern
(3) large inorganic subunits that form chains that interlock with each other
(4) four bases that make up the folded structure   13_____

14. The diagrams below represent portions of the genes that code for wing structure in two organisms of the same species. Gene 1 was taken from the cells of a female with normal wings, and gene 2 was taken from the cells of a female with abnormal wings.

Gene 1   **Gene 2**

G ▭ ▮ C   G ▭ ▮ C
A ▭ ▨ T   A ▭ ▨ T
A ▭ ▨ T   T ▨ ▭ A
T ▨ ▭ A   T ▨ ▭ A
T ▨ ▭ A   C ▮ ▭ G
C ▮ ▭ G

The abnormal wing structure was most likely due to

(1) an insertion   (3) a deletion
(2) a substitution   (4) normal replication

          14_____

15. Which situation would most directly affect future generations naturally produced by a maple tree?

(1) Ultraviolet radiation changes the DNA sequence within some leaves of the tree.
(2) Ultraviolet radiation changes the DNA sequence within the gametes of some flowers of the tree.
(3) An increase in temperature reduces the number of cell divisions in the roots.
(4) Rapidly growing cells just under the bark are exposed to radiation, causing changes in genetic material.   15_____

16. Some steps involved in DNA replication and protein synthesis are summarized in the table below.

Step A	DNA is copied and each new cell gets a full copy.
Step B	Information copied from DNA moves to the cytoplasm.
Step C	Proteins are assembled at the ribosomes.
Step D	Proteins fold and begin functioning.

In which step would a mutation lead directly to the formation of an altered gene?

(1) *A*   (3) *C*
(2) *B*   (4) *D*   16_____

17. During meiosis, crossing-over (gene exchange between chromosomes) may occur. Crossing-over usually results in

(1) the production of an extra amino acid
(2) the formation of an extra chromosome
(3) the formation of identical twins
(4) new combination of inheritable traits

          17_____

18. Which phrases best identify characteristics of asexual reproduction?

   (1) one parent, union of gametes, offspring similar to but not genetically identical to the parent

   (2) one parent, no union of gametes, offspring genetically identical to parents

   (3) two parents, union of gametes, offspring similar to but not genetically identical to parents

   (4) two parents, no union of gametes, offspring genetically identical to parents

                         18 _____

19. To determine the identity of their biological parents, adopted children sometimes request DNA tests. These tests involve comparing DNA samples from the child to DNA samples taken from the likely parents. Possible relationships may be determined from these tests because the

   (1) base sequence of the father determines the base sequence of the offspring

   (2) DNA of parents and their offspring is more similar than the DNA of nonfamily members

   (3) position of the genes on each chromosome is unique to each family

   (4) mutation rate is the same in closely related individuals   19 _____

20. One way to produce large numbers of genetically identical offspring is by

   (1) cloning

   (2) fertilization

   (3) changing genes by agents such as radiation or chemicals

   (4) inserting a DNA segment into a different DNA molecule   20 _____

21. The diagram below shows a process that affects chromosomes during meiosis.

This process can be used to explain

   (1) why some offspring are genetically identical to their parents

   (2) the process of differentiation in offspring

   (3) why some offspring physically resemble their parents

   (4) the origin of new combinations of traits in offspring   21 ____

22. Even though human proteins are synthesized from only 20 different amino acids, there are thousands of different proteins found in human cells. This great variety of proteins is possible because the

   (1) size of a specific amino acid can vary within a protein

   (2) chemical composition of a specific amino acid can vary

   (3) sequence and number of amino acids can be different in each protein

   (4) same amino acid can have many different properties   22 ____

23. The diagram can be used to illustrate cellular changes.

Which row of terms in the chart below best completes the diagram?

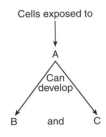

Row	A	B	C
(1)	atmospheric oxygen	mutations	increased mitochondria
(2)	radiation	cancer	mutations
(3)	salt water	more cytoplasm	two nuclei
(4)	less sunlight	extra genes	decreased mutations

                         23 ____

24. Mustard gas removes guanine (G) from DNA. For developing embryos, exposure to mustard gas can cause serious deformities because guanine

(1) stores the building blocks of proteins
(2) supports the structure of ribosomes
(3) produces energy for genetic transfer
(4) is part of the genetic code   24 _____

25. Three structures are represented in the diagram below.

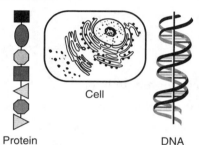

Protein   DNA

What is the relationship between these three structures?

(1) DNA is made up of proteins that are synthesized in the cell.
(2) Protein is composed of DNA that is stored in the cell.
(3) DNA controls the production of protein in the cell.
(4) The cell is composed only of DNA and protein.   25 _____

26. The human liver contains many specialized cells that secrete bile. Only these cells produce bile because

(1) different cells use different parts of the genetic information they contain
(2) cells can eliminate the genetic codes that they do not need
(3) all other cells in the body lack the genes needed for the production of bile
(4) these cells mutated during embryonic development   26 _____

27. The Y-chromosome carries the SRY gene that codes for the production of testosterone in humans. Occasionally a mutation occurs resulting in the SRY gene being lost from the Y-chromosome and added to the X-chromosome, as shown in the diagram below.

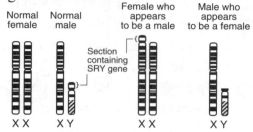

Based on the diagram, which statement is correct?

(1) The production of testosterone influences the development of male characteristics.
(2) Reproductive technology has had an important influence on human development.
(3) Normal female characteristics develop from a single X-chromosome.
(4) Male characteristics only develop in the absence of X-chromosomes.   27 _____

28. The sequence of subunits in a protein is most directly dependent on the

(1) region in the cell where enzymes are produced
(2) DNA in the chromosomes in a cell
(3) type of cell in which starch is found
(4) kinds of materials in the cell membrane   28 _____

29. If 15% of a DNA sample is made up of thymine, T, what percentage of the sample is made up of cytosine, C?

(1) 15%   (3) 70%
(2) 35%   (4) 85%   29 _____

30. Which sequence best represents the relationship between DNA and the traits of an organism?

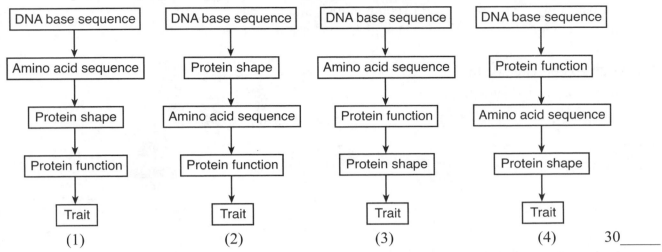

(1)   (2)   (3)   (4)   30_____

31. Which row in the chart best describes what happens when some DNA bases are deleted from a gene?

Row	Gene	Trait Controlled By the Original DNA
(1)	is not changed	is never changed
(2)	is not changed	may be changed
(3)	is changed	is never changed
(4)	is changed	may be changed

31_____

32. The diagram represents stages in the development of an embryo. The process of mitosis is involved in all shown steps.

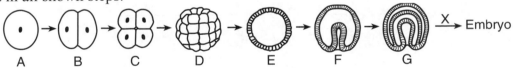

If cell *A* has 46 chromosomes, how many chromosomes will most likely be found in each cell of stage *G*?

(1) 23   (2) 46   (3) 69   (4) 92   32_____

33. Four different segments of a DNA molecule are represented.

There is an error in the DNA molecule in

(1) segment 1, only
(2) segment 3, only
(3) segments 2 and 3
(4) segments 2 and 4

Segment 1
T–A–G–G–C
A–T–C–C–G

Segment 2
G–G–T–G–A
C–C–A–C–T

Segment 3
G–A–T–T–A
C–C–A–A–T

Segment 4
C–A–A–T–G
G–T–T–A–C

33____

34. DNA replication occurs in preparation for
    (1) mitosis, only
    (2) meiosis, only
    (3) both mitosis and meiosis
    (4) neither mitosis nor meiosis

    34 _____

35. Give an appropriate title for the accompanying diagram.

    _____

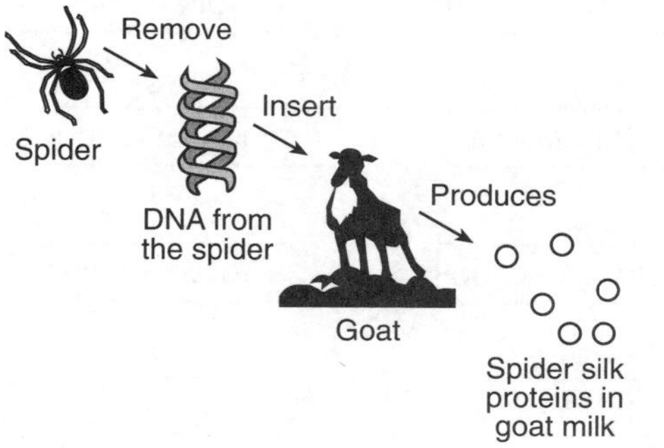

36. Place the correct phase number inside the appropriate box of the flowchart below.

    Phase 1 – Increased chance of cancer
    Phase 2 – Exposure of cells to radiation
    Phase 3 – Increase rate of mutation

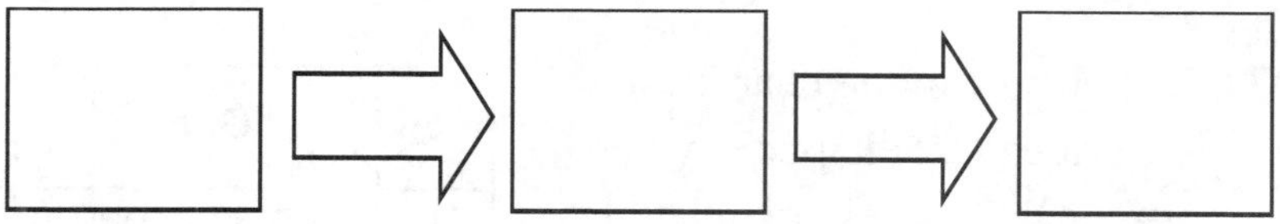

    Base your answers to question 37 on the statement below.

    Selective breeding has been used to improve the racing ability of horses.

37. *a)* Define selective breeding and state how it would be used to improve the racing ability of horses.

    Selective breeding:_____

    Improvement:_____

    b) State one disadvantage of selective breeding.

    _____

38. Compare asexual reproduction to sexual reproduction. In your comparison, be sure to include:

    a) Which type of reproduction results in offspring that are usually genetically identical to the previous generation and explain why this occurs.

    Type of reproduction: _____

    Explanation:_____

    b) Give one other way these methods of reproduction differ.

    _____

39. The diagram illustrates some of the changes that occur during gamete formation. Give a statement on the amount of DNA in stage 1 cell compared to the amount of DNA in stage 4 cell.

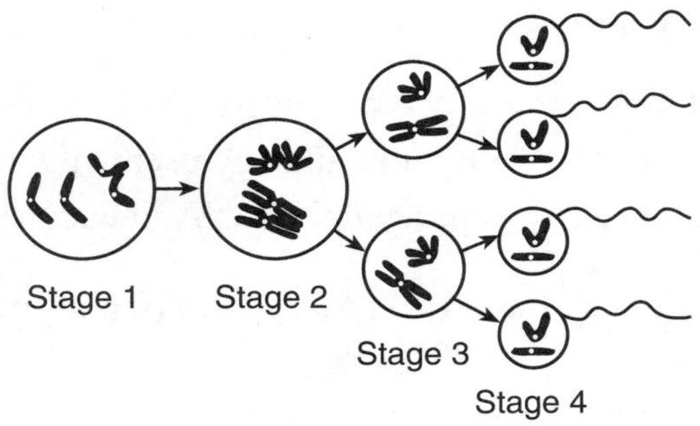

_____

_____

Stage 1   Stage 2   Stage 3   Stage 4

Base your answers to question 40 on the diagram below, which illustrates some steps in genetic engineering.

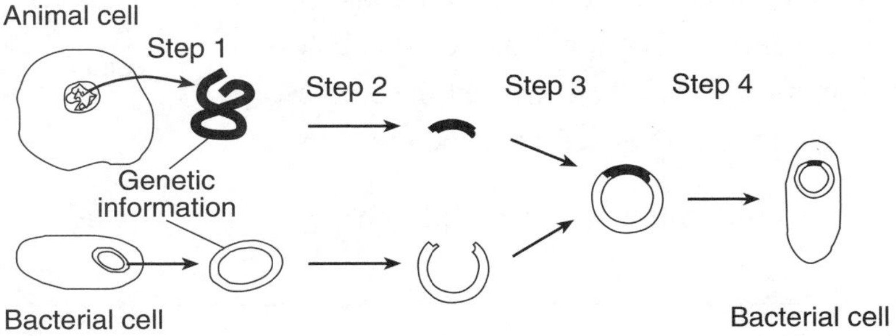

Animal cell   Step 1   Step 2   Step 3   Step 4

Genetic information

Bacterial cell   Bacterial cell

40. *a)* What is the result of step 3? _____

b) State one way that enzymes are used in step 2. _____

_____

c) State one possible reason why a gene for the production of a human hormone would be placed in bacterial DNA.

_____

Base your answers to question 41 on the information below.

To demonstrate techniques used in DNA analysis, a student was given two paper strip samples of DNA. The two DNA samples are shown below.

Sample 1: ATTCCGGTAATCCCGTAATGCCGGATAATACTCCGGTAATATC

Sample 2: ATTCCGGTAATCCCGTAATGCCGGATAATACTCCGGTAATATC

The student cut between the C and G in each of the shaded CCGG sequences in sample 1 and between the As in each of the shaded TAAT sequences in sample 2. Both sets of fragments were then arranged on a paper model of a gel.

41. *a)* The action of what kind of molecules was being demonstrated when the DNA samples were cut?

_____

b) State one way the arrangement of the two samples on the gel model would be different.

_____

Base your answers to question 42 on the information and diagram below.

DNA samples were collected from four children. The accompanying diagram represents the results of a procedure that separated the DNA in each sample.

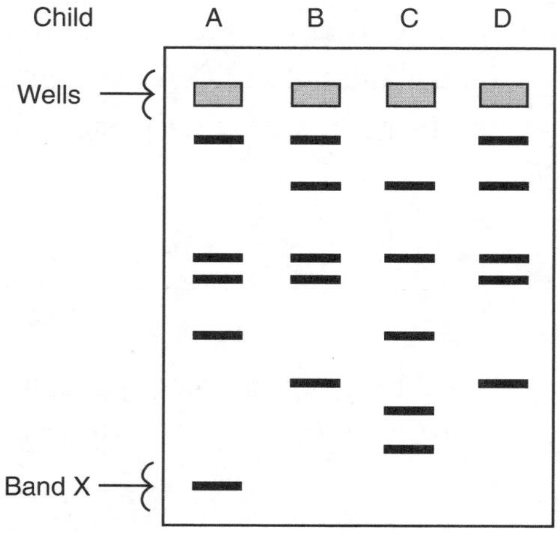

42. *a)* Identify the procedure used to obtain these results.

_____

b) Band *X* represents the
(1) largest fragment of DNA that traveled the fastest
(2) smallest fragment of DNA that traveled the fastest
(3) largest fragment of DNA that traveled the slowest
(4) smallest fragment of DNA that traveled the slowest

b _____

c) The DNA is most similar in which two children? _____ and _____

Support your answer._____

_____

d) State one way information obtained from this procedure can be used.

_____

e) Identify another substance other than DNA that can be analyzed by this technique.

_____

43. A sample of body cells and samples of sex cells received from four members of a species are screened for the presence of a specific gene mutation. The results of the gene-testing procedure conducted on the cells are shown in the table below.

Species Member Tested	Type of Cells Tested and the Result (+ = mutation present, – = mutation absent)		
	Body Cells	Sperm	Egg
1	+		+
2	+	+	
3	–		+
4	+	–	

Which species member would be unlikely to pass the gene mutation on to its offspring? _____

Explain your choice: _____

44. In the past, diabetics used horse or cow insulin to control their glucose levels. Today, as a result of genetic engineering, human insulin can be synthesized by bacteria. State one advantage for a person with diabetes to receive genetically engineered insulin rather than insulin taken from a horse or cow.

_____

45. A small village that is heavily infested with mosquitoes was sprayed with an insecticide once a week for several months. Changes in the size of the mosquito population are shown in the accompanying graph.

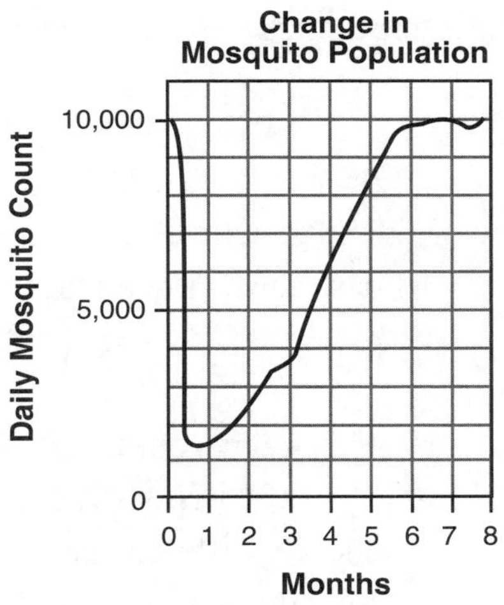

State one way that the population of mosquitoes present 7 months after spraying differs genetically from the population of mosquitoes present before the spraying began.

_____

_____

Base your answers to question 46 on the information below.

The sequences below represent the same portions of a DNA molecule from the same gene used by a student to study the relationship between two plant species. A biological catalyst that recognizes the CCGG site is used to cut the DNA molecules into pieces. The catalyst cuts the DNA between the C and G of the site.

46. *a)* Draw lines in the sequences below for species 1 and species 2 to show where the catalyst would cut the DNA.

Species 1: T A C C G G A T T A G T T A T G C C G G A T C G

Species 2: T A C G G A T G C C G G A T C G G A A A T T C G

b) Complete the data table below to show the results of the action of the catalyst.

Results of Catalyst Action

	Number of Cuts	Number of Resulting Pieces of DNA
Species 1		
Species 2		

c) Are the two species of plants closely related? _____

Support your answer._____

_____

47. An alteration of genetic information is shown below.

A-G-T-A-C-C-G-A-T → A-G-T-G-A-T

This type of alteration of the genetic information is an example of _____

48. Explain how using cloning to produce a single crop could actually lead to a loss of the entire crop.

_____

1. 2   The genetic code for all living things is found within the molecular bases of DNA. Each molecular base forms a sequence that can code for a particular protein. These proteins will be made during the process of protein synthesis.

2. 3   Many environmental factors can influence whether a gene is read (transcribed and translated). Identical twins, whose DNA is identical, may show variance in height, weight, intelligence, etc., due to differences in gene expression resulting from environmental differences, such as diet and education.

3. 4   The process of choosing animals with desirable characteristics or traits for breeding purposes is called selective breeding. This process is used to produce not only dog breeds but many desirable agricultural animals and plants.

4. 3   By recombining genes through fertilization, new combinations of genetic information can occur. These new gene combinations may result in genetic variation and may be inherited through gametes during sexual reproduction.

5. 1   During the process of meiosis, crossing over can lead to a chromosomal change. This process can lead to new variations through different genetic combinations found in the offspring.

6. 4   Genetically engineered insulin is produced as a result of the human insulin gene being inserted into circular rings of DNA within the bacteria. The bacteria then reads this inserted DNA and produces human insulin. The insulin produced is much less likely to produce side effects because it is genetically human based.

7. 1   Cloning is the production of identical organisms from one cell. By removing a cell from a mature plant and promoting growth of the cell into mature plants, the process of cloning can be achieved.

8. 3   Within a cell's nucleus are found thin strands of genetic material known as chromosomes. These chromosomes are composed of many smaller segments known as genes.

9. 1   This molecule represents a double helix of DNA. The patterned number sequences represent paired molecular bases (A-T, C-G). The patterns or sequences of these bases set up the genetic code for all living things.

10. 1   In asexual reproducing organisms, hereditary information is passed from a parent organism to resulting offspring through DNA. DNA consists of coded instructions using sequences of 4 molecular bases – A,T,C, and G. The sequence of these four bases determines the structure of proteins in new organisms.

11. 1   Meiosis is the process which allows for the production of sperm and egg. During this process, the chromosome number reduces to half that of the original body cell amount. When the genetic information found in the chromosomes of the sperm and the egg unite during fertilization, the original chromosome number is restored in the next generation.

12. 1   The process of genetic engineering allows for the transfer of a section of DNA encoded for a specific protein into another cell, usually a bacteria. Upon insertion, this section of DNA is now part of the bacterial DNA. When the bacteria reproduces (asexually), it will produce new bacteria with exact copies of DNA found in parent cell. The new cells will be able to produce the protein coded for by the inserted section of DNA, in this case insulin.

13. 1   A change in base unit sequence (like TAA → TAC) will lead to a change in the DNA and may alter proteins. These alterations or mutations can lead to genetic variation.

14. 2   Genes can be "turned on" so that particular genetic traits can be expressed. Environmental factors can trigger this expression of genes. In plants, the environmental factor of light triggers production of chlorophyll.

15. 2   Within a cell, protein synthesis occurs when coded genetic information is copied and transferred from nucleus to ribosomes. In the ribosomes, amino acids are assembled, based on the copied code, into particular sequences that make up a specific protein. This would not occur if the ribosomes were damaged or destroyed.

16. 1   Asexual reproduction produces offspring that are genetically identical to the parent. This is accomplished by various types of cell divisions where the chromosomes in offspring are exact copies of the parent. Therefore, under normal circumstances, there would be no genetic variations.

17. 3   The sequence of molecular bases in DNA code for specific amino acids. When the genetic code is changed, it will change the sequence of amino acids that are linked together to form a protein. Therefore, a change in DNA could lead to a change in a respiratory protein.

18. 4   In sexual reproduction, when a change or alteration occurs in the egg or sperm, and if fertilization occurs, the change will be expressed as a new trait within the offspring of that species.

19. 2   During genetic engineering, the insertion of a gene into another organism or into another organism's DNA is aided by the action of specific enzymes that join two segments of DNA together with the portion of the inserted gene at a particular location.

20. 2   During this procedure, known as gel electrophoresis, DNA fragments that are positioned in the wells are moved through a gel using electric currents. The smallest fragments travel the farthest and fastest; this would be the DNA fragment band X.

21. 3   Inheritable characteristics must be passed through sex cells known as gametes. When a change or alteration occurs in genes passed on by the gametes, these alterations will be expressed as new characteristics within the offspring of that species.

22. 3   Meiosis produces gametes or sex cells that contain only half the amount of genetic information as the parent. When combined at fertilization, these two half amounts of genetic material (chromosomes) will restore the original chromosome number for that species, but contain different combinations of genetic information.

23. 3   The reproductive cells represented in this diagram are sperm cells. Sperm cells are produced by a division process known as meiosis where the resulting cells contain half the chromosome number as the parent cell. When fertilization takes place, the sperm will provide half the genetic material, and the egg will provide the other half.

24. 2   Inheritance of a mutation must take place through a change in the DNA in a sex cell or gamete. A DNA base substitution in gametes that occurred during meiosis would be carried to the offspring by that gamete. All other choices relate to types of body cells that do not take part in reproduction or inheritance of genes.

25. 4   During asexual reproduction, genetic information from the parent cell (*A*) is passed to daughter cells (*B* and *C*) through mitosis. The genes for protein *X* were present in cell *A*, and when mitosis occurred, the gene for protein *X* got passed to each new cell *B* and *C*.

26. 1   Letter X represents the four molecular bases (A,T,C,G) that form different sequences known as genes. These genes are found within the DNA of chromosomes. Chromosomes are located in the nucleus of a cell.

27. 2   In order for a mutation to be passed from parent to offspring, the change must occur in the gametes or sex cells of the parent. The mismatched DNA (a mutation) found in a sperm or egg would be transferred from parent to offspring. All other choices relate to types of body cells that do not take part in reproduction or inheritance of genes.

28. Answer: Offspring are not identical to either parent because they receive:
    genetic material from each parent   *or*   half of their genes or DNA
    or chromosomes from each parent *or*   genetic information from each parent

    Explanation: The recombination of genetic information that occurs during fertilization of egg by sperm leads to variation and explains why offspring resemble but are not identical to either parent. Each sex cell has genetic material from one parent.

29. Answer: 30%

    Explanation: In a DNA sequence, C is linked with G and A is linked with T. Therefore, C and G must constitute 40% of the sample (20%+20%). The remaining 60% must be A and T, of which A will be 30%.

30. Answer: Largest   nucleus
                 ↓   chromosome
              Smallest   gene

    Explanation: See answer for question #26.

31. *a)* Answer: 3

Explanation: Based on the information presented in the chart, we can convert the DNA base sequence given into its representative amino acids. Amino acids are coded using a group of three molecular bases known as a codon. Taking the first three bases of the given code, CAA, and using the chart, one can determine that CAA codes for valine (Val). The second group of three bases, GTT, codes for glutamine (Glu), and continuning with the rest of the base code sequence, leads to a chain of amino acids (Val –Glu –Phe – Asp – Asp – Thr).

b) Answer: ultraviolet light *or* radiation *or* x-rays *or* chemicals.

Explanation: All of the above are considered environmental mutagenic agents. Mutagenic agents have the ability to alter the base sequence in the DNA code, leading to a mutation – a sudden change in the genetic code.

c) Acceptable responses include but are not limited to: The amino acid sequence would be changed. *or* The protein would contain threonine instead of proline. *or* The shape of the protein would change. *or* The protein produced may not function properly or function at all.

Explanation: The base sequence of DNA determines what the identity of a protein is, its shape, and its function. If the original code or base sequence is altered, then the amino acid sequence will also be changed, and therefore the protein produced. If the protein is changed, its original shape and function may not be the same.

32. Answer: No

Supporting statement: Any mutation to skin cells will not be passed on to offspring. Gametes are the only cells responsible for the passing of genetic information. The mutation would have to occur to these sex cells in order to get passed to the offspring.

33. Acceptable responses include, but are not limited to:

a) Nondisjunction could have occurred. *or* A mutation might have taken place.
or The child may have inherited two recessive alleles (genes).
or A mutation or genetic change in a parent's DNA could be passed through a gamete or sex cell to the offspring during sexual reproduction and then be reflected in its genetic makeup.

Explanation: Both parents could carry the recessive gene, but it would not be expressed. If their child inherited this pair of recessive genes, that recessive disorder would then be fully expressed.

b) amniocentesis *or* karyotyping *or* blood screening *or* electrophoresis

Explanation: All of these processes involve the removal and analysis of genetic material. Through that analysis, geneticists can determine if a child may have inherited a genetic disorder.

c) Acceptable responses include, but are not limited to:
down syndrome *or* sickle-cell anemia *or* hemophilia (Other answers are possible.)

Explanation: Genetic disorders occur when a gene sequence is altered and the proteins that are normally coded for are not synthesized, leading to deficiencies. Disorders can also occur when there are irregular numbers of chromosomes due to nondisjunction – a failure of chromosomes to separate during meiosis.

34. Acceptable responses include, but are not limited to:

a) There would be no variation. *or* All would be identical genetic copies, unlike noncloned herds, where much genetic diversity would be present. *or* All sheep would be the same.

Explanation: Cloning is a process using biotechnology where the resulting offspring are genetically identical to the organism that donated its DNA to be cloned.

b) All sheep would have one or more desired trait that the original individual possessed.

Explanation: By choosing the donor DNA cell, farmers and researchers can clone organisms with desired genetic traits. All cloned organisms would have that trait.

c) Because all are the same, the entire flock could be lost if a disease to which they have no resistance were to infect them. *or* The sheep may have a genetic flaw. *or* shorter life span

Explanation: When there is no variation, the flock could be susceptible to a disease or illness, because they may lack a genetic variation that may allow them to fight that disease. The identical clones would all be affected by that disease or illness. This could result in death of the animals and monetary loss for the farmer.

d) They would all be the same sex, so they could not mate with each other.

Explanation: When sheep or cattle are cloned, the donor genetic material will determine what the sex of the clones will be. All clones will be the same gender as the donor, so sexual reproduction between cloned members would be impossible.

e) Both parents contribute genes to the offspring. *or* Different gene combinations will result.

Explanation: The unrelated sheep would have a different genetic makeup than that of the cloned sheep, so when an unrelated sheep and a cloned sheep reproduce, new genetic variations occur through the recombination of each animal's genetic material.

35. Answer: environmental factors

Explanation: The expression of genetic material can be influenced by outside factors such as the environment. These factors can "turn on" or "turn off" genes so that their information will be expressed or not expressed. Twins, while having the same genetic makeup, could express different characteristics if they were exposed to different factors. For example, if one twin is exposed to sunlight and the other gets no exposure, the twin with sun exposure will exhibit a darkening of the skin that the other twin will not.

36. a) Answer: gel electrophoresis

Explanation: Gel electrophoresis is a procedure in which samples of DNA are placed into wells situated in a thin layer of gel. An electrical current is passed through the gel separating the DNA fragments, causing them to migrate through the gel. This procedure has many applications including criminal/forensic work, evolutionary relationships, and even identification of bodies.

b) Answer: electrical current *or* attraction of negative DNA fragments to positive pole
or charges on DNA   *or*   DNA has negative charge

Explanation: The electrophoresis equipment has a negative and positive end. Electrical current is run through the gel creating this difference in charge. DNA with its negative charge will move from the negative end (wells) to the positive end.

c) Answer: bands in different positions in each column
or different banding patterns *or* different number of bands in columns

Explanation: Each individual has DNA that is unique and different from everyone else. When DNA is broken into fragments and runs through the gel, these different fragments create different patterns, with fragments moving to different positions for each individual.

d) Answer: Enzymes *or* restriction enzymes

Explanation: Enzymes, derived from bacteria, are used to cut sections of DNA at a specific site. Each enzyme has a particular point upon which it acts.

37. *a)* Frequency: The above average leg strength trait would increase in frequency.

Explanation: If rabbits with stronger legs can escape predators, they will be available to reproduce and pass that favorable leg trait on to their offspring. Rabbits without the stronger trait may be preyed upon more often and not be as reproductively successful. Over time, the successful stronger leg trait frequency will increase within a population.

b) Answer: These rabbits will start to decrease in numbers. *or* They will be eaten by predators.

Explanation: The rabbits without the leg strength trait will be preyed upon more easily and will decrease in number.

38. Answer: Plant species *A* cuts: 1   Plant species *B* cuts: 0

Explanation: Plant species *A* will be cut by the restriction enzyme once at the
recognized sequence: ACCGCAGGG/ATTCGC

Plant Species *B* does not contain the recognized sequence and
therefore will receive 0 cuts.

39. *a)* Answer: Adenine and Thymine are present in equal numbers.
or There is the same number of molecule.

Explanation: Adenine (*A*) and Thymine (*T*) are complimentary base pairs. Due to this pairing, the amount of each base in the pair would be equal.

b) Answer: The molecule Uracil (U) would replace the thymine (T) molecule in the chart.

Explanation: RNA molecules contain the molecular base Uracil (U), in place of Thymine (T), and would pair with Adenine (A). The chart numbers would remain unchanged as U and A are complimentary base pairs.

40. *a*) Where: nucleus
   Specific molecule: DNA – where the information is found
   or
   Where: chromosome
   Specific molecule: DNA

   Explanation: Genetic information, composed of DNA, is stored within the nucleus of cells, tightly coiled into chromosome structures for integrity. This organization allows for continuity in DNA replication and error-free transcription or copying of the DNA code into RNA for protein synthesis.

   b) Cellular structure: ribosomes
   Molecules: amino acids

   Explanation: Protein synthesis occurs in the cellular organelle known as the ribosome. During this process in the ribosome, amino acids are assembled into proteins. The original genetic code found in DNA will determine the sequence of the amino acid chain and ultimately, the structure and function of that protein.

41. *a*) Acceptable responses include, but are not limited to:
   genetic engineering *or* genetic recombination *or* genetic manipulation *or* gene splicing
   Note: No credit for biotechnology. It is a field of science, not a technique.

   Explanation: Genetic engineering is a process that allows for the manipulation or movement of DNA from one organism into another. DNA is commonly cut and inserted using enzymes specific to DNA.

   b) Acceptable responses include, but are not limited to: a segment of DNA that codes for a protein *or* Genes control traits. *or* Genes carry genetic information from one generation to the next.

   Explanation: A gene is a section of DNA that codes for an amino acid sequence which becomes a protein. That protein will have a specific structure and function based on the order of amino acids.

   c) Acceptable responses include, but are not limited to:
   enzyme *or* restriction enzyme *or* biological catalyst

   Explanation: Restriction enzymes cut DNA at specific locations. They are used to remove desirable genes from one organism as well as cut the DNA of another organism receiving that gene. They then allow for the insertion of the gene into the other organism.

   d) Acceptable responses include but are not limited to: make medicines for humans *or* increase the yield of crops *or* introduce new traits/characteristics into an organism *or* use plants to produce vaccines *or* produce needed hormones (chemicals) for humans

   Explanation: The insertion of desirable genes into other organisms allow for the production of medicines such as hormones, insulin, antibiotics and vaccines. Organisms such as plants can be genetically manipulated to have become resistant to disease, pests or severe environmental factors such as heat, cold or drought.

EVOLUTION

Overview:

Evolution is an ongoing process of change in species over time. These changes have their origin in genetics. When changes in genes occur, the result is variation, which is the basis for evolution. Evolution within a species can include changes in structure, function, or even behavior over a period of time. A widely held mechanism for evolution involves a process known as *natural selection*. Natural selection is a process where certain organisms are selected based on their favorable genetic makeup. These organisms pass those successful genes on to future generations, ultimately changing the species. Evidence from fossils, anatomy, and biochemistry supports the concept of evolutionary change.

Essential Information:

Evolution Evidence – According to the basic evolutionary theory, species that exist on present day Earth evolved from earlier species that may have been distinctly different. Various types of evidence support this theory of change. The *fossil record* provides support that earlier species changed structurally into modern day species. Scientists have been able to piece together the history of a species by examining fossil evidence in successive layers of undisturbed *sedimentary rock*. By examining *vertebrate anatomy*, such as bone structures and embryo features, scientists have been able to conclude that certain species have a common ancestry based on shared characteristics. Scientists have used *biochemical similarities* in proteins and DNA to link species together and understand their evolutionary relationships and ancestry. Using biotechnology methods, such as *gel electrophoresis* and *DNA sequencing*, scientists can examine different species' DNA for common sequences. The more shared DNA sequences, the more closely related the species. Through various types of evidence, evolutionists have a more complete picture of the changes that occurred to species over time and the relationships that those species share.

Natural Selection – The most widely held mechanism for evolution is the process of natural selection. The concept of natural selection was developed by Charles Darwin through his visits to the Galapagos Islands and his study of variation among finch beaks, as well as other variations in animal species. The process is based on the concept that environments on Earth change. When changes occur, there may be fewer or different resources available for species to use. Because of this, species will either adapt or possibly become extinct. When resources are available, species' population numbers will increase until a point where *competition* occurs for those resources. Certain individuals with more desirable traits, will be more successful and their frequency will increase in population.

Within a population, there exists *genetic variation*. These variations may occur through several sources. *Mutations* occur when a gene sequence is suddenly changed. These changes may occur as a result of agents such as harmful chemicals or *radiation*. During sexual reproduction, *recombination* or *crossing over* can also lead to new variations of genetic information. These variations may be slight modifications of a structure, process, or behavior that allow for those individuals to be better competitors for *available resources* or be able to avoid predation successfully. This is sometimes called *survival of the fittest*. Variation is an important factor that ensures that at least some of the individuals within a species may survive when conditions are not favorable. Those that survive will continue to reproduce, passing that successful genetic variation on to their offspring. Over time, the genetic makeup of the population may change to reflect those successful variations. The percentage of individuals with the desirable variation will increase. Individuals with a genetic makeup that prevents them from competing will diminish in numbers and they may eventually become *extinct*. Most species that have lived on Earth are now extinct. As one can see, natural selection allows for a changing environment where individual members of populations that have successful genetic variations are selected for survival.

Modern Applications of Natural Selection – Antibiotic resistance in bacteria or insecticide resistance in insects occurs when a variation within the genetic makeup of an organism allows that organism to survive exposure to those chemicals. That organism passes that gene on to future generations and eventually a population becomes resistant to that chemical. The term "superbug" is a microbe that is resistant to the effects of medication previously used to treat that microbe.

Evolutionary Model – Scientists believe that life on Earth began with simple *unicellular* organisms. Billions of years later, today's complex multi-cellular organisms have evolved. To help explain what evolution looks like, scientists have suggested a *evolutionary model* that somewhat resembles the look of a tree. At the base of the tree are the simpler, less complex organisms from which modern day life evolved. As variation occurred and new, more complex life forms developed, branching began to occur, leading to new and different species. Some branches extend to the present, and species at the end of those branches exist today. Some branches do not reach present day, and those species have died out becoming extinct. Species that have had relatively minor changes throughout their existence will be represented by a single branch that extends to the present time. Species that are found on the same branches are more closely related than those on separate branches, as evidenced by their related DNA base sequences. The rate of reproduction may also influence how rapidly species can change and the number of branches that exist. Organisms with a short *reproductive cycle*, such as bacteria, have the capacity to develop many more evolutionary changes than those organisms with longer reproductive cycles. Thus, those rapidly reproducing species will have more branches in their part of the evolutionary model.

Additional Information:

- Variations in color can be a distinct advantage when avoiding predation. For example, changes in fur color in the pocket mouse has allowed the mouse to successfully adapt to geologic changes in its habitat and avoid predation by hawks in the southwest United States.

- Anole lizards have successfully adapted to specific niches in Puerto Rico based on the type and length of their legs allowing them to successfully navigate vegetative levels within their tropical habitat.

- As biotechnology continues to develop, more evidence is provided to create a clearer and more accurate picture of evolutionary relationships.

- The evolution theory is still a theory, and there exist other views/theories that conflict with evolution and deserve credence.

Diagrams:

1. **Evolutionary Model** – This model shows that evolution involves changes that give rise to a variety of organisms, some of which continue to change through time, while others die out. In this evolutionary model, all organisms have a common ancestral linkage to *A*. Organisms *F*, *I*, *H*, and *G* are still alive. Of these, *F* and *I* are most closely related and would have the most similar DNA base sequences. Organism *J* had insufficient adaptive characteristics for survival in a changing environment, thus became extinct.

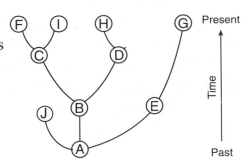

2. **Vertebrate Anatomy** – Vertebrate anatomy is often used to conclude common evolutionary linkage of organisms. In this diagram, bones of forearms of two animals that are alive today are so similar they most likely evolved from a common ancestor. Members of the original ancestral population may have been separated by natural events. Over time, changes to the forearms contribute to the survival of the organism in its new environment.

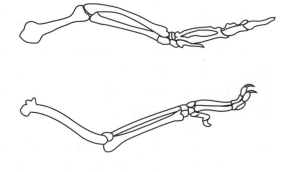

3. **Variation** – Variation within a species is important to the survival of that species, especially when conditions are not favorable. Species *A* has the best chance of survival because it has the most genetic diversity. Species C has the least chance of survival, as it lacks genetic diversity. Genetic diversity provides for the chance that a trait might help an organism adapt and survive a change in its environment.

Species A	Species B	Species C	Species D

4. **Variation of Finch's Beaks** – Darwin, through his visits to the Galapagos Islands, studied the variation in organisms on these islands, especially the variation in the beaks of finches. From his observations and research, he proposed the theory of natural selection.

5. **Links to a Common Ancestor** – Although variation exists within the many species of finches, each type of finch shares a common ancestor with the others. Different environments and food sources lead to natural selection and the development of many new species.

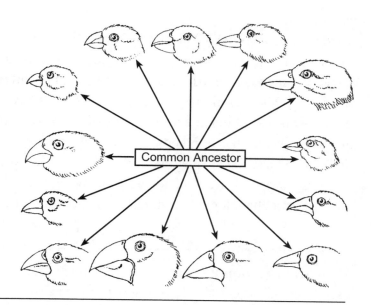

6. **Amino Acids and Biochemical Similarities** – Biochemical similarities in proteins and amino acids are used to link species together to understand their evolutionary relationships and ancestry. In this chart, amino acids sequences are being compared. The more shared amino acids sequences, the more closely related the species are to each other.

Species	Sequence of Four Amino Acids Found in the Same Part of the Hemoglobin Molecule of Species
human	Lys–Glu–His–Phe
horse	Arg–Lys–His–Lys
gorilla	Lys–Glu–His–Lys
chimpanzee	Lys–Glu–His–Phe
zebra	Arg–Lys–His–Arg

7. **Banding Pattern in Gel Electrophoresis** – This diagram represents the results of gel electrophoresis, where DNA fragments are moved through a gel creating a banding pattern. In this case, evolutionary relationships can be determined by comparing the banding pattern for species *A*, *B* and *C*. Species *A* and *C* are more closely related because they share more common bands with each other compared to species *B*.

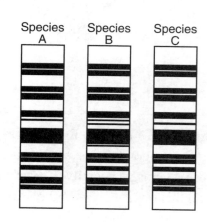

Evolution

Vocabulary Refresher

Group A   *Directions* - Match the correct definition for the following terms:

1. _____Natural selection

2. _____Vertebrate anatomy

3. _____Common ancestry

4. _____DNA sequencing

5. _____Genetic variation

6. _____Available resources

7. _____Gel electrophoresis

8. _____Fossil record

9. _____Biochemical similarities

10. _____Crossing over

11. _____Survival of the fittest

A. Different sets of genes that are expressed as different forms of a trait within a population.

B. A process where molecular base sequences of an individual's genetic code is determined.

C. Organisms having similar genetic traits that can be traced back to a shared ancestor.

D. A natural process where organisms that are best adapted to their environment survive and pass those favorable traits to the next generation.

E. Evidence found in sedimentary rocks that shows the existence and changes that have occurred within populations of organisms.

F. Having common sequences of DNA, amino acids, or common proteins or even sharing chemical processes.

G. Obtainable nutrients and materials that are essential for organisms to survive.

H. The term given when variations occur that allow for individuals to be better competitors for available resources and survive as of a result of this.

I. A biotechnology process that uses the movement of fragments of DNA to determine evolutionary or genetic relationships.

J. Physical features, such as bone structure, used to compare animals with backbones for evolutionary relationships.

K. The trading of sections of two homologous chromosomes during meiosis which leads to variation.

Group B *Directions* - Match the correct definition for the following terms:

1. _____Radiation

2. _____Extinct

3. _____Unicellular organisms

4. _____Evolution model

5. _____Reproductive cycles

6. _____Species

7. _____Evolution

8. _____Mutations

9. _____Recombination

10. _____Competition

A. A model containing branches coming from common ancestors that show the relationship between ancestral and modern day species.

B. The amount of time between reproduction in one generation and reproduction in the next generation.

C. Sudden changes within the genetic code or DNA that may contribute to evolutionary differences.

D. This occurs when individuals or populations go after the same food, space or mates.

E. These single cell organisms that have rapid reproductive cycles are more likely to exhibit genetic diversity among the offspring in a short period of time.

F. High energy waves or particles that can damage DNA molecules, which may lead to mutations.

G. A group of individuals that are able to interbreed and produce viable offspring.

H. A slow process of change in species, populations, or individuals across successive generations.

I. A species that could not successfully adapt to a changing environment or lacked needed variations for survival and died out.

J. The joining of genetic information from each gamete (sperm and egg), resulting in genetic variation.

Evolution

1. Natural selection and its evolutionary consequences provide a scientific explanation for each of the following except

   (1) the fossil record
   (2) protein and DNA similarities between different organisms
   (3) similar structures among different organisms
   (4) a stable physical environment   1 _____

2. Which statement represents the major concept of the biological theory of evolution?

   (1) A new species moves into a habitat when another species becomes extinct.
   (2) Every period of time in Earth's history has its own group of organisms.
   (3) Present-day organisms on Earth developed from earlier, distinctly different organisms.
   (4) Every location on Earth's surface has its own unique group of organisms.
                                           2 _____

3. Which situation would most likely result in the highest rate of natural selection?

   (1) reproduction of organisms by an asexual method in an unchanging environment
   (2) reproduction of a species having a very low mutation rate in a changing environment
   (3) reproduction of organisms in an unchanging environment with little competition and few predators
   (4) reproduction of organisms exhibiting genetic differences due to mutations and genetic recombinations in a changing environment   3 _____

4. Some behaviors such as mating and caring for young are genetically determined in certain species of birds. The presence of these behaviors is most likely due to the fact that

   (1) birds do not have the ability to learn
   (2) individual birds need to learn to survive and reproduce
   (3) these behaviors helped birds to survive in the past
   (4) within their lifetimes, birds developed these behaviors   4 _____

5. Which statement is not part of the concept of natural selection?

   (1) Individuals that possess the most favorable variations will have the best chance of reproducing.
   (2) Variation occurs among individuals in a population.
   (3) More individuals are produced than will survive.
   (4) Genes of an individual adapt to a changing environment.   5 _____

6. The diagrams how the bones in the forelimbs of three different organisms.

   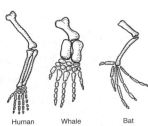

   Human   Whale   Bat

   Differences in the bone arrangements support the hypothesis that these organisms

   (1) are members of the same species
   (2) may have descended from the same ancestor
   (3) have adaptations to survive in different environments
   (4) all contain the same genetic information   6 _____

7. Which population of organisms would be in greatest danger of becoming extinct?

(1) A population of organisms having few variations living in a stable environment.
(2) A population of organisms having few variations living in an unstable environment.
(3) A population of organisms having many variations living in a stable environment.
(4) A population of organisms having many variations living in an unstable environment. 7 _____

8. The relationship of some mammals is indicated in the diagram below.

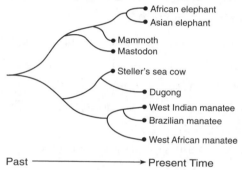

Which statement about the African elephant is correct?

(1) It is more closely related to the mammoth than it is to the West African manatee.
(2) It is more closely related to the West Indian manatee than it is to the mastodon.
(3) It is not related to the Brazilian manatee or the mammoth.
(4) It is the ancestor of Steller's sea cow. 8 _____

9. Which factor contributed most to the extinction of many species?

(1) changes in the environment
(2) lethal mutations
(3) inability to evolve into simple organisms
(4) changes in migration patterns 9 _____

10. A characteristic that an organism exhibits during its lifetime will only affect the evolution of its species if the characteristic

(1) results from isolation of the organism from the rest of the population
(2) is due to a genetic code that is present in the gametes of the organism
(3) decreases the number of genes in the body cells of the organism
(4) causes a change in the environment surrounding the organism 10 _____

11. Which statement best explains the significance of meiosis in the process of evolution within a species?

(1) The gametes produced by meiosis ensure the continuation of any particular species by asexual reproduction.
(2) Equal numbers of eggs and sperm are produced by meiosis.
(3) Meiosis produces eggs and sperm that are alike.
(4) Meiosis provides for variation in the gametes produced by an organism. 11 _____

12. Over time, data that support the successful evolution of a species would include observations that describe

(1) an increase in the genetic changes occurring in body cells
(2) a decrease in the genetic variety carried in sex cells
(3) an increase in the proportion of offspring that have favorable characteristics
(4) a decrease in the proportion of the population that has beneficial traits 12 _____

13. Which two processes result in variations that commonly influence the evolution of sexually reproducing species?

    (1) mutation and genetic recombination
    (2) mitosis and natural selection
    (3) extinction and gene replacement
    (4) environmental selection and selective breeding   13_____

14. The percent of DNA that species *A* has in common with species *B*, *C*, *D*, and *E* are shown in the graph below.

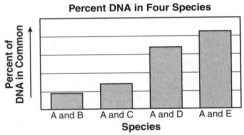

Percent DNA in Four Species

Which statement is a valid conclusion that can be drawn from this graph?

    (1) Species *A* is closely related to species *B*, but is not related to species *E*.
    (2) Fewer mutations have occurred in species *B* and *C* than in species *A*.
    (3) Species *A* and *E* have the greatest similarity in protein structure.
    (4) Environment influences the rate of evolution.   14_____

15. Woolly mammoths became extinct thousands of years ago, while other species of mammals that existed at that time still exist today. These other species of mammals most likely exist today because, unlike the mammoths, they

    (1) produced offspring that all had identical inheritable characteristics
    (2) did not face a struggle for survival
    (3) learned to migrate to new environments
    (4) had certain inheritable traits that enabled them to survive   15_____

16. Natural selection is best described as

    (1) a change in an organism in response to a need of that organism
    (2) a process of nearly constant improvement that leads to an organism that is nearly perfect
    (3) differences in survival rates as a result of different inherited characteristics
    (4) inheritance of characteristics acquired during the life of an organism   16_____

17. What will most likely occur as a result of changes in the frequency of a gene in a particular population?

    (1) ecological succession
    (2) biological evolution
    (3) global warming
    (4) resource depletion   17_____

18. Some evolutionary pathways are represented in the diagram below.

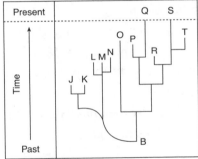

An inference that can be made from information in the diagram is that

    (1) many of the descendants of organism *B* became extinct
    (2) organism *B* was probably much larger than any of the other organisms represented
    (3) most of the descendants of organism *B* successfully adapted to their environment and have survived to the present time
    (4) the letters above organism *B* represent members of a single large population with much biodiversity   18_____

19. Which species in the chart below is most likely to have the fastest rate of evolution?

Species	Reproductive Rate	Environment
A	slow	stable
B	slow	changing
C	fast	stable
D	fast	changing

(1) A   (3) C

(2) B   (4) D   19_____

20. What is the most probable reason for the increase in the percentage of variety A in the population of the species shown in the graph below?

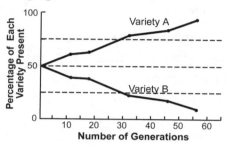

(1) There is no chance for variety A to mate with variety B.

(2) There is no genetic difference between variety A and variety B.

(3) Variety A is less fit to survive than variety B is.

(4) Variety A has some adaptive advantage that variety B does not have.

20_____

21. Which statement provides evidence that evolution is still occurring at the present time?

(1) The extinction rate of species has decreased in the last 50 years.

(2) Many bird species and some butterfly species make annual migrations.

(3) New varieties of plant species appear more frequently in regions undergoing climatic change.

(4) Through cloning, the genetic makeup of organisms can be predicted.

21_____

22. Which process is correctly matched with its explanation?

	Process	Explanation
(1)	extinction	adaptive characteristics of a species are not adequate
(2)	natural selection	the most complex organisms survive
(3)	gene recombination	genes are copied as a part of mitosis
(4)	mutation	overproduction of offspring takes place within a certain population

22_____

23. The table below shows adaptations in two organisms.

Environmental Adaptations

Organism	Environment	Adaptation
desert rat	hot and dry	comes out of burrow only at night
Arctic poppy plant	cold and windy	grows low to ground next to rocks

The presence of these adaptations is most likely the result of

(1) reproductive technology   (3) asexual reproduction

(2) natural selection   (4) human interference   23_____

Base your answers to question 24 on the diagram. Letters *A* through *L* represent different species of organisms. The arrows represent long periods of geologic time.

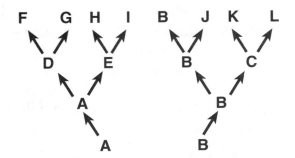

24. *a)* Which two species are the most closely related?

(1) *J* and *L*   (3) *F* and *H*

(2) *G* and *L*   (4) *F* and *G*   a _____

b) Which species was best adapted to changes that occurred in its environment over the longest period of time?

(1) *A*   (2) *B*   (3) *C*   (4) *J*   b_____

c) Which two species would most likely show the greatest similarity of DNA and proteins?

(1) *B* and *J*   (2) *G* and *I*   (3) *J* and *K*   (4) *F* and *L*   c_____

d) The pattern of these evolutionary pathways is most likely the result of alterations within which structure?

(1) vacuole   (2) cell membrane   (3) nucleus   (4) ribosome   d_____

Base your answers to question 25 on the information below.

Evolutionary changes have been observed in beak size in a population of medium ground finches in the Galapagos Islands. Given a choice of small and large seeds, the medium ground finch eats mostly small seeds, which are easier to crush. However, during dry years, all seeds are in short supply. Small seeds are quickly consumed, so the birds are left with a diet of large seeds. Studies have shown that this change in diet may be related to an increase in the average size of the beak of the medium ground finch.

25. *a)* The most likely explanation for the increase in average beak size of the medium ground finch is that the

(1) trait is inherited and birds with larger beaks have greater reproductive success
(2) birds acquired larger beaks due to the added exercise of feeding on large seeds
(3) birds interbred with a larger-beaked species and passed on the trait
(4) lack of small seeds caused a mutation which resulted in a larger beak   a _____

b) In exceptionally dry years, what most likely happens in a population of medium ground finches?

(1) There is increased cooperation between the birds.
(2) Birds with large beaks prey on birds with small beaks.
(3) The finches develop parasitic relationships with mammals.
(4) There is increased competition for a limited number of small seeds.   b _____

26. When Charles Darwin traveled to the Galapagos Islands, he observed 14 distinct varieties of finches on the islands. Darwin also observed that each finch variety ate a different type of food and lived in a slightly different habitat from the other finches. Darwin concluded that the finches all shared a common ancestor but had developed different beak structures.

The 14 varieties of finches are most likely the result of

(1) absence of biodiversity

(3) asexual reproduction

(2) biological evolution

(4) lack of competition

26_____

Base your answers to question 27 on the information below and on your knowledge of biology.

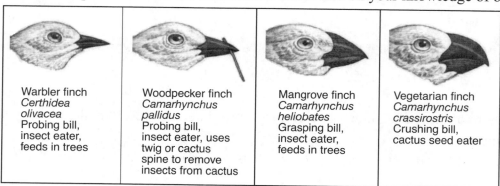

Source: http://taggart.glg.msu.edu/isb200/beagle.htm

27. *a)* The differences seen in the beaks of the four species of finches are most likely the result of

(1) gene expression and asexual reproduction

(3) migration and the need to adapt

(2) variation and natural selection

(4) heredity and a diet of seeds

a _____

b) A person expressed concern that the vegetarian finch may face greater competition when other finch populations increase. State whether the vegetarian finch will face competition if the populations of warbler finches, woodpecker finches, and mangrove finches increase. Support your answer.

Answer:_____

Supporting Statement:_____

28. The diagram represents possible evolutionary relationships between groups of organisms.

Which statement is a valid conclusion that can be drawn from the diagram?

(1) Snails appeared on Earth before corals.

(2) Sponges were the last new species to appear on Earth.

(3) Earthworms and sea stars have a common ancestor.

(4) Insects are more complex than mammals.

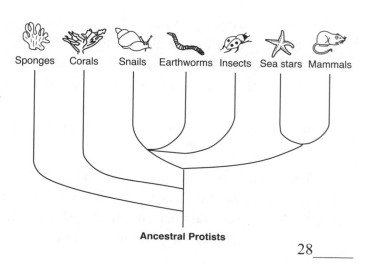

28_____

Base your answers to question 29 on the information below.

A plant known as caltrop is found on one of the Galapagos Islands. The caltrop plant produces seeds with tough, spiny coats. There is a bird species, *Geospiza fortis*, that can crack the tough seed coat and eat the contents inside. On one part of the island where there are many of these birds, the caltrop plants produce fewer seeds and the coats of the seeds have longer and more numerous spines. On another part of the island where there are few of these birds, the plants produce more seeds and the seed coats have fewer, shorter spines.

29. *a)* Identify one variation the caltrop seeds have for survival. _____

  b) Identify one process that can result in adaptations. _____

  c) Identify *one* adaptation, other than beak size and shape, a finch species might possess and state how that would aid in its survival.

  Adaptation: _____ Aid in survival: _____

30. The data table shows the number of amino acid differences in the hemoglobin molecules of several species compared with amino acids in the hemoglobin of humans.

Based on the information in the data table, write the names of the organisms from the table in their correct positions on the evolutionary tree below.

Amino Acid Differences

Species	Number of Amino Acid Differences
human	0
frog	67
pig	10
gorilla	1
horse	26

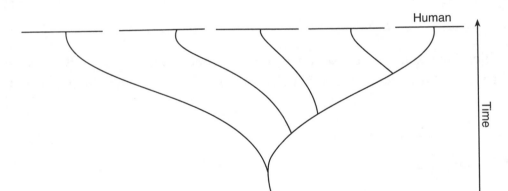

31. The evolutionary pathways of several species are represented in the accompanying diagram.

Which species was best adapted for survival in changing environmental conditions? Give a supporting statement for your answer.

Species: _____

Supporting statement:

_____

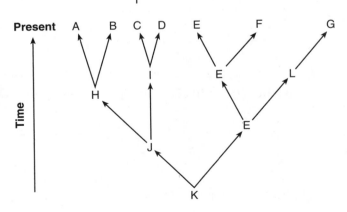

Base your answers to question 32 on the diagram that shows variations in the beaks of finches in the Galapagos Islands.

32. *a)* The diversity of species seen on the Galapagos Islands is mostly due to

(1) gene manipulation by scientists
(2) gene changes resulting from mitotic cell division
(3) natural selection
(4) selective breeding   a ____

b) Warbler finches are classified as

(1) producers
(2) herbivores
(3) carnivores
(4) decomposers   b ____

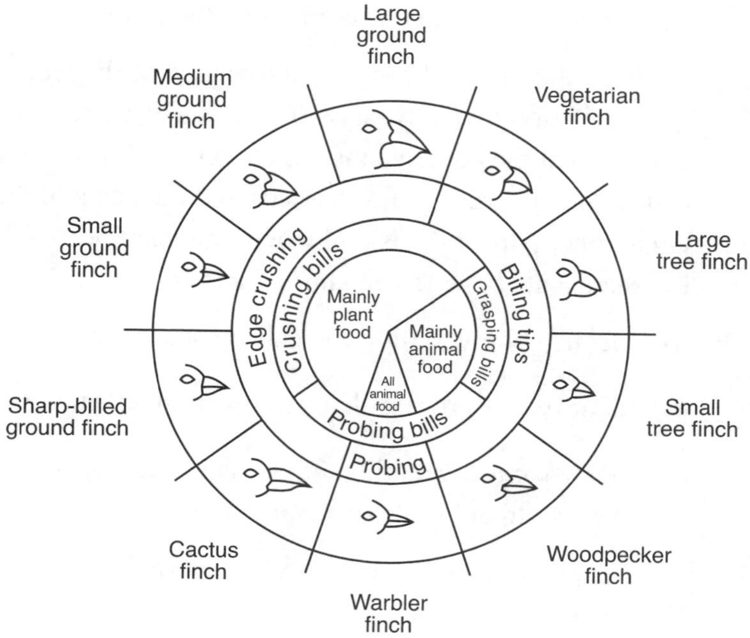

From: *Galapagos: A Natural History Guide*

c) Finches that eat mainly plant food are given what classification?_____

d) State one reason why large ground finches and large tree finches can coexist on the same island.

_____

_____

e) The cactus finch, warbler finch, and woodpecker finch all live on one island. Based on the information in the diagram, which one of these finches is least likely to compete with the other two for food?

Answer: _____

Support your answer with an explanation.

_____

_____

f) How would the introduction of another species of seed-eating ground finch to the Galapagos Islands most likely influence the medium ground finch?

_____

_____

g) Identify the term that describes the ecological role each finch performs within the Galapagos Islands.

_____

Base your answers to question 33 on the information below.

Scientists attempted to determine the evolutionary relationships between three different plant species, *A*, *B*, and *C*. In order to do this, they examined the stems and DNA of these species. Diagram 1 represents a microscopic view of the cross sections of the stems of these three species. DNA was extracted from all three species and analyzed using gel electrophoresis. The results are shown in diagram 2. Based on the data they collected, they drew diagram 3 to represent the possible evolutionary relationships.

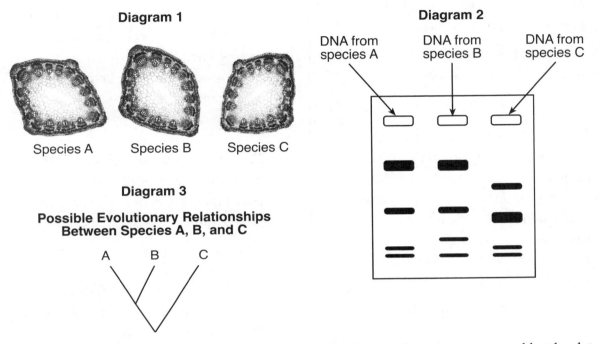

Diagram 1

Species A   Species B   Species C

Diagram 2

DNA from species A   DNA from species B   DNA from species C

Diagram 3

Possible Evolutionary Relationships Between Species A, B, and C

A   B   C

33. *a)* State why the evolutionary relationships shown in diagram 3 are not supported by the data provided by the stem cross sections in diagram 1.

_____

_____

b) Explain how the DNA banding pattern in diagram 2 supports the evolutionary relationships between the species shown in diagram 3.

_____

c) This technique used to analyze DNA involves the

(1) synthesis of new DNA strands from subunits
(2) separation of DNA fragments on the basis of size
(3) production of genetically engineered DNA molecules
(4) removal of defective genes from DNA

c _____

Set 1 – Evolution   **Page 77**

1. A certain plant species, found only in one particular stream valley in the world, has a very shallow root system. An earthquake causes the stream to change its course so that the valley in which the plant species lives becomes very dry. As a result, the species dies out completely. The effect of this change on this plant species is known as

   (1) evolution   (3) mutation
   (2) extinction   (4) succession   1 _____

2. Scientists in the United States, Europe, and Africa have now suggested that the hippopotamus is a relative of the whale. Earlier studies placed the hippo as a close relative of wild pigs, but recent studies have discovered stronger evidence for the connection to whales. This information suggests that

   (1) genetic engineering was involved in the earlier theories
   (2) structural evidence is the best evolutionary factor to consider
   (3) natural selection does not occur in hippopotamuses
   (4) scientific explanations are tentative and subject to change   2 _____

3. Exposure to cosmic rays, x rays, ultraviolet rays, and radiation from radioactive substances may promote

   (1) the production of similar organisms
   (2) diversity among organisms
   (3) an increase in population size
   (4) a change from sexual to asexual reproduction   3 _____

4. A species in a changing environment would have the best chance of survival as a result of a mutation that has a

   (1) high adaptive value and occurs in its skin cells
   (2) low adaptive value and occurs in its skin cells
   (3) high adaptive value and occurs in its gametes
   (4) low adaptive value and occurs in its gametes   4 _____

5. Certain antibacterial soaps kill 99% of the bacteria present on hands. Constant use of these soaps could be harmful over time because

   (1) more pathogens may be resistant to the soap
   (2) microbes prevent viral diseases
   (3) large populations of pathogens are beneficial to the hands
   (4) the soap stimulates skin cell division   5 _____

6. In 2007, scientists broke open a fossil of a dinosaur bone and found some preserved tissues. Analysis showed that some proteins in these tissues are very similar to proteins found in modern chickens. The conclusion that these dinosaurs are related to modern chickens is based on

   (1) molecular similarities
   (2) natural selection
   (3) similarities in behavior
   (4) the occurrence of mutations   6 _____

7. Thousands of years ago, giraffes with short necks were common within giraffe populations. Nearly all giraffe populations today have long necks. This difference could be due to

(1) giraffes stretching their necks to keep their heads out of reach of predators
(2) giraffes stretching their necks so they could reach food higher in the trees
(3) a mutation in genetic material controlling neck size occurring in some skin cells of a giraffe
(4) a mutation in genetic material controlling neck size occurring in the reproductive cells of a giraffe   7 _____

8. Which statement is most closely related to the modern theory of evolution?

(1) Characteristics that are acquired during life are passed to offspring by sexual reproduction.
(2) Evolution is the result of mutations and recombination, only.
(3) Organisms best adapted to a changed environment are more likely to reproduce and pass their genes to offspring.
(4) Asexual reproduction increases the survival of species.   8 _____

9. To determine evolutionary relationships between organisms, a comparison would most likely be made between all of the characteristics below except

(1) methods of reproduction
(2) number of their ATP molecules
(3) sequences in their DNA molecules
(4) structure of protein molecules present
9 _____

10. The diagram below represents a process involved in reproduction in some organisms.

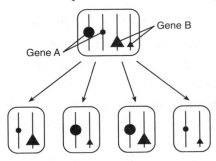

This process is considered a mechanism of evolution because
(1) mitosis produces new combinations of inheritable traits
(2) it increases the chances of DNA alterations in the parent
(3) it is a source of variation in the offspring produced
(4) meiosis prevents recombination of lethal mutations   10 _____

11. The first life-forms to appear on Earth were most likely

(1) complex single-celled organisms
(2) complex multicellular organisms
(3) simple single-celled organisms
(4) simple multicellular organisms
11 _____

12. The teeth of carnivores are pointed and are good for puncturing and ripping flesh. The teeth of herbivores are flat and are good for grinding and chewing. Which statement best explains these observations?

(1) Herbivores have evolved from carnivores.
(2) Carnivores have evolved from herbivores.
(3) The two types of teeth most likely evolved as a result of natural selection.
(4) The two types of teeth most likely evolved as a result of the needs of an organism.   12 _____

13. Which statement best describes a current understanding of natural selection?

(1) Natural selection influences the frequency of an adaptation in a population.
(2) Natural selection has been discarded as an important concept in evolution.
(3) Changes in gene frequencies due to natural selection have little effect on the evolution of species.
(4) New mutations of genetic material are due to natural selection.   13_____

14. Which statement describing a cause of extinction includes the other three?

(1) Members of the extinct species were unable to compete for food.
(2) Members of the extinct species were unable to conceal their presence by camouflage.
(3) Members of the extinct species lacked adaptations essential for survival.
(4) Members of the extinct species were too slow to escape from predators.   14_____

15. The bones in the forelimbs of three mammals are shown.

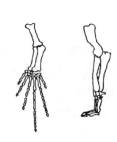

For these mammals, the number, position, and shape of the bones most likely indicates that they may have

(1) developed in a common environment
(2) developed from the same earlier species
(3) identical genetic makeup
(4) identical methods of obtaining food   15_____

16. In an area of Indonesia where the ocean floor is littered with empty coconut shells, a species of octopus has been filmed "walking" on two of its eight tentacles. The remaining six tentacles are wrapped around its body. Scientists suspect that, with its tentacles arranged this way, the octopus resembles a rolling coconut. Local predators, including sharks, seem not to notice the octopus as often when it behaves in this manner. This unique method of locomotion has lasted over many generations due to

(1) competition between octopuses and their predators
(2) ecological succession in marine habitats
(3) the process of natural selection
(4) selective breeding of this octopus species   16_____

17. The diagram below shows the effect of spraying a pesticide on a population of insects over three generations.

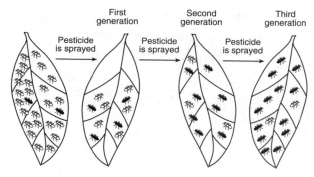

Which concept is represented in the diagram?

(1) survival of the fittest
(2) succession
(3) dynamic equilibrium
(4) extinction   17_____

18. Which statement is best supported by the theory of evolution?

(1) Genetic alterations occur every time cell reproduction occurs.
(2) The fossil record provides samples of every organism that ever lived.
(3) Populations that have advantageous characteristics will increase in number.
(4) Few organisms survive when the environment remains the same. 18 ____

19. A species that lacks the variation necessary to adapt to a changing environment is more likely to

(1) develop many mutated cells
(2) become extinct over time
(3) begin to reproduce sexually
(4) develop resistance to diseases 19 _____

20. The graph below shows the percent of variation for a given trait in four different populations of the same species. The populations inhabit similar environments.

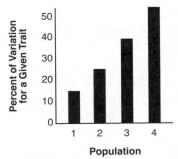

In which population will the greatest number of individuals most likely survive if a significant environmental change related to this trait occurs?

(1) 1   (3) 3
(2) 2   (4) 4   20 _____

21. A researcher recently discovered a new species of bacteria in the body of a tubeworm living near a hydrothermal vent. He compared the DNA of this new bacterial species to the DNA of four other species of bacteria. The DNA sequences came from the same part of the bacterial chromosome of all four species.

Species	DNA Sequence
unknown species	ACT GCA CCC
species I	ACA GCA CCG
species II	ACT GCT GGA
species III	ACA GCA GGG
species IV	ACT GCA CCG

According to these data, the unknown bacterial species is most closely related to

(1) species I   (3) species III
(2) species II   (4) species IV   21 _____

22. A population of animals is permanently split by a natural barrier into two separate populations in different environments. What will likely result after a long period of time?

(1) The evolution of the two populations will be identical.
(2) The production of variations will stop in the two populations.
(3) The two populations will evolve into separate species.
(4) Autotrophic nutrition will replace heterotrophic nutrition in the two populations.   22 _____

23. Which characteristics of a population would most likely indicate the lowest potential for evolutionary change in that population?

(1) sexual reproduction and few mutations
(2) sexual reproduction and many mutations
(3) asexual reproduction and few mutations
(4) asexual reproduction and many mutations

23 _____

24. In a certain species of insect, some individuals have flattened white disks on their bodies that protrude and interlock, resembling an orchid flower. This adaptation provides the insect with a better opportunity to capture its prey. If environmental conditions remain unchanged, it is most likely that, in future generations, the proportion of the population with this adaptation will

(1) increase, only
(2) decrease, only
(3) increase, then decrease
(4) decrease, then increase   24_____

25. Which statement is best supported by fossil records?

(1) Many organisms that lived in the past are now extinct.
(2) Species occupying the same habitat have identical environmental needs.
(3) The struggle for existence between organisms results in changes in populations.
(4) Structures such as leg bones and wing bones can originate from the same type of tissue found in embryos.

25_____

Researchers discovered four different species of finches on one of the Galapagos Islands. DNA analysis show ed that these four species, shown in the accompanying illustration, are closely related even though they vary in beak shape and size. It is thought that they share a common ancestor.

26. *a*) Which factor most likely influenced these differences in beak size and shape?

(1) Birds with poorly adapted beaks changed their beaks to get food.
(2) Birds with yellow beaks were able to hide from predators.
(3) Birds with successful beak adaptations obtained food and survived to have offspring.
(4) Birds with large, sharp beaks become dominant.   a_____

b) Which factors most likely had a role in the development of beak characteristics in these finches?

(1) mutation and cloning
(2) genetic engineering and selective breeding
(3) unchanging environment and the need to reproduce
(4) variation and recombination   b_____

c) Relationships between animal species may most accurately be determined by comparing the

(1) habitats in which they live   (3) base sequences of DNA
(2) structure of guard cells   (4) shape of these cells   c_____

27. Which concept is best illustrated in the flowchart?

Overproduction + limited niches ⟶ Struggle for existence + hereditary variation ⟶ Survival of the fittest + environmental change ⟶ Change of species or new species

(1) natural selection   (3) dynamic equilibrium
(2) genetic manipulation   (4) material cycles   27_____

28. Which evolutionary tree best represents the information in the chart?

Species	Sequence of Four Amino Acids Found in the Same Part of the Hemoglobin Molecule of Species
human	Lys–Glu–His–Phe
horse	Arg–Lys–His–Lys
gorilla	Lys–Glu–His–Lys
chimpanzee	Lys–Glu–His–Phe
zebra	Arg–Lys–His–Arg

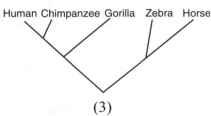

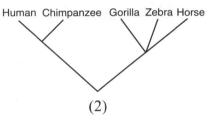  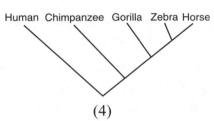

(1) (3)

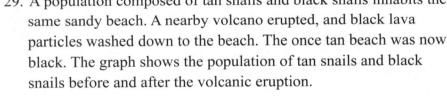

(2) (4) 28 _____

29. A population composed of tan snails and black snails inhabits the same sandy beach. A nearby volcano erupted, and black lava particles washed down to the beach. The once tan beach was now black. The graph shows the population of tan snails and black snails before and after the volcanic eruption.

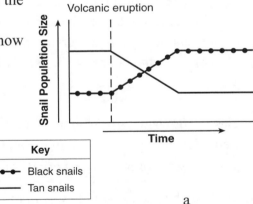

a) Which statement concerning the snails is correct?

(1) The lava particles turned the tan snails black.
(2) The tan snails will become extinct.
(3) The black snails had an adaptive advantage.
(4) The tan snails preyed on the black snails.

a _____

b) The increase in the number of black snails can best be explained by

(1) natural selection after an environmental change
(2) climatic change followed by ecological succession
(3) increased stability due to a decrease in variation
(4) an increase in mutation rate

b _____

c) Variation in snail color is an example of

(1) environmental stability   (3) equilibrium
(2) a natural limitation   (4) diversity

c _____

30. A farmer growing potatoes notices aphids, a type of insect, feeding on the plants. An insecticide was sprayed on the plants several times over a two-year period. The graph represents samples of three different generations of insecticide-resistant and nonresistant aphids over this time period.

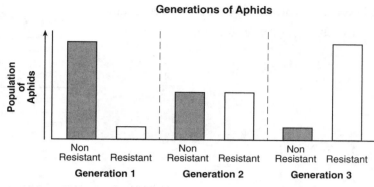

a) The resistance gene was present in the aphid population as a result of

(1) the need of the potatoes to become resistant to the insecticide
(2) changes in the aphids' local habitat by the insecticide
(3) a recombination of the proteins in the potato cells
(4) a random change in the aphids' DNA sequence

a_____

b) In year three, the farmer discontinued the use of the insecticide. Which statement would best predict the population in generation 4?

(1) The nonresistant aphid would become extinct.
(2) The nonresistant aphid population would likely increase.
(3) The resistant aphid would mutate to a nonresistant aphid.
(4) The plants would be free of insect populations.

b_____

c) One negative consequence of using an insecticide is that it

(1) selects for insecticide-resistant organisms
(2) keeps a balance of organic compounds
(3) encourages biodiversity in plants
(4) gives the nonresistant aphids a survival advantage

c_____

Base your answers to question 31 on the diagram. Letters *A* through *E* represent different species of organisms. The arrows represent long periods of geologic time.

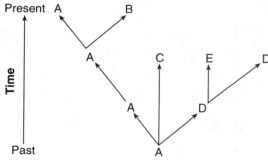

31. *a*) Which species would most likely show the greatest similarities in their amino acid sequences?

(1) *A* and *E*   (3) *B* and *D*
(2) *A* and *B*   (4) *C* and *E*   a _____

b) Which species is the common ancestor to all of the other species? _____

c) Identify one species that was not able to adapt to its environment. _____

Support your answer:_____

_____

32. When Charles Darwin was developing his theory of evolution, he considered variations in a population important. However, he could not explain how the variations occurred. Name two processes that can result in variation in a population. Explain how these processes actually cause variation.

First process:_____

Explanation:_____

Second process:_____

Explanation:_____

Base your answers to question 33 on the finch diversity chart, which contains information concerning the finches found on the Galapagos Islands.

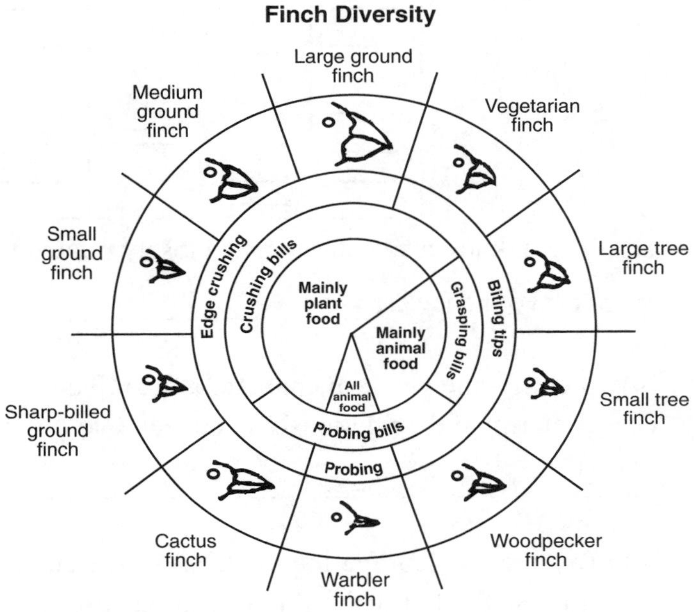

Finch Diversity

33. *a*) Identify one bird that would most likely compete for food with the large tree finch. Support your answer.

Bird: _____

Supporting statement: _____

_____

_____

b) Identify one trait, other than beak characteristics, that would contribute to the survival of a finch species and state one way this trait contributes to the success of this species.

Trait:_____   Statement:_____

_____

c) Three different species of finch inhabit one particular Galapagos Island. All three species of finch prefer plant food and have edge-crushing bills. Explain how all three species of finch can live successfully on the same island.

_____

34. For many years, health officials had encouraged using antibacterial hand soap. Today, many scientists recommend using hand soap with no added antibacterial substances. State one reason why using antibacterial hand soap may no longer be recommended.

_____

35. Scientists found members of a plant species they did not recognize. They wanted to determine if the unknown species was related to one or more of four known species, *A*, *B*, *C*, and *D*. The relationship between species can be determined most accurately by comparing the results of gel electrophoresis of the DNA from different species.
The chart below represents the results of gel electrophoresis of the DNA from the unknown plant species and the four known species.

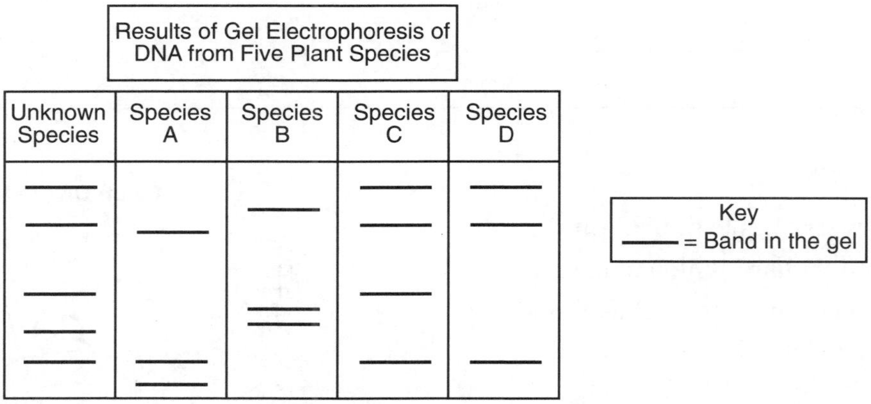

Results of Gel Electrophoresis of DNA from Five Plant Species				
Unknown Species	Species A	Species B	Species C	Species D

Key
—— = Band in the gel

a) The unknown species is most closely related to which of the four known species? _____

Support your answer:_____

b) Identify one physical characteristic of plants that can be readily observed and compared to help determine the relationship between two different species of plants.

_____

c) Explain why comparing the DNA of the unknown and known plant species is probably a more accurate method of determining relationships than comparing only the physical characteristic you identified in question *b*.

_____

d) Of the 4 known species (*A*, *B*, *C* and *D*), which two are most closely related? _____ and _____

e) Identify one additional way to determine the evolutionary relationship of these plants.

_____

36. *R*, *S*, and *T* are three species of birds. Species *S* and *T* show similar coloration. The enzymes found in species *R* and *T* show similarities. Species *R* and *T* also exhibit many of the same behavioral patterns.

Show the relationship between species *R*, *S*, and *T* by placing the letter representing each species at the top of the appropriate branch on the diagram.

Base your answers to question 37 on the information below.

In the Beaks of Finches laboratory activity, students were each assigned a tool to use to pick up seeds. In round one, students acting as birds used their assigned tools to pick up small seeds from their own large dishes (the environment) and place them in smaller dishes (their stomachs). The seeds collected by each student were counted. Some students were able to collect many seeds, while others collected just a few.

In round two, students again used their assigned tools to collect seeds. This time several students were picking up seeds from the same dish of seeds.

37. *a*) Explain how this laboratory activity illustrates the process of natural selection.

_____

_____

b) One factor that influences the evolution of a species that was not part of this laboratory activity is
(1) struggle for survival   (3) competition
(2) variation   (4) overproduction ___   b_____

c) Identify one trait, other than beak characteristics, that could contribute to the ability of a finch to feed successfully. _____

Base your answer to question 38 on the information and data table.

Body Structures and Reproductive Characteristics of Four Organisms

38. *a*) Explain why it would be difficult to determine which one of the other three organisms from the table should be placed in box 1.

Organism	Body Structures	Reproductive Characteristics
pigeon	feathers, scales 2 wings, 2 legs	lays eggs
A	scales 4 legs	lays eggs
B	fur 2 leathery wings, 2 legs	gives birth to live young provides milk for offspring
C	fur 4 legs	lays eggs provides milk for offspring

Evolutionary Tree

_____

_____

b) Identify and describe a technique that could help determine which organism belongs in box 1.

_____

_____

1. 4   A stable physical environment is not explained or defined by evolution or natural selection. Natural selection and evolutionary consequences result in changes in organisms over the course of time. This is evident in the fossil record.

2. 3   The biological theory of evolution is based on the concept that modern organisms developed through a series of adaptations from early species.

3. 4   Natural selection is the process where new species develop over time based on favorable adaptations. These adaptations may be a result of mutation, genetic variation, or genetic recombination; therefore, the higher the number of mutations or genetic variations, the higher the rate of natural selection.

4. 3   Favorable behavioral adaptations that allowed birds to survive within an environment can be genetically programmed into a bird's genetic code due to the fact that the surviving birds with favorable traits will pass these traits on to their offspring.

5. 4   Genes themselves do not adapt. Genes provide the means, through variation, for the organism to adapt to environmental change. Statements 1, 2, and 3 are all important concepts within the process of natural selection.

6. 3   Each of these organisms inhabits different environments and uses its forelimbs for a different function. In order to survive within their environment, these organisms accumulated adaptations within their bone structure. Even though there are similarities in bone structure suggesting common ancestry, each organism's bones reflect changes due to adaptation to its environment.

7. 2   In an unstable environment, an organism is much more likely to experience stress on its population that could lead to extinction. By having few variations, the population would be less likely to adapt to any changes or diseases within their environment, thus leading to possible extinction.

8. 1   The diagram shows the evolutionary relationships between different mammals. A single origin position to the left represents a common ancestor in the past for all these organisms. The African elephant is more closely related to mammals that follow its evolutionary pathway. Therefore, the African and Asian elephants would be more closely related to the mammoth and mastodon than to any of the other named mammals.

9. 1   Changing environments place pressure on a species. If species adapt to the changing environment through natural selection, they will survive. Species that do not adapt are destined to become extinct. Many factors can influence the environment, such as climate, weather, natural occurrences, and even man.

10. 2   Genes provide the means through variation for an organism to adapt and evolve. In order for a trait to be passed on to the next generation, it must be present in the gametes of that organism. Those successful genes that are passed on will allow that organism to adapt to environmental change.

11. 4   During the process of meiosis, genes are shuffled and crossing over may occur, leading to variation in the resulting gametes. Each sex cell or gamete contains one half the amount of genetic material as the parent cell and will recombine during sexual reproduction, resulting in variation.

12. 3   Natural selection is a process where individuals with favorable traits or characteristics survive and pass those characteristics on to future generations. The proportion (frequency) of that favorable trait within the population will increase over time.

13. 1   Variations are the result of a change in the genetic code brought on by a mutation or by recombination of genes produced when sex cells or gametes come together. Remember that sexually reproducing species produce sex cells by means of meiosis, and each cell contains only half of the genetic material. At fertilization, new combinations of genes may occur.

14. 3   Based on the graph, species A and E have the most DNA in common. Since DNA provides the code for amino acids and the building of proteins, species A and E would also have the greatest similarity in protein structure.

15. 4   Present existing mammals species are successful today because they inherited traits that allowed them to adapt to and evolve in a changing environment. The woolly mammoth did not inherit successful traits and was unable to survive, leading to its extinction. Environmental changes such as climate, weather changes, natural occurrences, and even humans may have contributed towards the extinction of this mammal.

16. 3   Natural selection is a process where individuals with favorable traits or characteristics survive and pass those characteristics on to future generations. The proportion (frequency) of that favorable trait within the population will increase over time.

17. 2   Changes in gene frequency lead to variation within a population. Variation can lead to biological evolution if environmental conditions change. Genetic variation can be brought about by a change within the gene sequence, many times resulting in a mutation.

18. 1   All of the shown evolutionary pathways originated from the ancestral organism B. Only organism Q and S successfully adapted to changing environments and have reached the Present time. The other organisms did not successfully adapt and are now extinct.

19. 4   Organisms that have fast reproductive rates and live in changing environments would show fast evolutionary rates. Evolution reflects an organism's ability to adapt to changes in an environment. Certain genetic traits that allow organisms to survive and therefore adapt are passed reproductively from one generation to the next. If an organism has a rapid or fast reproductive rate, those adaptive genes will be passed faster, thus allowing for a faster evolution rate.

20. 4   Variety A is increasing while B is decreasing. This shows that variety A has successfully adapted to its environment and has some favorable variations that have been passed along many generations. Variety B does not have these favorable variations and is heading to extinction, as shown by the graph.

21. 3   Evolution is a change in a population over time as a result of a change in the environment. Climate change in a region may allow for changes in the plant populations. Those with favorable characteristics would survive, perhaps leading to new varieties of plants. This region undergoing climate changes would show more evidence of evolution based on more plant varieties.

22. 1   In unfavorable conditions, if the adaptive characteristics of a species are not adequate, the species faces extinction.

23. 2   Through natural selection, the desert rat and the Arctic poppy plant have adapted differently to their environments. These adaptations have allowed them to survive in their harsh environment, reproduce, and pass those favorable traits on to the next generation, ensuring continual survival of the species.

24. *a*) 4   Species *F* and *G* would be most closely related because they both share the most recent common ancestor *D*.

    b) 2   Species *B* was best adapted to environmental change. Species *B* started as an ancestral species and survived through each period of geologic time to the most recent time period.

    c) 1   Both *B* and *J* share a common ancestor – species *B*. Because they share this common ancestor, they both will have some DNA related to ancestral species *B*. Remember, DNA serves as a template in protein synthesis.

    d) 3   Within the nucleus is found DNA. If a mutation occurs and alters the DNA within a gamete, it may be expressed as new characteristics within the offspring of that species and possibly lead to genetic variation.

25. *a*) 1   Due to a decrease in the numbers of small seeds during the dry years, those finches with the larger beak trait were able to survive and reproduce. The large beak trait was then passed on to future generations. This is an example of natural selection.

    b) 4   Due to a diminished amount of seeds, there will be competition for whatever food is available. Those finches that have a better adapted trait, such as a larger beak, can outcompete other finches, survive, and reproduce, passing that trait on.

26. 2   Biological evolution is defined as a slow change over time. As the finches moved to different islands, they adapted to different habitats and foods, evolving beak variations. Over time, the finches with the best adapted beaks for that island survived and formed a particular variety of finch. Eventually 14 different varieties of finches evolved. This is the process described by Charles Darwin as natural selection.

27. *a*) 2   Based on the information provided in the diagram, the differences in beaks of the four finches are most likely a result of variation and natural selection. Each finch beak type has a different structure based on genetic variation which allowed that finch to be successful in a specific niche. The process of natural selection occurs when individuals with successful variations survive in changing environments.

    b) No
Supporting statement: The vegetarian finches eat seeds and would not face competition from the insect finches. *or* No, the other finches eat insects and the vegetarian finches eats seeds. *or* they eat different foods.

Yes
Supporting statement: As the finches population increases there will be competition for nesting sites.

28. 3 Based on the diagram, earthworms and sea stars have a common ancestor. This common ancestor is found directly up from the ancestral protists where the straight line branches left and right. The left branch leads to the earthworm and the right branch leads to the sea star. By sharing a common ancestor, the earthworm and sea star are evolutionarily related.

29. a) Answer: tough seed coats *or* spiny seed coats

    Explanation: The caltrop plants are producing seeds that contain tough spiny coats. These adaptations on the seeds have evolved as a means of protection against being eaten by the bird species – *Geospiza fortis*.

    b) Answer: natural selection *or* mutation *or* sexual reproduction

    Explanation: All of the above processes will create variations within species. These variations, if favorable to the species, will be passed on to future generations making the species better adapted to the environment in which they live.

    c) Adaptation: fast flight speed — to escape predators *or* camouflage — to hide from predators *or* eyesight— to locate food *or* mating behavior (songs)— to attract mates

30. 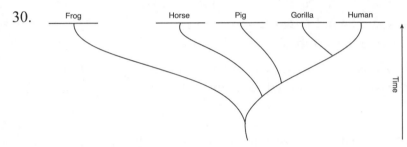 Explanation: One method of determining evolutionary position is to compare proteins or amino acid sequences of various organisms. Those organisms with a greater number of common amino acids are more closely related. Evolutionary relationships can be expressed in the form of an evolutionary tree, which shows how organisms evolved and when new species appeared. For example, the gorilla has only one amino acid different from humans and would be placed on the branch closest the human. The frog which has the greatest number of differences would be placed on a branch farthest from the human – to the far left.

31. Answer: Species *E*

    Supporting statement: Species *E* is best adapted for changing environments because it has survived as species *E* through a long period of time and not changed, whereas other species have changed or become extinct. In the evolutionary tree, species *E* continues through time to present day indicating that it has favorable characteristics that enable it to survive.

32. a) 3 Natural selection is a process where organisms adapt to changes in their environment. Genetic variability due to mutations led to particular individuals being more successful on different islands. Those organisms survived while others did not. The Galapagos Islands provide varying habitats with varying food sources for many organisms, leading to diversity through natural selection.

    b) 3 Carnivores are organisms that feed exclusively on other animals.

    c) Answer: herbivores

    Explanation: Herbivores are organisms that feed exclusively on producers.

d) Acceptable responses include but are not limited to:
Large ground finches eat mainly plant food, and large tree finches eat mainly animal food.
or They do not compete for the same resources.
or They occupy different niches.

Explanation: Using the diagram, locate the large ground finch and large tree finch and move directly in towards the center, noting the type of food they eat. Since these birds feed on different food types (plant vs. animal), they will not be competing for the same resources, allowing each bird to be successful. Remember that two organisms cannot successfully occupy the same niche at the same time; one will outcompete the other.

e) Answer: Cactus finch   Supporting statement: Because it eats mainly plant food whereas the other two finches eat mostly animal food.

Explanation: A niche is a role that an organism plays in an ecosystem. The diagram shows that the cactus finch feed mainly on plant food, while the warbler and woodpecker finch feed on animal food. Since the cactus finch has a different food source, it occupies a different niche and would not compete with the other two types of finch.

f) Answer: The medium ground finch would face increase competition for seeds.
or The food resources for these birds would be in limited supply.
or One of these bird species might be outcompeted for food and become extinct.

Explanation: Since both of these finches have a diet of seeds, competition will take place. The above given answers are resulting consequences for animals that compete for the same food.

g) Answer: Niche

Explanation: A niche is the role that an organism plays within an ecosystem. Most niches on the Galapagos are based on the nutritional habits of the finches.

33. *a*) Acceptable responses include but are not limited to:
or According to diagram 3, *C* should look different from *A* and *B*, but it does not.
or Stem cross sections in diagram 1 show that *A*, *B* and *C* have similar stem structures, indicating that they are most likely related.
or Diagram 3 shows only *A* and *B* as being closely related.

Explanation: All the stems in diagram 1 are very similar. It is not possible from this diagram to tell the evolutionary relationship that might exist among them.

b) Answer: Species *A* and *B* have the most bands in common.

Explanation: Species that are closely related will share similar DNA sequences. When the DNA is subjected to gel electrophoresis, species with close evolutionary links will have more bands in common. In diagram 2, species *A* and *B* share three bands in common, while *C* shares one band in common with *B* and two with *A*.

c) 2   Gel electrophoresis is a process that separates DNA fragments that have been cut up by restriction enzymes. The DNA is placed in a gel, and an electric current is applied. The DNA migrates through the gel as a result of the electric current, with the smallest fragments moving the farthest. It can then be analyzed for similarities.

$C_6H_{12}O_6$  **ATP**

Overview:

In order to carry out life functions, living organisms require chemical compounds that can be broken down for energy and synthesized for structure and function. Organisms use the processes of photosynthesis and respiration to create molecules that can be used as energy molecules for life functions. These chemical compounds and processes are universally used by all living organisms to maintain life.

Essential Information:

Chemical Compounds – Living organisms, in order to function successfully within their environment, require specific compounds. Inorganic compounds, such as water and carbon dioxide, are necessary for vital cellular functions. Organic compounds contain the basic elements of carbon and hydrogen and can also be enhanced with the addition of oxygen, nitrogen, sulfur, and phosphorus. Different combinations of these elements result in various types of organic compounds such as:

- *Carbohydrates* include complex sugars and starches that can be broken down into simple sugars like *glucose* to provide energy. Some carbohydrates, like cellulose, serve as part of the structure of the cell wall in plants.
- *Proteins* are compounds that are composed of sequences of *amino acids* – the building blocks of proteins. Proteins are essential for both structure and function in living things. An important class of proteins includes enzymes, which are necessary for many reactions to proceed.
- *Nucleic acids* include both the genetic molecules DNA and RNA. They are made of smaller subunits called nucleotides. Nucleic acids function to provide a means to store genetic information and provide a template for the synthesis of proteins.
- *Lipids* are large molecules that include fats, which store energy, and oils and waxes that prevent water loss. Lipids also are an important component of the cell membrane.

Enzymes – In order to synthesize or break down organic compounds, *enzymes* or biological catalysts are needed. Enzymes have a defined structure based on the sequence of amino acids used to construct them. This structure is important to their function of speeding up chemical reactions. Enzymes have a special location known as the *active site* where *substrates*, substances that enzymes act on, can bind and enter into a reaction. Therefore, enzymes are said to be *substrate specific* because they bind to a particular substrate that fits into the active site like a puzzle piece. This enzyme substrate binding is described as a *lock and key model* (see diagram 2). It is important to understand that an enzyme's shape determines its function.

Each enzyme will work to either synthesize substrates into a more complex compound or to break down a substrate into a simpler and usable form. Several factors can influence enzyme action. Each enzyme has an *optimum temperature* at which it functions. Enzyme action or rate of reaction will increase as temperature increases. When an enzyme reaches a temperature where its reaction rate has peaked, that is said to be the optimum. At a certain point, temperatures become too high, and this causes the enzyme's shape or structure to distort. A change in the enzyme's structure may decrease the function of that enzyme or stop it altogether. Another factor that influences enzyme action is pH, or the measure of acidity or alkalinity of an environment. Each enzyme has an *optimum pH* where it maximizes its function. As the pH value moves away from that optimum value, the function diminishes due to changes in the enzymes structure.

Energy Needs – All living organisms require energy to carry out life functions. Organisms use organic compounds that are cycled through the processes of *photosynthesis* and *respiration* to provide that energy. *Autotrophs*, or producers, such as plants, are able to convert energy from visible light into chemical energy during the process of photosynthesis, within an organelle known as the *chloroplast*. Within the membrane of the chloroplasts, light energy is captured, and this begins the process of synthesizing simple sugar – like glucose. This glucose is then synthesized and used by both heterotrophs (consumers) and autotrophs (producers) for energy. Certain compounds are necessary for this synthesis to take place: water, which enters the plant through the root system, and carbon dioxide, which enters through tiny openings called *stomata* located on the underside of leaves. Stomata are surrounded by guard cells. These cells regulate the opening and closing of the stomata. Through the stomata, gas exchange takes place, with carbon dioxide entering and oxygen being released. As a result of photosynthesis, sugar molecules such as glucose are produced along with the byproduct, oxygen, which exits through the stomata. Certain factors can influence the rate of photosynthesis, including light intensity, amount of available water, and temperature.

Respiration – *Respiration* is a process where the energy held in the chemical bonds of glucose is released to produce an energy molecule, *ATP*. Respiration can occur in two ways depending on the presence or absence of oxygen. Without oxygen, respiration takes place in the form of *fermentation* or *anaerobic respiration*. This process typically takes place in yeast and bacteria where the incomplete breakdown of glucose yields small amounts of ATP, carbon dioxide, and alcohol. This process can also take place in muscles when they lack enough oxygen. It results in the buildup of lactic acid leading to muscle fatigue. Cellular respiration or *aerobic respiration* occurs in the presence of oxygen and takes place in the cell structure known as the *mitochondria*. In cellular respiration, glucose is broken down into carbon dioxide, water, and larger amounts of ATP. The inner folds of the mitochondria provide a surface area for this process to occur. ATP can be used for many activities, such as active transport, synthesis of complex molecules, and locomotion or muscle movement.

A cyclic relationship exists between the processes of photosynthesis and respiration where molecules of carbon dioxide, oxygen, and glucose are shuttled back and forth in and between living organisms. Producers carry out photosynthesis, providing oxygen and glucose for all living things to utilize in respiration. Carbon dioxide, the byproduct of respiration, is then used by plants to build glucose molecules.

Additional Information:

- Enzymes are unchanged by the reactions which they participate in and leave the reaction ready to act again.

- Plants have many structural modifications that allow them to be efficient at photosynthesis. Their flat, broad leaves allow for maximum surface area to absorb light energy. Stomata on the bottom of each leaf prevent excessive evaporation or water loss. Most of the chloroplasts are located on the upper portions of the leaf to capture the most sunlight.

- There are 20 different amino acids that are used to build proteins. Each protein has a different variation of types and sequences of those amino acids.

Diagrams:

1. **Lock and Key Model of Enzymes** – Molecule *A* represents an enzyme, while molecule *B* represents a substrate. These two molecules fit together in a way that is sometimes referred to as a Lock and Key Model.

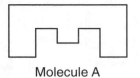

Molecule A   Molecule B

2. **Enzyme Substrate Reaction** – This diagram shows the structures of a substrate and enzyme as they bind together at the active site. In this reaction, the substrate, a dipeptide or protein is broken down into its amino acid products. Notice the enzyme is unchanged by the reaction and ready to act again.

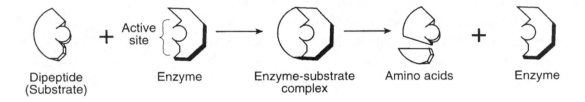

Dipeptide (Substrate)   Enzyme   Enzyme-substrate complex   Amino acids   Enzyme

3. **Optimum pH** – The activity of two different enzymes, trypsin and pepsin are shown in this graph. Each enzyme has an optimum pH at which it performs at peak rate. pH is a measure of how acidic or basic conditions are within a system or environment.

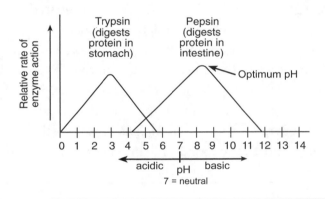

4. **Photosynthesis** – Photosynthetic activity in aquatic plants can be measured by the production of oxygen bubbles, collected in an inverted test tube. As the rate of photosynthesis increases, so will the rate of bubble production until optimum level is reached.

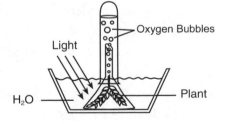

5. **Fermentation** – This diagram illustrates the process of fermentation where yeast cells are carrying out anaerobic respiration (without oxygen). Yeast, glucose and water are placed in the shown apparatus. During the process of fermentation, carbon dioxide is released and collects in the tube. The rate of respiration can be measured by the amount of carbon dioxide collected in the tube.

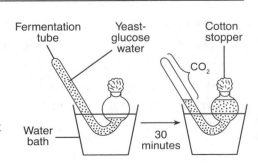

6. **Energy Flow** – This diagram shows a cyclic relationship of the flow of energy and gases between plants and animals. Plants, through photosynthesis, produce glucose ($C_6H_{12}O_6$), water and oxygen. Glucose and oxygen are then used by animals during respiration to produce the energy molecule ATP, while releasing water and carbon dioxide, which are again used by plants.

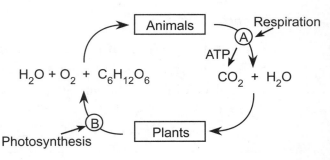

7. **Mitochondrion and ATP** – The cell part pictured here is the mitochondrion, where the process of cellular respiration takes place. The arrows represent the production of the energy molecule, ATP, and the byproduct, CO_2. The inner folds of the mitochondrion provide a surface for this process to take place.

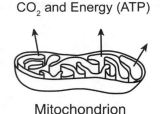

Mitochondrion

8. **Energy Production in Cells** – When compared to Cell *B*, Cell *A* contains a larger number of mitochondria and is able to carry out more cellular respiration and therefore, produce more ATP. These ATP or energy molecules may be used in the process of active transport. Cells that require much energy for function, such as muscle cells, contain more mitochondria than other cells.

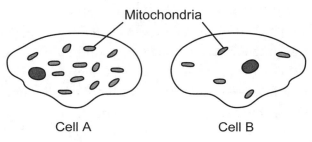

9. **Stomata and Guard Cells** – The diagrams show a cross-sectional view and a microscopic view of a leaf. In the cross-sectional view, the stomata opening is surrounded by guard cells on the bottom of the leaf surface. The pointer in the microscopic view is directed at guard cells that surround the darkened stomata opening. The stomata provides a location for the exchange of gases. Carbon dioxide enters the plant and oxygen exits. Because water can also exit the plant through the stomata, guard cells regulate the opening and closing to maintain homeostasis within the plant.

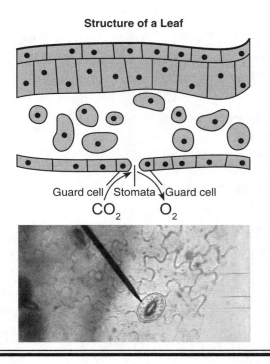

Chemistry and Energy for Life

Group A *Directions* - Match the correct definition for the following terms:

1. _____Substrate

2. _____Guard cell

3. _____Organic compounds

4. _____Optimum pH

5. _____Active site

6. _____Nucleotides

7. _____Aerobic

8. _____Photosynthesis

9. _____Autotroph

10. _____Nucleic acids

11. _____Amino acids

12. _____Enzymes

13. _____Carbohydrates

A. Special proteins that speed up the rate of chemical reactions in living things.

B. The process by which some organisms are able to capture light energy to produce sugar from carbon dioxide and water.

C. Molecules necessary for life that contain both hydrogen and carbon atoms. Carbohydrates are an example of this type of molecule.

D. The basic building block of DNA and RNA, composed of a sugar, phosphate and a nitrogen base.

E. Compounds that the body can break down into simple sugars, like glucose to use for energy.

F. A level of acidic, neutral, or basic condition in which an enzyme functions most efficiently.

G. An organism that produces its own food; the source of energy for all other living things.

H. Specialized cells that control the opening and closing of the pores (stomata) on the surface of a leaf.

I. An environment with the presence of oxygen.

J. A location on an enzyme where the substrate fits closely with that enzyme.

K. The molecule or compound that an enzyme binds to in a reaction.

L. Any one of several building blocks of protein.

M. Large, complex organic molecules that contain the genetic instructions needed to carry out cellular life processes.

Group B *Directions* - Match the correct definition for the following terms:

1. _____Respiration

2. _____Chloroplast

3. _____ Substrate specific

4. _____ Lock and key model

5. _____Optimum temperature

6. _____Mitochondrion

7. _____Lipids

8. _____Proteins

9. _____Anaerobic

10. _____Glucose

11. _____Inorganic compounds

12. _____ATP

13. _____ Stomata

14. _____Fermentation

A. Any one of a group of organic compounds that includes oils, fats, and waxes.

B. A small pore found on the underside of most leaves.

C. A favored condition of temperature, in which an enzyme functions most efficiently.

D. A compound that stores energy in cells; a high energy molecule which supplies energy for cells.

E. A simple carbohydrate that is a major source of energy for cells.

F. An environment where there is little or no oxygen is present.

G. The process by which the chemical bond energy stored in nutrients like glucose is released to produce ATP in cells.

H. Organic compounds composed of sequences of amino acids.

I. Organelles that contain enzymes used to extract energy from nutrients; site of cellular respiration.

J. A way to describe the fit of an enzyme with its specific substrate.

K. An anaerobic process where glucose is partially broken down by bacteria or yeast, yielding limited supplies of ATP, while releasing CO_2.

L. A green organelle that contains chlorophyll where photosynthesis occurs.

M. Describes the close relationship between an enzyme's shape and the molecules that it acts on.

N. Compounds such as water and carbon dioxide that are involved in vital processes like photosynthesis and cellular respiration.

Chemistry and Energy for Life

1. Which process usually uses carbon dioxide molecules?

   (1) cellular respiration
   (2) asexual reproduction
   (3) active transport
   (4) autotrophic nutrition   1 _____

2. Which phrase best describes cellular respiration, a process that occurs continuously in the cells of organisms?

   (1) removal of oxygen from the cells of an organism
   (2) conversion of light energy into the chemical bond energy of organic molecules
   (3) transport of materials within cells and throughout the bodies of multicellular organisms
   (4) changing of stored chemical energy in food molecules to a form usable by organisms   2 _____

3. In heterotrophs, energy for the life processes comes from the chemical energy stored in the bonds of

   (1) water molecules
   (2) oxygen molecules
   (3) organic compounds
   (4) inorganic compounds   3 _____

4. Energy from organic molecules can be stored in ATP molecules as a direct result of the process of

   (1) cellular respiration
   (2) cellular reproduction
   (3) diffusion
   (4) digestion   4 _____

5. Eating a sweet potato provides energy for human metabolic processes. The original source of this energy is the energy

   (1) in protein molecules stored within the potato
   (2) from starch molecules absorbed by the potato plant
   (3) made available by photosynthesis
   (4) in vitamins and minerals found in the soil   5 _____

6. In what way are photosynthesis and cellular respiration similar?

   (1) They both occur in chloroplasts.
   (2) They both require sunlight.
   (3) They both involve organic and inorganic molecules.
   (4) They both require oxygen and produce carbon dioxide.   6 _____

7. A small piece of black paper was folded in half and used to cover part of the top and bottom portions of a leaf on a living geranium plant. After the plant was kept in sunlight for several days, the paper was removed. The leaf was then boiled in alcohol to remove the chlorophyll and placed in Lugol's iodine solution, which turns blue-black in the presence of starch. Only the part of the leaf that had not been covered turned blue-black. This investigation was most likely testing the hypothesis that

   (1) light is necessary for photosynthesis to occur
   (2) alcohol plus chlorophyll forms Lugol's iodine solution
   (3) green plants use carbon dioxide in photosynthesis
   (4) plants use alcohol in the production of chlorophyll   7 _____

8. The diagram represents events associated with a biochemical process that occurs in some organisms.

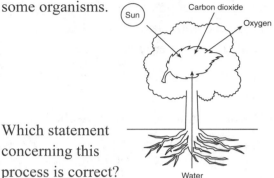

Sun
Carbon dioxide
Oxygen
Water

Which statement concerning this process is correct?

(1) The process represented is respiration and the primary source of energy for the process is the Sun.
(2) The process represented is photosynthesis and the primary source of energy for the process is the Sun.
(3) This process converts energy in organic compounds into solar energy which is released into the atmosphere.
(4) This process uses solar energy to convert oxygen into carbon dioxide. 8 _____

9. Carbon dioxide makes up less than 1 percent of Earth's atmosphere, and oxygen makes up about 20 percent. These percentages are maintained most directly by

(1) respiration and photosynthesis
(2) the ozone shield
(3) synthesis and digestion
(4) energy recycling in ecosystems 9 _____

10. Which process uses energy to combine inorganic molecules to synthesize organic molecules?

(1) respiration   (3) photosynthesis
(2) digestion   (4) decomposition

10 _____

11. The table shows the rate of water loss in three different plants.

Plant	Liters of Water Lost Per Day
Cactus	0.02
Potato plant	1.00
Apple tree	19.00

One reason each plant loses a different amount of water is that each has

(1) different guard cells adapted to maintain homeostasis
(2) different types of insulin-secreting cells that regulate water levels
(3) the same number of chloroplasts but different rates of photosynthesis
(4) the same rate of photosynthesis but different numbers of chloroplasts 11 _____

12. In the leaf of a plant, guard cells help to

(1) destroy atmospheric pollutants when they enter the plant
(2) regulate oxygen and carbon dioxide levels
(3) transport excess glucose to the roots
(4) block harmful ultraviolet rays that can disrupt chlorophyll production 12 _____

13. The failure to regulate the pH of the blood can affect the activity of

(1) enzymes that clot blood
(2) red blood cells that make antibodies
(3) chlorophyll that carries oxygen in the blood
(4) DNA that controls starch digestion in the blood 13 _____

14. The temporary storage of energy in ATP molecules is part of which process?

(1) cell division
(2) cellular respiration
(3) protein synthesis
(4) DNA replication 14 _____

Set 1 – Chemistry and Energy for Life

15. Enzymes have an optimum temperature at which they work best. Temperatures above and below this optimum will decrease enzyme activity. Which graph best illustrates the effect of temperature on enzyme activity?

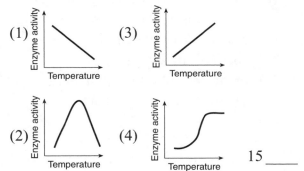

(1)   (3)

(2)   (4)

15 _____

16. Most of the starch stored in the cells of a potato is composed of molecules that originally entered these cells as

(1) enzymes   (3) amino acids
(2) simple sugars (4) minerals   16 _____

17. Organisms that have the ability to use an atmospheric gas to produce an organic nutrient are known as

(1) herbivores   (3) carnivores
(2) decomposers   (4) autotrophs   17 _____

18. Which statement concerning proteins is not correct?

(1) Proteins are long, usually folded, chains.
(2) The shape of a protein molecule determines its function.
(3) Proteins can be broken down and used for energy.
(4) Proteins are bonded together, resulting in simple sugars.   18 _____

19. The diagram below represents a series of reactions that can occur in an organism.

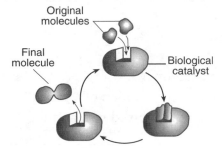

This diagram best illustrates the relationship between

(1) enzymes and synthesis
(2) amino acids and glucose
(3) antigens and immunity
(4) ribosomes and sugars   19 _____

20. A process that occurs in the human body is shown in the diagram below.

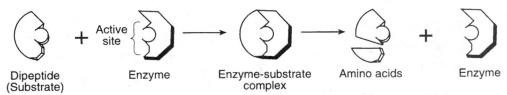

What would happen if a temperature change caused the shape of the active site to be altered?

(1) The dipeptide would digest faster.
(2) The dipeptide would digest slower or not at all.
(3) The amino acids would combine faster.
(4) The amino acids would combine slower or not at all.   20 _____

21. The diagram below represents the synthesis of a portion of a complex molecule in an organism.

Building blocks → Product

Which row in the chart could be used to identify the building blocks and product in the diagram?

Row	Building Blocks	Product
(1)	starch molecules	glucose
(2)	amino acid molecules	part of protein
(3)	sugar molecules	ATP
(4)	DNA molecules	part of starch

21 _____

22. The diagram below represents a beaker containing a solution of various molecules involved in digestion.

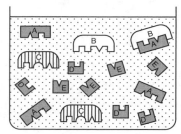

Which structures represent products of digestion?

(1) A and D   (3) B and E
(2) B and C   (4) D and E   22 _____

23. Many biological catalysts, hormones, and receptor molecules are similar in that, in order to function properly, they must

(1) interact with each other at a high pH
(2) interact with molecules that can alter their specific bonding patterns
(3) contain amino acid chains that fold into a specific shape
(4) contain identical DNA base sequences   23 _____

24. The production of energy-rich ATP molecules is the direct result of

(1) recycling light energy to be used in the process of photosynthesis
(2) releasing the stored energy of organic compounds by the process of respiration
(3) breaking down starch by the process of digestion
(4) copying coded information during the process of protein synthesis   24 _____

25. Two proteins in the same cell perform different functions. This is because the two proteins are composed of

(1) chains folded the same way and the same sequence of simple sugars
(2) chains folded the same way and the same sequence of amino acids
(3) chains folded differently and a different sequence of simple sugars
(4) chains folded differently and a different sequence of amino acids   25 _____

26. Which process is most closely associated with the regulation of water loss from the leaves of trees?

(1) digestion of water within the cytoplasm in the leaf cells of the trees
(2) synthesis of protein by the chloroplasts in the leaf cells of the trees
(3) movement of water through leaf openings controlled by the guard cells
(4) absorption of nitrogen through leaf openings controlled by the guard cells   26 _____

27. A single-celled organism is represented in the diagram below. An activity is indicated by the arrow.

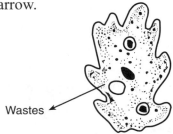

Wastes

If this activity requires the use of energy, which substance would be the source of this energy?

(1) DNA   (3) a hormone
(2) ATP   (4) an antibody   27 _____

Base your answers to question 28 on the information in the diagram below.

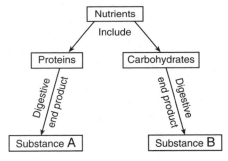

28. *a)* In an autotrophic organism, substance *B* functions as a

(1) source of energy
(2) hormone
(3) vitamin
(4) biotic resource   a _____

b) In a heterotrophic organism, substance *A* could be used directly for

(1) photosynthesis
(2) synthesis of enzymes
(3) a building block of starch
(4) a genetic code   b _____

29. Three days after an organism eats some meat, many of the organic molecules originally contained in the meat would be found in newly formed molecules of

(1) glucose   (3) starch
(2) protein   (4) oxygen   29 _____

30. A fully functioning enzyme molecule is arranged in a complex three-dimensional shape. This shape determines the

(1) specific type of molecule it interacts with during a reaction
(2) rate at which the enzyme breaks down during a reaction it regulates
(3) pH of all body systems
(4) temperature of the products of the reaction it regulates   30 _____

31. An investigation was carried out and the results are shown below. Substance *X* resulted from a metabolic process that produces ATP in yeast (a single-celled fungus).

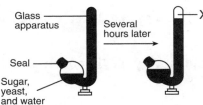

Which statement best describes substance *X*?

(1) It is oxygen released by protein synthesis.
(2) It is glucose that was produced in photosynthesis.
(3) It is starch that was produced during digestion.
(4) It is carbon dioxide released by respiration.   31 _____

32. Explain how carbohydrates provide energy for life functions.

_____

_____

33. Enzyme molecules are affected by changes in conditions within organisms.

Explain how a prolonged, excessively high body temperature during an illness could be fatal to humans. Your answer must include:

a) the role of enzymes in a human

_____

b) the effect of this high body temperature on enzyme activity

_____

Base your answers to question 34 on the diagram below. The arrows in the diagram represent biological processes.

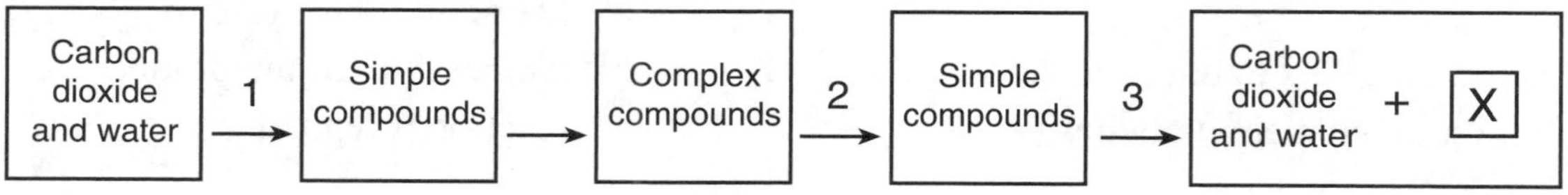

| Carbon dioxide and water | 1 → | Simple compounds | → | Complex compounds | 2 → | Simple compounds | 3 → | Carbon dioxide and water | + | X |

34. *a*) Identify *one* type of organism that carries out process 1. _____

b) Explain why process 2 is essential in humans.

_____

_____

c) Identify process 3. _____

d) Identify what letter *X* represents. _____

35. Explain why it is important for plants to "hold enzymes in their functional shapes."

_____

_____

36. *a*) The diagram represents a cell of a green plant. Which letter points to an organelle that uses solar energy to produce energy-rich compounds?

_____

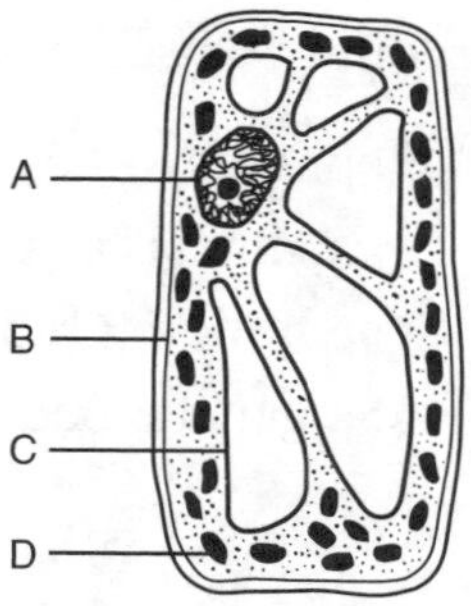

b) Which letter allows for the diffusion of carbon dioxide and water into the cell? _____

Base your answers to question 37 on the diagram below which represents a cell found in some complex organisms. The enlarged section represents an organelle, labeled *X*, found in this cell.

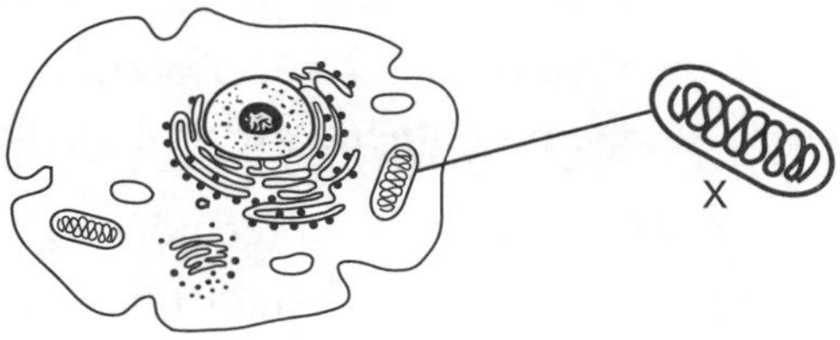

Describe the function of organelle *X* and explain how it is important to the survival of the cell. In your answer, be sure to:

37. *a*) identify organelle *X* _____

b) state the process that this organelle performs

_____

c) identify the *two* raw materials that are needed for this process to occur

_____ and _____

d) identify one molecule produced by this organelle and explain why it is important to the organism

Molecule: _____

Importance: _____

38. In some land plants, guard cells are found only on the lower surfaces of the leaves. In some water plants, guard cells are found only on the upper surfaces of the leaves. Explain how guard cells in both land and water plants help maintain homeostasis. In your answer be sure to:

a) identify one function regulated by the guard cells in leaves _____

b) explain how guard cells carry out this function

_____

c) give one possible evolutionary advantage of the position of the guard cells on the leaves of land plants

_____

Base your answers to question 39 on the summary equation of the process below.

Photosynthesis

water + carbon dioxide $\xrightarrow{\text{enzymes}}$ glucose + oxygen + water

39. *a*) Identify the source of the energy in this process. _____

b) Identify where the energy ends up at the completion of that process.

_____

c) State one reason why this process is important to living things.

_____

d) Identify the cell organelle where this process takes place. _____

1. Organisms that are able to manufacture organic nutrients from substances in the abiotic environment are classified as

    (1) heterotrophs (3) predators
    (2) fungi (4) autotrophs 1 _____

2. In nature, during a 24-hour period, green plants continuously use

    (1) carbon dioxide, only
    (2) both carbon dioxide and oxygen
    (3) oxygen, only
    (4) neither carbon dioxide nor oxygen
    2 _____

3. Which process is directly used by autotrophs to store energy in glucose?

    (1) diffusion (3) respiration
    (2) photosynthesis (4) active transport
    3 _____

4. Starch molecules present in a maple tree are made from materials that originally entered the tree from the external environment as

    (1) enzymes (3) amino acids
    (2) simple sugars (4) inorganic compounds
    4 _____

5. Which substance is an inorganic molecule?

    (1) starch (3) water
    (2) DNA (4) fat 5 _____

6. All cells of an organism are engaged in many different chemical reactions. This fact is best supported by the presence in each cell of thousands of different kinds of

    (1) enzymes (3) chloroplasts
    (2) nuclei (4) organelles 6 _____

7. The equation below represents a summary of a biological process.

    carbon dioxide + water → glucose + water + oxygen

    This process is completed in

    (1) mitochondria (3) cell membranes
    (2) ribosomes (4) chloroplasts 7 _____

8. Much of the carbon dioxide produced by green plants is not excreted as a metabolic waste because it

    (1) can be used for photosynthesis
    (2) is too large to pass through cell membranes
    (3) is needed for cellular respiration
    (4) can be used for the synthesis of proteins 8 _____

    Base your answers to question 9 on the diagram below, which represents stages in the digestion of a starch.

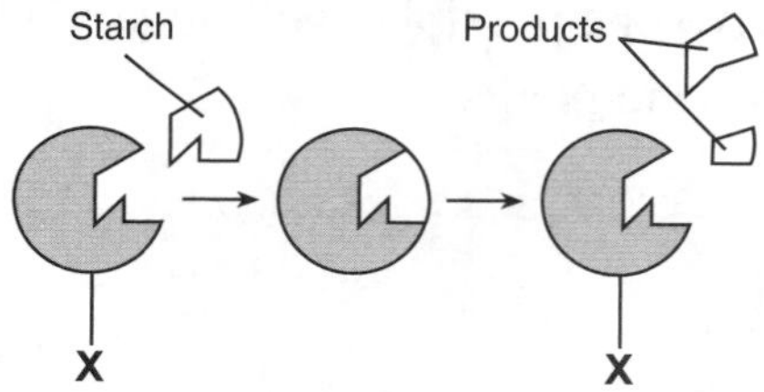

9. *a*) The products would most likely contain

    (1) simple sugars
    (2) fats
    (3) amino acids
    (4) minerals a _____

    b) The structure labeled **X** most likely represents

    (1) an antibody
    (2) a receptor molecule
    (3) an enzyme
    (4) a hormone b _____

10. Which statement describes all enzymes?

   (1) They control the transport of materials.
   (2) They provide energy for
       chemical reactions.
   (3) They affect the rate of chemical reactions.
   (4) They absorb oxygen from
       the environment.   10 _____

11. Enzyme molecules normally interact with
    substrate molecules. Some medicines work
    by blocking enzyme activity in pathogens.
    These medicines are effective because they

   (1) are the same size as the enzyme
   (2) are the same size as the substrate
       molecules
   (3) have a shape that fits into the enzyme
   (4) have a shape that fits into all
       cell receptors   11 _____

12. The diagram
    represents a cross
    section of part
    of a leaf.

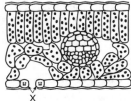

    Which life functions are directly regulated
    through feedback mechanisms associated
    with the actions of the structures labeled X?

   (1) excretion and immunity
   (2) digestion and coordination
   (3) circulation and reproduction
   (4) respiration and photosynthesis   12 _____

13. Luciferin is a molecule that, when broken
    down in fireflies, produces heat and light.
    The rate at which luciferin is broken down
    in cells is controlled by

   (1) a carbohydrate (3) an enzyme
   (2) a simple sugar (4) a complex fat
                                            13 _____

Base your answers to question 14 on the
diagram below, which represents a chemical
reaction that occurs in the human body.

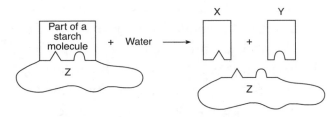

14. *a)* Substances X and Y are examples
         of which kind of molecule?

   (1) simple sugar   (3) fat
   (2) amino acid   (4) hormone   a _____

   b) Which statement describes a
         characteristic of molecule Z?

   (1) Molecule Z will function at any
       temperature above 20°C.
   (2) Molecule Z is composed of a string
       of molecular bases represented by
       A, T, G, and C.
   (3) Molecule Z will function best
       at a specific pH.
   (4) Molecule Z is not specific, so this
       reaction can be controlled by any
       other chemical in the body.   b _____

15. The shape of a protein is most directly
    determined by the

   (1) amount of energy available for synthesis
       of the protein
   (2) kind and sequence of amino acids
       in the protein
   (3) type and number of DNA molecules
       in a cell
   (4) mistakes made when the DNA
       is copied   15 _____

16. A student performed an experiment to demonstrate that a plant needs chlorophyll for photosynthesis. He used plants that had green leaves with white areas. After exposing the plants to sunlight, he removed a leaf from each plant and processed the leaves to remove the chlorophyll. He then tested each leaf for the presence of starch. Starch was found in the area of the leaf that was green, and no starch was found in the area of the leaf that was white. He concluded that chlorophyll is necessary for photosynthesis.

Which statement represents an assumption the student had to make in order to draw this conclusion?

(1) Starch is synthesized from the glucose produced in the green areas of the leaf.
(2) Starch is converted to chlorophyll in the green areas of the leaf.
(3) The white areas of the leaf do not have cells.
(4) The green areas of the leaf are heterotrophic.   16 _____

17. The graph below shows the effect of temperature on the relative rate of action of enzyme X on a protein.

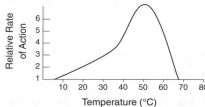

Which change would not affect the relative rate of action of enzyme X?

(1) the addition of cold water when the reaction is at 50°C
(2) an increase in temperature from 70°C to 80°C
(3) the removal of the protein when the reaction is at 30°C
(4) a decrease in temperature from 40°C to 10°C   17 _____

18. A biological process that occurs in both plants and animals is shown below.

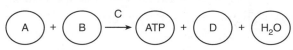

Which row in the chart below identifies the lettered substances in this process?

Row	A	B	C	D
(1)	O_2	CO_2	glucose	enzymes
(2)	glucose	O_2	enzymes	CO_2
(3)	enzymes	O_2	CO_2	glucose
(4)	glucose	CO_2	enzymes	O_2

18 _____

19. Living organisms must be able to obtain materials, change the materials into new forms, remove poisons, and move needed material from one place to another. Many of these activities directly require

(1) energy released from ATP
(2) carbohydrates formed from receptor molecules
(3) the synthesis of DNA
(4) the breakdown of energy-rich inorganic molecules   19 _____

20. The flow of energy through an ecosystem involves many energy transfers. The diagram below summarizes the transfer of energy that eventually powers muscle activity.

$$\text{Sun} \xrightarrow{A} \text{Food} \xrightarrow{B} \text{ATP} \xrightarrow{C} \text{Muscle Activity}$$

The process of cellular respiration is represented by

(1) arrow A, only
(2) arrow B, only
(3) arrow C, only
(4) arrows A, B, and C 20 _____

21. A word equation is shown below.

Starch molecules $\xrightarrow{\text{(biological catalyst)}}$ Simple sugars

This reaction is most directly involved in the process of

(1) reproduction
(2) protein synthesis
(3) replication
(4) heterotrophic nutrition   21 _____

22. All life depends on the availability of usable energy. This energy is released when

(1) organisms convert solar energy into the chemical energy found in food molecules
(2) respiration occurs in the cells of producers and high-energy molecules enter the atmosphere
(3) cells carry out the process of respiration
(4) animal cells synthesize starch and carbon dioxide   22 _____

23. Which statement concerning simple sugars and amino acids is correct?

(1) They are both wastes resulting from protein synthesis.
(2) They are both building blocks of starch.
(3) They are both needed for the synthesis of larger molecules.
(4) They are both stored as fat molecules in the liver.   23 _____

24. Which row in the chart below contains correct information concerning synthesis?

Row	Building Blocks	Substance Synthesized Using the Building Blocks
(1)	glucose molecules	DNA
(2)	simple sugars	protein
(3)	amino acids	enzyme
(4)	molecular bases	starch

24 _____

25. Which words best complete the lettered blanks in the two sentences below?

Organic compounds, such as proteins and starches, are too *A* to diffuse into cells. Proteins are digested into *B* and starches are digested into *C*.

(1) *A*—large, *B*—simple sugars, *C*—amino acids
(2) *A*—small, *B*—simple sugars, *C*—amino acids
(3) *A*—large, *B*—amino acids, *C*—simple sugars
(4) *A*—small, *B*—amino acids, *C*—simple sugars   25 _____

26. The function of most proteins depends primarily on the

(1) type and order of amino acids
(2) environment of the organism
(3) availability of starch molecules
(4) nutritional habits of the organism   26 _____

27. Which statement best describes the flow of energy and the movement of chemical compounds in an ecosystem?

(1) Energy flows into living organisms and remains there, while chemical compounds are transferred from organism to organism.
(2) Chemical compounds flow in one direction in a food chain and energy is produced.
(3) Energy is transferred from organism to organism in a food chain and chemical compounds are recycled.
(4) Energy flows out of living organisms and is lost, while chemical compounds remain permanently inside organisms.   27 _____

28. What substance could be represented by the letter X in the diagram?

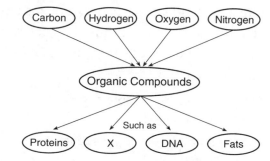

(1) carbohydrades   (3) ozone
(2) carbon dioxide   (4) water   28 _____

29. The rate at which all organisms obtain, transform, and transport materials depends on an immediate supply of

(1) ATP and enzymes
(2) solar energy and carbon dioxide
(3) carbon dioxide and enzymes
(4) ATP and solar energy   29 _____

30. A biological process that occurs in plants is represented below.

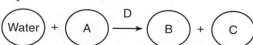

Which row in the chart below identifies the lettered substances in this process?

Row	A	B	C	D
(1)	enzymes	oxygen	carbon dioxide	glucose
(2)	carbon dioxide	glucose	oxygen	enzymes
(3)	glucose	enzymes	oxygen	carbon dioxide
(4)	oxygen	glucose	carbon dioxide	enzymes

30 _____

31. The diagram represents a plant cell. Which process takes place in structure A?

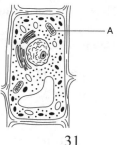

(1) cellular respiration
(2) heterotrophic nutrition
(3) digestion of fats
(4) protein synthesis   31 _____

32. The diagram represents a process that occurs in a structure of a specialized cell.

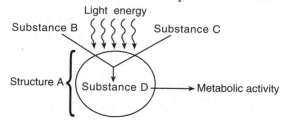

Which row in the chart correctly identifies the letters in the diagram?

Row	A	B	C	D
(1)	ribosome	oxygen	carbon dioxide	water
(2)	mitochondrion	water	oxygen	protein
(3)	nucleus	nitrogen	carbon	starch
(4)	chloroplast	carbon dioxide	water	glucose

32 _____

33. The enzyme amylase will affect the breakdown of carbohydrates, but it will not affect the breakdown of proteins. The ability of an enzyme molecule to interact with specific molecules is most directly determined by the

(1) shapes of the molecules involved
(2) number of molecules involved
(3) sequence of bases present in ATP
(4) amount of glucose present in the cell

33 _____

34. Which cell structure is mainly responsible for releasing energy from food molecules in some single-celled organisms?

(1) ribosome   (3) cell membrane
(2) chloroplast   (4) mitochondrion   34 _____

35. Which set of terms best identifies the letters in the diagram below?

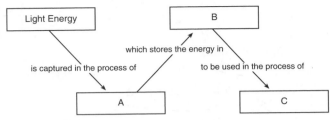

	A	B	C
(1)	photosynthesis	inorganic molecules	decomposition
(2)	respiration	organic molecules	digestion
(3)	photosynthesis	organic molecules	respiration
(4)	respiration	inorganic molecules	photosynthesis

35 _____

36. The diagram below represents a cell organelle involved in the transfer of energy from organic compounds.

The arrows in the diagram could represent the release of

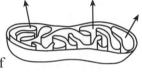

(1) ATP from a chloroplast carrying out photosynthesis

(2) oxygen from a mitochondrion carrying out photosynthesis

(3) glucose from a chloroplast carrying out respiration

(4) carbon dioxide from a mitochondrion carrying out respiration

36 _____

37. Maple trees and tulips are classified as autotrophs because they both

(1) produce gametes by the process of mitosis

(2) produce carbon dioxide and water as metabolic wastes

(3) are able to obtain complex organic materials from the environment

(4) are able to synthesize organic molecules from inorganic raw materials

37 _____

38. The diagram below represents a biological process.

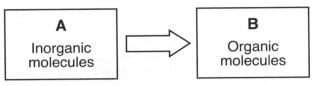

Which set of molecules is best represented by letters A and B?

(1) A: oxygen and water
    B: glucose

(2) A: glucose
    B: carbon dioxide and water

(3) A: carbon dioxide and water
    B: glucose

(4) A: glucose
    B: oxygen and water

38 _____

39. The swordfish contains a heat generating organ that warms its brain and eyes up to 14°C above the surrounding ocean water temperature. Which structures are most likely to be found at relatively high concentrations within the cells of this heat generating organ?

(1) nuclei   (3) chromosomes

(2) chloroplasts (4) mitochondria

39 _____

40. A student prepared a test tube containing yeast, glucose, and water. After 24 hours, the test tube was analyzed for the presence of several substances. What substance would the student expect to find if respiration occurred in the test tube?

(1) a hormone   (3) nitrogen

(2) starch   (4) carbon dioxide

40 _____

Base your answers to question 41 on the diagram below.

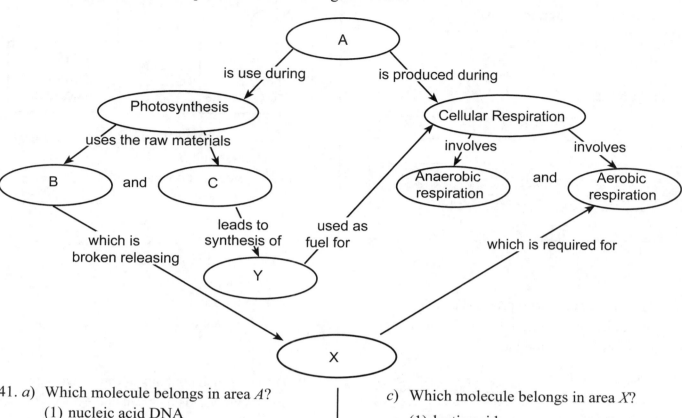

41. *a)* Which molecule belongs in area *A*?
   (1) nucleic acid DNA
   (2) energy molecule ATP
   (3) glucose
   (4) oxygen   a_____

b) In which organelle do the reactions
   that belong in area *B* and *C* occur?

   (1) mitochondrion
   (2) chloroplast
   (3) nucleus
   (4) Golgi complex   b_____

c) Which molecule belongs in area *X*?

   (1) lactic acid
   (2) carbon dioxide
   (3) water
   (4) oxygen   c_____

d) Which molecule belongs in area *Y*?

   (1) water
   (2) oxygen
   (3) glucose
   (4) hydrogen   d_____

42. Which phrase, if placed in box *X*, would correctly complete the flowchart shown below?

   | Exposed to sunlight | → | Increased use of CO_2 | → | X |

(1) Increased use of starch in root cells
(2) Increased concentration of glucose in leaf cells
(3) Decreased ATP in root cells
(4) Decreased concentration of oxygen in leaf cells   42_____

43. The pH of the internal environment of lysosomes (organelles that contain digestive enzymes) is approximately 4.5, while the pH of the surrounding cytoplasm is approximately 7. The average pH of the human stomach during digestion is approximately 2.5, while the average pH of the small intestine during digestion is about 8. The graph shows how pH affects the enzyme activity of four different enzymes, A, B, C, and D.

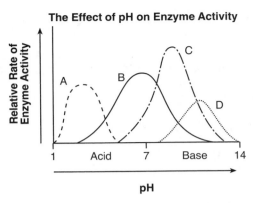

The Effect of pH on Enzyme Activity

a) What will most likely happen to the action of an enzyme from the small intestine if it is placed in an environment similar to the environment in which enzyme C functions best?

(1) It would no longer be able to function because the environment is too acidic.

(2) It would adapt to the new environment and start carrying out the same function as enzyme C.

(3) It would continue to function because it is able to modify the pH of the environment.

(4) It would be able to function because the pH of the environment is similar to that of the intestine.

a_____

b) Lysosomes break open during the process of digestion, releasing enzymes into the cytoplasm. Which statement may explain why the entire cell may not be digested?

(1) The acidic environment of the cytoplasm destroys the enzymes.

(2) Antibodies in the cytoplasm break down foreign enzymes.

(3) The pH of the cytoplasm causes the enzymes to function less effectively.

(4) Enzymes can function only in the location where they are synthesized.

b_____

c) Which enzyme functions best in a pH environment most similar to that of human stomach enzymes?

(1) A   (2) B   (3) C   (4) D

c_____

44. The diagram represents changes in the sizes of openings present in leaves as a result of the actions of cells X and Y.

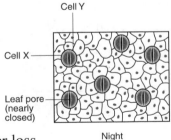
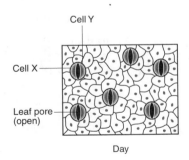

The actions of cells X and Y help the plant to

(1) maintain homeostasis by controlling water loss

(2) store excess heat during the day and remove the heat at night

(3) absorb light energy necessary for cellular respiration

(4) detect changes in the biotic factors present in the environment

44_____

45. If a starch-digesting enzyme were added to a sports gel that lists starch as an ingredient, which substance would increase in concentration?

(1) fat   (2) glucose   (3) amino acids   (4) water

45_____

46. Carbon exists in a simple organic molecule in a leaf and in an inorganic molecule in the air humans exhale.

   a) Identify the simple organic molecule formed in the leaf and the process that produces it.

   Molecule:_____ Process: _____

   b) Identify the carbon-containing molecule that humans exhale and the process that produces it.

   Molecule:_____ Process: _____

Base your answers to question 47 on the diagram that represents a human enzyme and four types of molecules present in a solution in a flask.

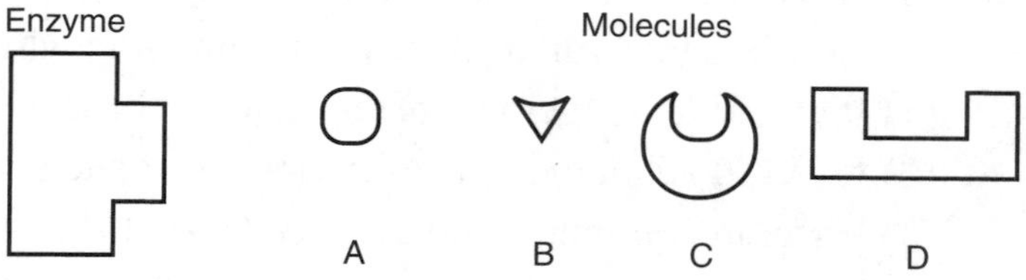

Enzyme   Molecules

A   B   C   D

47. a) Which molecule would most likely react with the enzyme? _____

   b) Explain your answer to question a.

   _____

   c) State what would most likely happen to the rate of reaction if the temperature of the solution in the flask were increased gradually from 10°C to 30°C.

   _____

48. Describe the cycling of carbon in an ecosystem. In your answer be sure to:

   a) identify the inorganic carbon compound that is obtained by plants from the environment _____

   b) identify the process plants use to form more complex organic molecules from this carbon compound

   _____

   c) describe how herbivores use these complex organic molecules

   _____

   d) identify the process herbivores use to return carbon to the environment _____

49. Name an organic molecule that is used during cellular respiration in the mitochondria?

   _____

50. Organelles carry out specific processes involving chemical reactions. In the chart, 3 organelles are given. For each, identify a process involving chemical reactions that occur there. Describe one specific way each process is important to the functioning of the organism.

Organelle	Process Involving Chemical Reactions that Occur in the Organelle	How the Process is Important to the Functioning of the Organism
mitochondrion		
chloroplast		
ribosome		

51. In the diagrams of the two different cells shown, only cell *A* produces substance *X*. Both cells *A* and *B* use substance *X*.

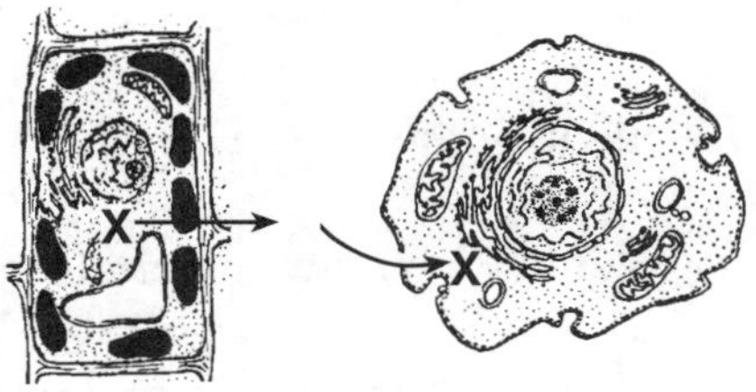

Cell A   Cell B

a) Identify substance *X*. _____

b) Identify the type of organelle in cell *A* that produces substance *X*._____

c) Identify the type of organelle found in both cell *A* and cell *B* that uses substance *X*. _____

Base your answers to question 52 on the summary equation of the process.

Respiration

glucose + oxygen $\xrightarrow{\text{enzymes}}$ water + carbon dioxide

52. a) Identify the source of the energy in this process. _____

b) Identify where the energy ends up at the completion of that process. _____

c) State one reason why this process is important to living things.

_____

53. Cardinals are birds that do not migrate but spend the winter in New York State. Many people feed these birds sunflower seeds during the winter months. Explain how the starches present in the sunflower seeds help the cardinals to survive. In your answer, be sure to:

a) identify the building blocks of starches _____

b) identify the process used to produce these building block _____

c) state one way cardinals use these building blocks to survive

_____

Base your answers to question 54 on the diagram of a cell.

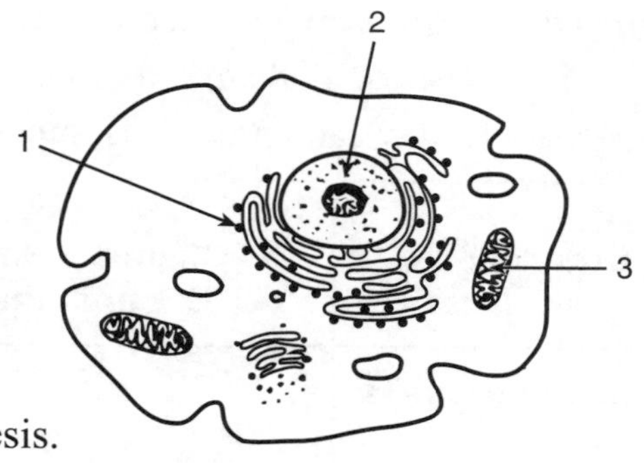

54. *a)* Describe how structures 1 and 2 interact in the process of protein synthesis.

_____

_____

b) Describe how structure 3 aids in the process of protein synthesis.

_____

55. Photosynthesis and respiration are two important processes. Discuss one of these processes and explain its importance to an organism. In your answer, be sure to:

a) identify the process being discussed _____

b) identify the organelle where this process occurs _____

c) identify two raw materials necessary for this process

1) _____

2) _____

d) identify one energy-rich molecule that is produced by this process _____

e) state how organisms use the energy-rich molecule that is produced

_____

f) state how a gas produced by this process is recycled in nature

_____

56. The accompanying diagram represents a change in guard cells that open and close pores in a plant.

This change directly helps to regulate what?

_____

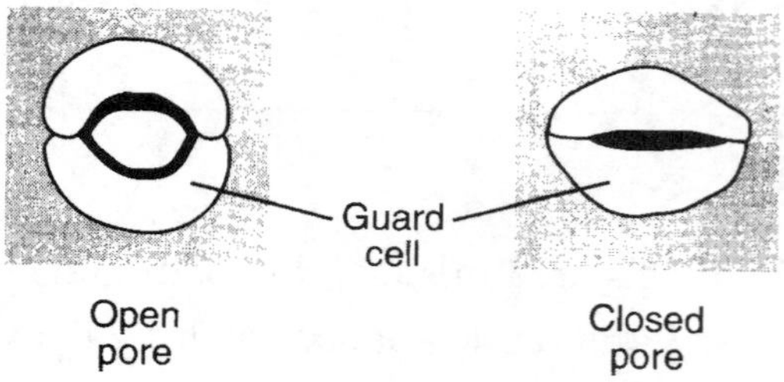

Guard cell

Open pore   Closed pore

57. State one reason why muscle tissues are likely to be affected by mitrochondrial diseases.

_____

1. 4   Carbon dioxide is used during autotrophic nutrition. Autotrophs carry out a process known as photosynthesis which uses carbon dioxide as a raw material for the synthesis of required nutrients.

2. 4   Respiration uses the stored chemical energy found in glucose. With oxygen, glucose will produce the energy needed for living organisms, while releasing carbon dioxide.

3. 3   Heterotrophs are organisms that must obtain preformed organic molecules or compounds that they can then break down into useful energy or building blocks. Generally these organic molecules are produced as a result of photosynthesis performed by autotrophs.

4. 1   The process of cellular respiration produces ATP molecules within the mitochondria of the cell. This energy is stored in the chemical bonds of ATP molecules. Remember that cells use simple sugars like glucose and oxygen to produce ATP molecules.

5. 3   In food, the original source of energy is sunlight. Through the process of photosynthesis, producers convert light energy, CO_2 and water into glucose and O_2.

6. 3   Photosynthesis and respiration both involve the following molecules: glucose which is organic, and water, oxygen, and carbon dioxide which are inorganic. Photosynthesis uses light energy, CO_2 and water to produce glucose and O_2. Respiration uses glucose and O_2 to produce CO_2 and energy.

7. 1   The section of the leaf that was covered was not exposed to sunlight and therefore could not undergo the process of photosynthesis. Lacking this process, no starch would be created. Remember that glucose, a product of photosynthesis, is converted into starch for storage purpose.

8. 2   In plants, the process of photosynthesis uses the energy of the Sun to convert carbon dioxide into the chemical energy of sugar (glucose), while giving off oxygen as a by-product.

9. 1   Respiration and photosynthesis are processes that maintain oxygen and carbon dioxide levels. Respiration, the energy producing process, uses oxygen and releases carbon dioxide to create the energy molecule, ATP. Photosynthesis uses carbon dioxide to produce sugars while releasing oxygen. Through each of these processes, carbon dioxide and oxygen levels in the atmosphere are maintained.

10. 3   The process of photosynthesis uses the inorganic compounds water and carbon dioxide to synthesize the organic compound, glucose. Plants use the energy of sunlight to initiate the mechanisms of this process.

11. 1   Each plant has adapted to the climate and surroundings that make it possible to survive. One mechanism for this survival is to control the water loss that occurs through the stomata. This is controlled by the guard cells that regulate the size of the stomata opening. Cactus plants, being desert plants, would have to reduce their water loss to the lowest level in order to maintain homeostasis.

12. 2   Guard cells surround and regulate the leaf openings called stomata. The atmospheric gases, carbon dioxide and oxygen enter and leave the plant respectively, through these stomata. By regulating the opening and closing of the stomata, the guard cells regulate oxygen and carbon dioxide levels. Transpiration or loss of water is also regulated through the activity of guard cells.

13. 1   In order for enzymes to function properly, they require a certain range of pH (specific to each enzyme). In the blood, if pH is not regulated, enzymes that clot blood may be impacted. Remember that an enzyme's shape determines its function. If pH changes and alters enzyme shape, the enzyme may not be able to function properly.

14. 2   Cellular respiration is a process where the chemical energy in a glucose (sugar) molecule is converted through chemical reactions to stored energy in a molecule of ATP. This process, which takes place in the mitochondria of a cell, also requires oxygen.

15. 2   The peak of graph 2 represents the optimum temperature for the enzyme. As the temperature range decreases or increases from this optimum temperature, the enzyme activity decreases. This relationship is shown in graph 2.

16. 2   Simple sugars are the building blocks of starch. Sugars, produced by photosynthesis, are converted to starch for storage purposes. This starch can be used at a later time for available energy.

17. 4   In the process of photosynthesis, autotrophs (producers) take in carbon dioxide (CO_2) for the synthesis of organic nutrients.

18. 4   Proteins do not bond together to form simple sugars. Sugars belong to the organic compound group, carbohydrates. Proteins, made up of folded chains of amino acids, may link together to form structural components of living organisms. On occasion, proteins may be broken down and used for energy.

19. 1   Enzymes are biological catalysts which speed up chemical reactions. They have a specific location where the reaction takes place (active site). In this diagram, the reaction taking place is synthesis, where simple or original molecules are combined using the biological catalyst to form complex or final molecules.

20. 2   In this reaction, dipeptide (a protein) is broken down into the amino acid products by an enzyme. Enzyme activity occurs within a specific temperature and pH range. If any one of these two factors is out of its functioning range, the enzyme changes shape. This change in shape alters the enzyme's active site, thus causing enzyme activity to slow down or not function at all.

21. 2   Amino acid molecules are simple building blocks that are used to synthesize more complex molecules called proteins (the shown product). These complex molecules of protein then could be used for a structural or digestive function.

22. 4   Digestion is the process where nutrients are broken down into a usable form for cellular use. Structures B and C represent enzymes which may speed up digestive processes. Structure A represents a substrate (nutrient) and structures D and E are the broken-down products of structure A as a result of the digestive action of B.

Copyright © 2017
Topical Review Book Company

23. 3   Catalysts, certain hormones, and receptor's molecules are all proteins. As with all proteins, the shape directly affects the function. The folding of the protein's amino acid chains creates specific shapes that determine specific function. Remember that proteins are composed of building blocks called amino acids.

24. 2   ATP molecules are produced by the process of cellular respiration. During respiration, glucose, an organic compound, is broken down, and the energy released is converted into ATP.

25. 4   Proteins are composed of building blocks called amino acids. The amino acids link together in a particular sequence to give the protein a specific shape. In proteins, shape relates to function. So, if proteins are shaped or folded differently, they will have different functions.

26. 3   The opening and closing of guard cells regulates the size of the stomata pore and allows plants to control the amount of water exiting, thus maintaining internal water balance.

27. 2   The use of energy to pass waste products across a cell membrane involves the energy molecule, ATP. Remember ATP is produced by the process of cellular respiration in living organisms.

28. *a)* 1   Substance *B* is a simple sugar like glucose, which serves as a source of energy. Carbohydrates are composed of sugars, like glucose, and when digested, break down into these molecules. Simple sugars are used to power the process of respiration which produces ATP.

   b) 2   Substance *A* is an amino acid. Amino acids are the building blocks of proteins such as enzymes. When proteins are digested, amino acids result and are available for synthesis processes, such as building enzymes.

29. 2   Meat mainly consists of protein. After an organism eats the meat, its digestive system breaks that protein down into building blocks called amino acids. These amino acids are distributed to cells to be used to synthesize needed proteins.

30. 1   The shape of an enzyme molecule is specific. Each enzyme has a site on its molecule that binds with a substrate to facilitate a particular reaction.

31. 4   The metabolic process represented in this investigation is anaerobic respiration, which occurs in the organism yeast. Respiration uses the energy in sugar to produce ATP and the waste product carbon dioxide. Substance X represents carbon dioxide that bubbled to the top displacing the water.

32. Answer: Energy in carbohydrate molecules is transferred to ATP.
   or Carbohydrates have energy in their bonds that can be used to make ATP for carrying on life functions.

   Explanation: Cellular respiration uses enzymes to break down molecules of glucose, a carbohydrate. As a result, the released energy is used to form molecules of ATP for future energy needs of the cell or organism.

33. *a*) Enzyme roles: catalyze chemical reactions *or* affect rates of reaction *or* help synthesize proteins *or* speed up digestion

b) Effect of high body temperature: Enzyme activity will slow down. *or* Enzyme will not function at all. *or* Enzymes will not catalyze reactions quickly.

Explanation: Enzymes are protein molecules which speed up chemical reactions within organisms. Enzyme activity can be affected by several factors, one of which is temperature. Above certain temperatures, enzymes change shape. This change in shape alters the enzyme's active site (site of reaction where substrate binds to enzyme) thus causing enzyme activity to slow down or not function at all. If enzymes don't function, many life activities, such as respiration or digestion, would not operate correctly, possibly leading to death.

34. *a*) Answer: plants *or* autotrophs *or* producers

Explanation: Process 1 is photosynthesis where the raw materials of carbon dioxide and water are being synthesized into simple sugar compounds. Organisms that carry out this process include all forms of autotrophs (plants).

b) Answer: so that energy can be released *or* to make food molecules small enough to be transported (or diffused)

Explanation: Process 2 is digestion. Digestion is necessary for humans to break down large complex compounds into usable simple compounds. These smaller molecules, usually building blocks of organic compounds, must be able to diffuse or move into the circulatory system so they can be transported to the cells. These molecules are essential for the cell to maintain homeostasis.

c) Answer: respiration

Explanation: Respiration is an energy-producing process that takes simple compounds and converts them to a usable form of energy (ATP). By-products of respiration are carbon dioxide and water.

d) Answer: ATP *or* energy

Explanation: As stated in the explanation for *c*, respiration is an energy-producing process, and the compound that is synthesized is ATP. ATP can be used for such activities as transport movement and cell division.

35. Answer and explanation: Enzymes are protein molecules that have a specific shape needed for proper functioning. An alteration of this shape deteriorates the enzyme's ability to function (see explanation #33).

36. *a*) Answer: *D*

Explanation: Letter *D* represents a chloroplast where photosynthesis takes place producing glucose. Glucose is a major source of energy for cells.

b) Answer: *B*

Explanation: The cell membrane allows for transport of nutrients into the cell.

37. Acceptable responses include but are not limited to:
   a) *Organelle:* mitochondrion
   b) *Process:* respiration/cellular respiration *or* aerobic respiration *or* releases energy (ATP)
   c) *Raw materials:* sugar/glucose *or* oxygen
   d) *Molecule produced:* ATP *or* water *or* carbon dioxide

   Importance: provides energy for life processes *or* chemical reaction
   or waste product that must be removed to maintain homeostasis

   Explanation: Organelle *X* is a mitochondrion, a cellular organelle that produce ATP (an energy molecule) as a result of cellular respiration. Glucose and oxygen are raw materials necessary for the process of respiration to take place. Carbon dioxide is produced as a waste product and must be removed from the cell to maintain homeostasis both within the cell and within the organism.

38. a) *Function:* gas exchange *or* respiration *or* photosynthesis *or* controls transpiration

   Explanation: The guard cells on a leaf surround the stomata and serve to open and close the stomata. The stomata allow for the exchange of gases (CO_2 and O_2) into and out of the plant. This movement of gases allows for important life processes, such as respiration and photosynthesis, to occur by providing necessary ingredients. Transpiration or loss of water is also regulated through the activity of guard cells.

   b) *Carry out function:* Guard cells change shape.
   or Guard cells change the size of the leaf opening (stomata).

   Explanation: Guard cells can change their shape through the movement of water. When a guard cell takes in water, the cell becomes plump and bends like a crescent. This shape change pulls open the stomata or leaf opening. Likewise, when the guard cell loses water, the stomata opening decreases or closes.

   c) *Evolution advantage:* prevents evaporation on a sunny day
   or   prevents the entrance of some pollutants

   Explanation: Guard cells, located on the bottom of the leaf, will experience less direct sunlight and therefore lower temperatures. This may be an advantage to land plants because excess water will not evaporate on hot, sunny days. The location of the guard cells on the bottom of the leaf also may prevent airborne pollutant particles from getting into the stomata from above.

39. a) Answer: sunlight   Explanation: Photosynthesis needs light as an energy source.

   b) Answer: glucose (carbohydrates or monosaccharide) *or* sugar *or* chemical bonds *or* $C_6H_{12}O_6$
   Explanation: Photosynthesis uses sunlight, CO_2, and water to produce glucose and O_2.

   c) Answer: Photosynthesis produces a simple sugar (glucose), which is a source of energy needed by all organisms. *or* Oxygen is produced by this processes.
   or Photosynthesis changes light energy into chemical energy.

   Explanation: See explanation for questions 16 and 17, page 118.

   d) Answer: Chloroplast   Explanation: In plants, photosynthesis takes place within the chloroplast.

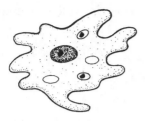  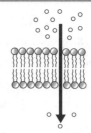

Overview:

Living organisms are composed of a small basic unit called the cell. Cells carry out basic life functions using various cell parts or *organelles*. The more complex the cell, the more defined the cell structure and more interrelated the cell parts. It is important to understand that what happens at the cellular level can be reflected throughout the whole organism. The discovery and development of the microscope has led to greater understanding of the cell's structure and function.

Essential Information:

Basic Cell Understanding – Understanding of the cell's importance as a basic unit of life came about with advancements in the use of the microscope. Today's microscopes are able to examine and give precise details about the workings of a cell. Two microscopes are commonly used in cell studies. The *compound light microscope* provides adequate magnification for students to begin to gain an appreciation for the cell as a unit of life. *Electron microscopes*, more commonly found at universities and in research facilities, provide a detailed look at cells with great magnification.

Various early cell biologists identified important concepts, which are collectively known as the *Cell Theory*. This theory states that animals and plants are composed of cells; cells are the basic unit of structure and function; and all cells come from preexisting cells. The exceptions are the first cell that ever existed and viruses. Cells are the basis for organization in living things. Cells that are grouped together by function are known as *tissues*. Tissues with similar function collectively form an *organ*. When organs are grouped together based on their function, they are organized into an *organ system*.

Cell Structures – Cell structures can be found in the simple unicellular organisms as well as in the cells of more complex multi-cellular organisms. Structures common to all cells are cytoplasm and the cell membrane. *Cytoplasm* is a liquid medium that serves to suspend various cell parts and may also play a role in cell transport. The *cell membrane* provides a barrier between the inside contents of the cell and its outside environment.

All cells have a region that contains genetic information. In most complex animal and plant cells, genetic information is held within the *nucleus*. The nucleus is membrane bound and contains tightly coiled DNA in *chromosomes*. Genetic information is transferred to *ribosomes*, small structures located in the cytoplasm that act as factories, synthesizing proteins by linking together amino acids. Organelles called *vacuoles* are involved in storage of nutrients. Energy processes are located within specific cell organelles. Cellular respiration takes place in the mitochondrion in all multicellular organisms. Photosynthesis is carried out in the chloroplast of plant cells only. Plant cells also differ from animal cells in that they also contain a cell wall. The cell wall is located outside the cell membrane. It is made of cellulose and acts to provide flexible support for the cell. Also note, in plant cells is a *large central vacuole* for the storage of water and nutrients.

Cell Membrane – The membrane of a cell has a specific structure consisting of a *lipid bi-layer*, which is a double layer of lipid molecules arranged to provide a barrier between the cell's contents and the outside environment. The membrane is represented by a model known as the *Fluid Mosaic Model*. This model helps to explain movement of materials in and out of the cell, as well as communication between cells. There are several types of proteins found in the membrane. *Channel proteins* allow for the flow of small molecules without the expenditure of energy. *Carrier proteins* are able to move larger molecules with the use of energy. *Receptor proteins*, found on the surface of the cell membrane, bind with specific molecules to activate a reaction or process within the cell using shape specific molecules. These proteins allow for communication between cells. Both hormones and nerve impulses involve the use of receptor proteins. Finally, *cell recognition proteins* allow a cell to identify other cells as self or foreign. This process is essential to the proper function of the immune system and the role of specialized white blood cells to fight infections.

Cellular Transport Processes – Movement across a membrane can be classified into two categories: *Passive transport* which requires no energy and *active transport* that requires energy for the movement of molecules or materials. Passive transport can be further divided into the processes of diffusion and osmosis. *Diffusion* is the movement of small molecules from regions of high concentration to regions of lower concentration. *Osmosis* is the diffusion of water from an area of higher water content to a region of lower water content based on the concentration of the solution on both sides of the cell membrane. Both processes are important for the maintenance of homeostasis within a cell. Some molecules diffuse easily through a membrane, others do not. The size of a molecule will determine the rate of diffusion. Smaller molecules, like water, readily move through a membrane, whereas larger molecules like starch may not diffuse at all. Active transport requires energy, usually ATP, for movement. It usually involves the movement of larger molecules, or the movement of molecules from regions of low concentration to regions of higher concentration. Active transport can also involve a process where the cell membrane engulfs or surrounds molecules or materials to bring into the cell. White blood cells use active transport to engulf foreign proteins and pathogens to protect the body from disease and infection.

Additional Information:

- Indicators such as iodine (starch indicator solution) and Benedict's solution (glucose indicator solution) can be used to verify the movement of molecules in laboratory settings. Iodine changes from an amber brown to a blue-black color in the presence of starch. Benedict's solution turns from a blue color to brick red in a warm water bath in the presence of glucose.

- When looking at cells under the microscope, more definition can be obtained when stains are added. The stain (like methylene blue or iodine) allows certain cell organelles to be more visible, making cell study easier and more efficient.

- Cells also contain several other organelles:
  - The endoplasmic reticulum, involved in protein transport
  - The Golgi apparatus, involved in marking and preparing proteins for dispersal into the cell
  - Lysosomes, involved in cellular digestive processes.

Diagrams:

1. **Unicellular** – This diagram represents an unicellular organism. It is a simple one-celled animal carrying out basic life functions. Each cell part of a unicellular organism performs a specific function, much like an organ would do in a multi-cellular organism.

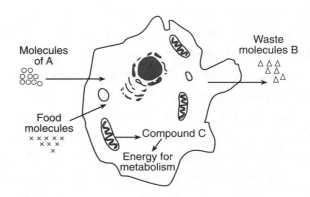

2. **Animal Cell Organelles** – All cells have organelles or cell parts that carry out necessary functions. This animal cell shows five such organelles. Part 1 is a ribosome where proteins are synthesized; part 2 is a nucleus that directs and stores genetic information; part 3 is a mitochondrion that is the site of cellular respiration; and part 4 is a vacuole used to store materials; part 5 is a cell membrane, which provides a barrier between the cell's contents and the outside environment.

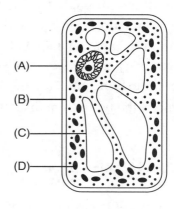

3. **Plant Cell Organelles** – In this diagram, a plant cell has three distinct cell parts that are different from an animal cell. The plant cell has a cell wall (*A*) that provides support and structure; large vacuoles (*C*), storage sites that consist of mainly water; and chloroplasts (*D*) where photosynthesis takes place. A cell membrane (*B*) is found in all animal and plant cells.

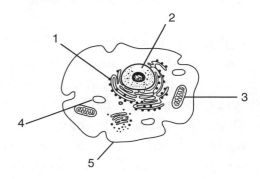

4. **Movement Across a Cell Membrane** – In this diagram, method *A* represents simple diffusion (passive transport) where molecules are moving from an area of higher to lower concentration. Method *B* shows facilitated diffusion where a protein molecule in the cell membrane enables the movement of molecules across the membrane. Method *C* illustrates active transport where molecules are moved from a region of low concentration to one of higher concentration with the help of membrane proteins and the use of ATP (energy).

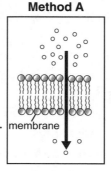
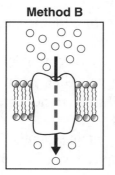
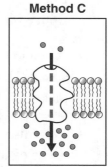

Cells and Cell Processes

Copyright © 2017
Topical Review Book Company

5. **Receptor Protein** – One type of proteins found within the cell membrane is a receptor protein. Receptor proteins, as seen in the diagram, are shape specific and bind with a specific molecule that fits into that receptor. This is shown in diagram where Signal 1 fits into rounded receptor of Cell *A* and Signal 2 fits into "V" shaped receptor of Cell *B*. When one type of protein molecule binds, it initiates a specific reaction within that cell.

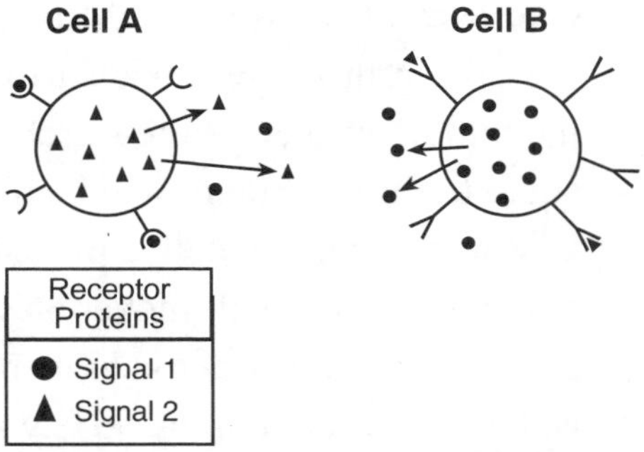

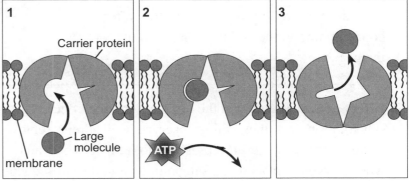

Cell A   Cell B

Receptor Proteins
● Signal 1
▲ Signal 2

6. **Carrier Protein** – Carrier proteins are membrane proteins that function to move molecules across the membrane. They usually require the input of energy in the form of ATP. They are needed when molecules may be too large or when moving molecules against a gradient (from low to high concentration) during active transport.

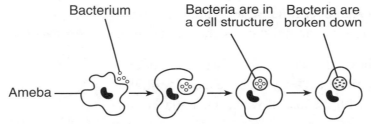

1   2   3

Carrier protein

Large molecule

membrane

ATP

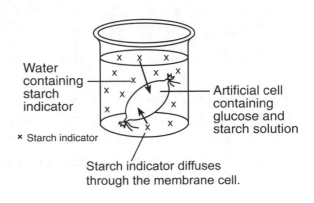

Bacterium

Bacteria are in a cell structure   Bacteria are broken down

Ameba

7. **Heterotrophic Nutrition** – Certain cells are able to engulf food, microbes and other molecules as a way to bring them into the cell. Once surrounded, the particles become enclosed in a vacuole. This process involves ATP, and is also evident during and immune response with white blood cells engulfing pathogens or antigen pieces.

8. **Diffusion** – Molecules may move or diffuse based on their concentration (from high to low concentration) until there is an equal distribution of molecules both in and out of the cell. To help model the process of diffusion, artificial cells are used to show movement of molecules across a membrane. In the diagram, the artificial cell contains both the molecules glucose and starch, while the outside of the artificial cell contains starch indicator. The starch indicator will diffuse into the cell causing a color change in the cell.

Water containing starch indicator

Artificial cell containing glucose and starch solution

× Starch indicator

Starch indicator diffuses through the membrane cell.

Note: The starch molecules will not diffuse through the cell membrane due to their large size, but the glucose being a smaller molecule will diffuse through the cell membrane

9. **Osmosis** – Osmosis, the diffusion of water, is dependent on the solute concentration both in and out of the cell. In this diagram, an artificial cell is placed in varying starch concentrations. When placed in the middle beaker where starch concentration is equal to the cell, there will be no net movement of water. When the cell is placed in the beaker to the left, water will move into the cell as the concentration of water is higher in the 100% water beaker than in the 95% water cell. When placed into the beaker on the far right, osmosis will cause the cell to lose water as the water concentration in the cell is higher than that of the beaker.

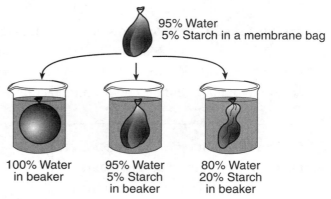

95% Water
5% Starch in a membrane bag

100% Water
in beaker

95% Water
5% Starch
in beaker

80% Water
20% Starch
in beaker

10. **Effect of Salt Water** – In the top diagram, the effect of a salt solution on a plant cell is observed. Cell *A* represents a normal plant cell. Cell *B* represents both the loss of water when the cell is placed in a salt solution and the subsequent effects on the cell membrane. Notice that the cell membrane has pinched in and pulled away from the cell wall. If cell *B* is placed in distilled water, over time, water will diffuse back into the cell and return to its original state as shown in cell *A*.

The lower diagram shows the movement of water out of an animal cell. Because animal cells do not have a cell wall, the whole cell will shrink with the loss of water when placed in a salt solution.

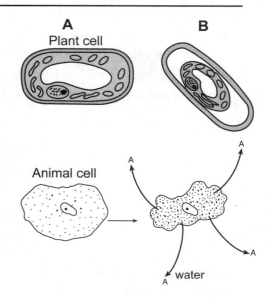

A

B

Plant cell

Animal cell

water

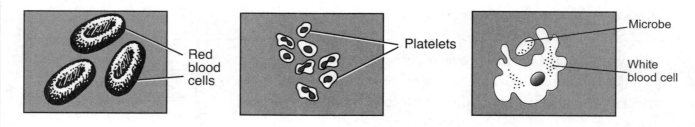

Red
blood
cells

Platelets

Microbe

White
blood cell

11. **Blood Cells and Function** – Blood cells perform specific functions that aid in maintaining homeostasis. Red blood cells transport oxygen throughout the body via the circulatory system. Platelets are small fragments of cell that aid in the clotting process, and white blood cells are involved in the bodies defense system by engulfing microbes for destruction.

Vocabulary Refresher

Group A   *Directions* - Match the correct definition for the following terms:

1. _____Compound light microscope

2. _____Active transport

3. _____Cell Theory

4. _____Tissues

5. _____Channel proteins

6. _____Organ system

7. _____Cytoplasm

8. _____Cell membrane

9. _____Nucleus

10. _____Ribosomes

11. _____Chloroplasts

12. _____Organelles

13. _____Vacuoles

A. Composed of cells that are grouped together by function.

B. The liquid portion of the cell that serves to suspend cell parts and also may aid in transportation.

C. An organelle responsible for holding the genetic information of the cell in tightly packed coils of DNA.

D. Uses a mirror, light, and magnifying lenses to produce magnification for student's classroom use.

E. A site for the storage of nutrients.

F. Proteins that allow for the flow of small molecules using no energy.

G. Structures within the cell that have specific functions.

H. This states that animals and plants are composed of cells that are the basic unit of structure and function, and that all cells come from preexisting cells.

I. Small structures located in the cytoplasm that carry out protein synthesis by facilitating the linking of amino acids into a chain.

J. Cell structures found only in plant cells that are responsible for photosynthesis.

K. Requires energy for the movement of molecules or materials.

L. The outer portion of the cell that provides a barrier between the inside contents of the cell and its outside environment.

M. Organs that are grouped together, based on a common function.

Group B   *Directions* - Match the correct definition for the following terms:

1. _____Large central vacuole

2. _____Electron microscope

3. _____Cell wall

4. _____Osmosis

5. _____Lipid bi-layer

6. _____Passive transport

7. _____Organ

8. _____Carrier protein

9. _____Mitochondrion

10. _____Receptor protein

11. _____Diffusion

12. _____Cell recognition protein

13. _____Fluid Mosaic Model

14. _____Unicellular

A. Provide flexible support for a plant cell; composed of cellulose.

B. An organelle that stores water and nutrients; commonly found in plants.

C. An organelle which produces energy through the process of respiration.

D. Requires no energy for the movement of molecules or materials through or across a membrane.

E. A model of the cell membrane that is used to explain movement and communication associated with the membrane.

F. A structure that contains various tissues all with similar function.

G. The diffusion of water from an area of higher water content to a region of lower water content; dependent on solution concentrations.

H. A protein that is able to distinguish between a foreign protein or cells and non-foreign protein or cells.

I. Makes up the cell membrane along with various proteins.

J. An instrument capable of great magnification that can produce a detailed view of cells parts. Usually used with nonliving specimens.

K. An organism consisting of a single cell.

L. The movement of small molecules from regions of high concentration to regions of lower concentration; requires no additional energy.

M. A protein that binds with specific molecules, activating a reaction or process within the cell.

N. A protein that uses a form of energy to move larger molecules through the membrane.

Cells and Cell Processes

1. Which diagram best represents the levels of organization in the human body?

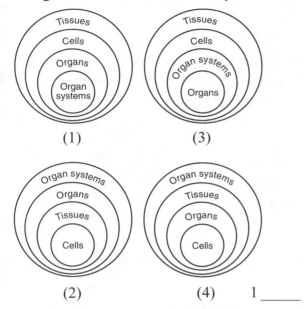

(1)   (3)

(2)   (4)   1 _____

2. Which statement describing the cells in a body system is correct?

   (1) Each cell in the system is identical to the other cells in the system, and each cell works independently of the other cells.
   (2) Some cells in the system may be different from the other cells in the system, but all cells are coordinated and work together.
   (3) Each cell in the system is different from the other cells in the system, and each cell works independently of the other cells.
   (4) All cells in the system are identical to each other and work together.   2 _____

3. What is the main function of a vacuole in a cell?

   (1) storage   (3) synthesis of molecules
   (2) coordination   (4) release of energy

3 _____

4. Humans require organ systems to carry out life processes. Single-celled organisms do not have organ systems and yet they are able to carry out life processes. This is because

   (1) human organ systems lack the organelles found in single-celled organisms
   (2) a human cell is more efficient than the cell of a single-celled organism
   (3) it is not necessary for single-celled organisms to maintain homeostasis
   (4) organelles present in single-celled organisms act in a manner similar to organ systems   4 _____

5. Which organelle is correctly paired with its specific function?
   (1) cell membrane—storage of hereditary information
   (2) chloroplast—transport of materials
   (3) ribosome—synthesis of proteins
   (4) vacuole—production of ATP   5 _____

6. Which structures carry out life functions within cells?

   (1) tissues   (3) organelles
   (2) organ systems   (4) organs   6 _____

7. The largest amount of DNA in a plant cell is contained in

   (1) a nucleus
   (2) a chromosome
   (3) a protein molecule
   (4) an enzyme molecule   7 _____

8. The current knowledge concerning cells is the result of the investigations and observations of many scientists. The work of these scientists forms a well-accepted body of knowledge about cells. This body of knowledge is an example of a

(1) hypothesis
(2) controlled experiment
(3) theory
(4) research plan   8 _____

9. In a cell, information that controls the production of proteins must pass from the nucleus to the

(1) cell membrane   (3) mitochondria
(2) chloroplasts   (4) ribosomes   9 _____

10. Which set of functions is directly controlled by the cell membrane?

(1) protein synthesis, respiration, digestion of food molecules
(2) active transport, recognition of chemical messages, protection
(3) enzyme production, elimination of large molecules, duplication of DNA codes
(4) release of ATP molecules, regulation of cell reproduction, food production
                                  10 _____

11. An enzyme known as rubisco enables plants to use large amounts of carbon dioxide. This enzyme is most likely active in the

(1) nucleus   (3) mitochondria
(2) vacuoles   (4) chloroplasts   11 _____

12. Homeostasis in unicellular organisms depends on the proper functioning of

(1) organelles   (3) guard cells
(2) insulin   (4) antibodies   12 _____

13. Which letter indicates a cell structure that directly controls the movement of molecules into and out of the cell?

(1) A
(2) B
(3) C
(4) D

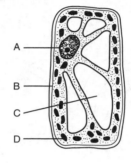

                                  13 _____

14. An organelle that releases energy for metabolic activity in a nerve cell is the

(1) chloroplast   (3) mitochondrion
(2) ribosome   (4) vacuole   14 _____

15. The function of a cell depends primarily on its

(1) life span   (3) structure
(2) color   (4) movement   15 _____

16. In the cell shown below, which lettered structure is responsible for the excretion of most cellular wastes?

(1) A
(2) B
(3) C
(4) D

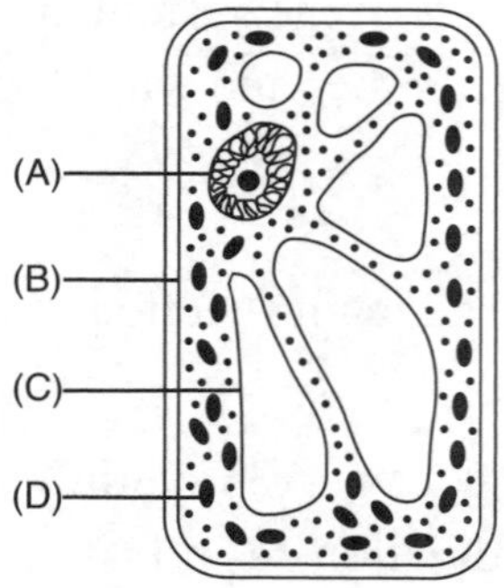

(A)
(B)
(C)
(D)

                                  16 _____

17. In the human body, oxygen is absorbed by the lungs and nutrients are absorbed by the small intestine. In a single-celled organism, this absorption directly involves the

(1) nucleus   (3) cell membrane
(2) chloroplasts   (4) chromosomes   17 ____

18. Damage to which structure will most directly disrupt water balance within a single-celled organism?

(1) ribosome   (3) nucleus
(2) cell membrane   (4) chloroplast   18 ____

19. The diagram below shows the relative concentration of molecules inside and outside of a cell.

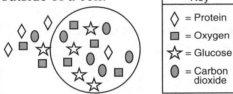

Key
◇ = Protein
■ = Oxygen
☆ = Glucose
◖ = Carbon dioxide

Which statement best describes the general direction of diffusion across the membrane of this cell?

(1) Glucose would diffuse into the cell.
(2) Protein would diffuse out of the cell.
(3) Carbon dioxide would diffuse out of the cell.
(4) Oxygen would diffuse into the cell.   19 ____

20. In a cell, all organelles work together to carry out

(1) diffusion
(2) active transport
(3) information storage
(4) metabolic processes   20 ____

21. The process of active transport requires the most direct use of

(1) carbon dioxide   (3) ATP
(2) amino acids   (4) glucose   21 ____

22. Which cell structure contains information needed for protein synthesis?

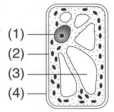

(1) ———
(2) ———
(3) ———
(4) ———

22 ____

23. Which row in the chart below best describes the active transport of molecule X through a cell membrane?

Row	Movement of Molecule X	ATP
(1)	high concentration → low concentration	used
(2)	high concentration → low concentration	not used
(3)	low concentration → high concentration	used
(4)	low concentration → high concentration	not used

23 ____

24. Which sequence represents the correct order of levels of organization found in a complex organism?

(1) cells → organelles → organs → organ systems → tissues
(2) tissues → organs → organ systems → organelles → cells
(3) organelles → cells → tissues → organs → organ systems
(4) organs → organ systems → cells → tissues → organelles   24 ____

25. Which statement regarding the functioning of the cell membrane of all organisms is not correct?

(1) The cell membrane forms a boundary that separates the cellular contents from the outside environment.
(2) The cell membrane is capable of receiving and recognizing chemical signals.
(3) The cell membrane forms a barrier that keeps all substances that might harm the cell from entering the cell.
(4) The cell membrane controls the movement of molecules into and out of the cell. 25 _____

26. A red onion cell has undergone a change, as represented in the diagram below.

This change is most likely due to the cell being placed in

(1) distilled water   (3) salt water
(2) light   (4) darkness   26 _____

27. When using a compound light microscope, the most common reason for staining a specimen being observed is to

(1) keep the organism from moving around
(2) make the view more colorful
(3) determine the effects of chemicals on the organism
(4) reveal details that are otherwise not easily seen   27 _____

28. Recently, researchers from Stanford University have changed mouse skin cells into mouse nerve cells. This was accomplished by inserting genes that control the synthesis of certain proteins into the skin cells. This type of research is often successful in advancing knowledge regarding the functioning of human cells because

(1) cells present in humans often function in similar ways to cells present in other organisms
(2) cells from different types of organisms function differently when transplanted into humans
(3) the cells in all complex organisms contain the same genes and function in similar ways
(4) cellular research using mice can always be applied to human cells since all complex organisms produce the same proteins   28 _____

29. The diagram below represents two cells, X and Y.

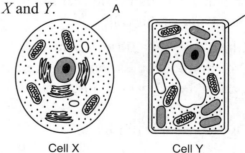

Cell X   Cell Y

Which statement is correct concerning the structure labeled A?

(1) It aids in the removal of metabolic wastes in both cell X and cell Y.
(2) It is involved in cell communication in cell X, but not in cell Y.
(3) It prevents the absorption of CO_2 in cell X and O_2 in cell Y.
(4) It represents the cell wall in cell X and the cell membrane in cell Y. 29 _____

30. The diagram below shows molecules represented by *X* both outside and inside of a cell.

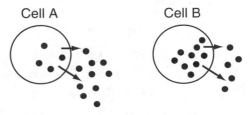

A process that would result in the movement of these molecules out of the cell requires the use of

(1) DNA   (3) antigens

(2) ATP   (4) antibodies   30 _____

31. The diagram below represents a portion of a cell membrane.

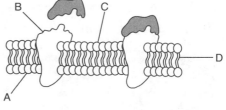

Which structure may function in the recognition of chemical signals?

(1) *A*   (3) *C*

(2) *B*   (4) *D*   31 _____

32. In the diagram, the dark dots indicate small molecules. These molecules are moving out of the cells, as indicated by the arrows. The number of dots inside and outside of the two cells represents the relative concentrations of the molecules inside and outside of the cells.

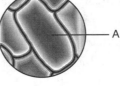

a) ATP is being used to move the molecules out of the cell by

(1) cell *A*, only   (3) both cell *A* and cell *B*

(2) cell *B*, only   (4) neither cell *A* nor cell *B*   a _____

b) Identify the structure responsible for the synthesis of ATP. _____

Base your answers to question 33 on the information and diagram.

A wet mount of red onion cells as seen with a compound light microscope is shown to the right.

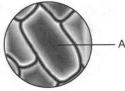

33. *a*) Using the accompanying circle, sketch what cell *A* would look like after the addition of the salt.

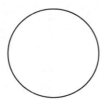

b) Which substance would most likely be used to return the cell to its original condition?

(1) starch indicator   (3) glucose indicator solution

(2) dialysis tubing   (4) distilled water   b _____

34. The diagram represents a plant cell in tap water as seen with a compound light microscope.

Which diagram best represents the appearance of the cell after it has been placed in a 15% salt solution for two minutes?

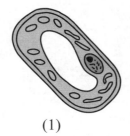 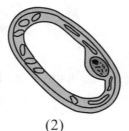 

(1)   (2)   (3)   (4)   34_____

35. Arrows *A*, *B*, and *C* in the diagram below represent the processes necessary to make the energy stored in food available for muscle activity.

Food $\xrightarrow{A}$ Simpler molecules $\xrightarrow{B}$ Mitochondria $\xrightarrow{C}$ ATP in muscle cells

The correct sequence of processes represented by *A*, *B*, and *C* is

(1) diffusion → synthesis → active transport

(2) digestion → diffusion → cellular respiration

(3) digestion → excretion → cellular respiration

(4) synthesis → active transport → excretion   35_____

36. An investigation was set up to study the movement of water through a membrane. The results are shown in the diagram.

Based on these results, which statement correctly predicts what will happen to red blood cells when they are placed in a beaker containing a water solution in which the salt concentration is much higher than the salt concentration in the red blood cells?

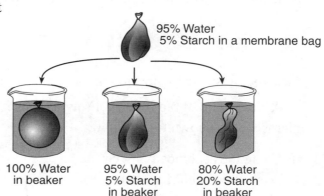

95% Water
5% Starch in a membrane bag

100% Water in beaker   95% Water 5% Starch in beaker   80% Water 20% Starch in beaker

(1) The red blood cells will absorb water and increase in size.

(2) The red blood cells will lose water and decrease in size.

(3) The red blood cells will first absorb water, then lose water and maintain their normal size.

(4) The red blood cells will first lose water, then absorb water, and finally double in size.   36_____

37. *a*) On the diagram, label the location
of each of the cell structures listed.

cell wall
cytoplasm
cell membrane

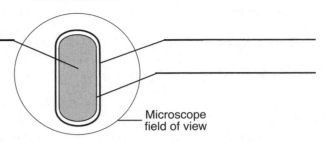

Microscope
field of view

b) Identify another cell structure,
not shown in the diagram, that
would also be found in an
autotrophic cell.

_____

38. Write the structures listed below in order from least complex to most complex.

organ   cell   organism   organelle   tissue

Least complex: _____

_____

_____

_____

Most complex: _____

39. Identify a specific structure in a single-celled organism. State how that structure is
involved in the survival of the organism.

Structure: _____

Statement: _____

40. The diagram represents a process
that is involved in the formation
of wrinkles. Complete the diagram
by drawing an appropriate structure
on the muscle cell membrane that
would allow the nerve cell to
communicate with the muscle cell.

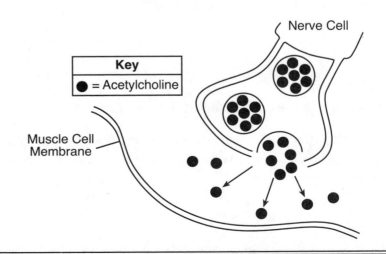

Nerve Cell

Key
● = Acetylcholine

Muscle Cell
Membrane

41. Data from two different cells are shown in the accompanying graphs.

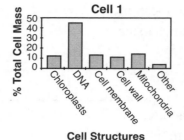

Cell 1

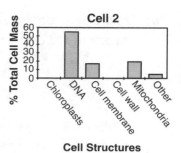

Cell 2

a) Which cell is most likely a plant cell?

_____

Support your answer.

_____

b) Almost all of the DNA of Cell 1 and 2 is located in what cell structure? _____

42. A laboratory setup using an artificial cell made from dialysis tubing is shown in the diagram.

Identify the process that would most likely be responsible for the movement of glucose from inside the artificial cell to the solution outside of the cell.

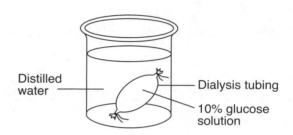

Distilled water — Dialysis tubing

10% glucose solution

_____

Base your answers to question 43 on the diagram, which represents a unicellular organism in a watery environment. The ▲s represent molecules of a specific substance.

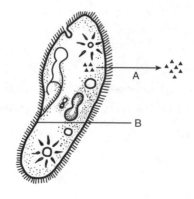

43. a) Arrow A represents active transport. State *two* ways that active transport is different from diffusion.

1. _____

2. _____

b) Identify the structure labeled B in the diagram. _____

c) In cells of multicellular organisms, structure B often contains molecules involved in cell communication. What specific term is used to identify these molecules?

_____

Base your answers to question 44 on the diagrams below. The diagrams represent two different cells and some of their parts. The diagrams are not drawn to scale.

44. *a*) Identify an organelle in cell *A* that is the site of autotrophic nutrition.

_____

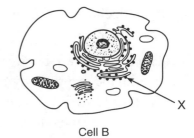

Cell A   Cell B

b) Identify the organelle labeled *X* in cell *B*.

_____

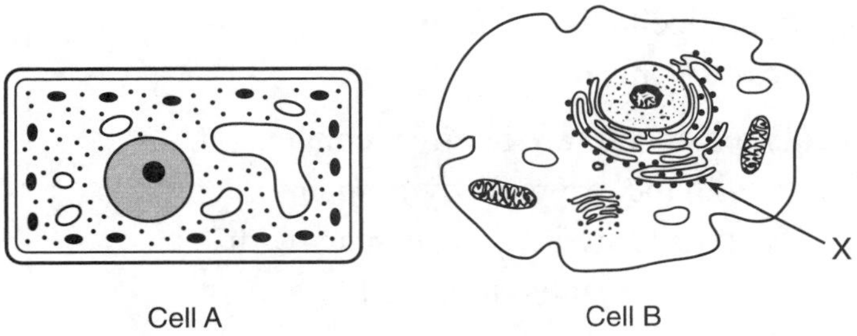

c) Which statement best describes these cells?

   (1) Cell *B* lacks vacuoles while cell *A* has them.
   (2) DNA would not be found in either cell *A* or cell *B*.
   (3) Both cell *A* and cell *B* use energy released from ATP.
   (4) Both cell *A* and cell *B* produce antibiotics.

c_____

Base your answers to question 45 on the experimental setup shown to the right.

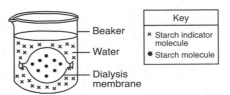

45. *a*) On the accompanying diagram, draw in the expected locations of the molecules after a period of one hour.

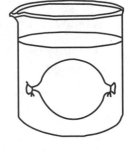

b) When starch indicator is used, what observation would indicate the presence of starch?

_____

c) State one reason why some molecules can pass through a certain membrane, but other molecules can not.

_____

46. *a*) In the accompanying diagram, which letter indicates the part of the cell that carries out a function most similar to a function of the human excretory system?   a _____

b) Which structure is responsible for the synthesis of ATP?

   (1) *A*   (2) *B*   (3) *C*   (4) *D*   b_____

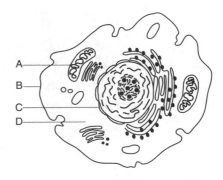

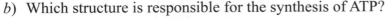

1. Specialized cells and organs are necessary in multicellular organisms because in these organisms

    (1) fewer cells are in direct contact with the external environment
    (2) all cells are in direct contact with the external environment
    (3) a body type evolved that relied on fewer body cells
    (4) a body type evolved that required larger sized cells   1 _____

2. The diagram represents levels of organization in living things.

    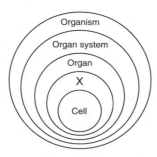

    Which term would best represent *X*?

    (1) human   (3) stomach
    (2) tissue   (4) organelle   2 _____

3. The diagram below represents a cell of a green plant.

    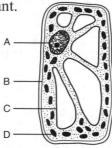

    Solar energy is used to produce energy-rich compounds in structure

    (1) *A*   (2) *B*   (3) *C*   (4) *D*   3 _____

4. The diagram below shows two different kinds of substances, *A* and *B*, entering a cell.

    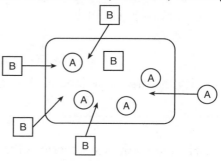

    ATP is most likely being used for

    (1) substance *A* to enter the cell
    (2) substance *B* to enter the cell
    (3) both substances to enter the cell
    (4) neither substance to enter the cell
                                                    4 _____

5. The calcium concentration in the root cells of certain plants is higher than in the surrounding soil. Calcium may continue to enter the root cells of the plant by the process of

    (1) diffusion   (3) active transport
    (2) respiration   (4) protein synthesis 5 _____

6. The ameba represented in the diagram is a single-celled organism.

    Which two processes are most closely associated with structure *A*?

    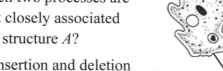

    (1) insertion and deletion
    (2) nervous regulation and circulation
    (3) active transport and diffusion
    (4) replication and photosynthesis   6 _____

7. The diagram below represents two single-celled organisms.

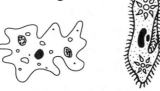

These organisms carry out the activities needed to maintain homeostasis by using specialized internal

(1) tissues   (3) systems
(2) organelles   (4) organs   7 _____

8. In the diagram below, which structure performs a function similar to a function of the human lungs?

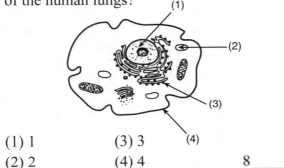

(1) 1   (3) 3
(2) 2   (4) 4   8 _____

9. Which sequence shows a decreasing level of complexity?

(1) organism → cells → organs → tissues
(2) organs → organism → cells → tissues
(3) cells → tissues → organs → organism
(4) organism → organs → tissues → cells

9 _____

10. Which structures are listed in order from the least complex to the most complex?

(1) plant cell, leaf, chloroplast, rose bush
(2) chloroplast, plant cell, leaf, rose bush
(3) chloroplast, leaf, plant cell, rose bush
(4) rose bush, leaf, plant cell, chloroplast

10 _____

11. The table below provides some information concerning organelles and organs.

Function	Organelle	Organ
gas exchange	cell membrane	lung
nutrition	food vacuole	stomach

Based on this information, which statement accurately compares organelles to organs?

(1) Functions are carried out more efficiently by organs than by organelles.
(2) Organs maintain homeostasis while organelles do not.
(3) Organelles carry out functions similar to those of organs.
(4) Organelles function in multicellular organisms while organs function in single-celled organisms.   11 _____

12. The diagram represents an autotrophic cell.

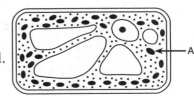

For the process of autotrophic nutrition, the arrow labeled *A* would most likely represent the direction of movement of

(1) carbon dioxide, water, and solar energy
(2) oxygen, glucose, and solar energy
(3) carbon dioxide, oxygen, and heat energy
(4) glucose, water, and heat energy

12 _____

13. All cells of an organism are engaged in many different chemical reactions. This fact is best supported by the presence in each cell of thousands of different kinds of

(1) enzymes (3) chloroplasts
(2) nuclei   (4) organelles   13 _____

14. If the ribosomes of a cell were destroyed, what effect would this most likely have on the cell?

    (1) It would stimulate mitotic cell division.

    (2) The cell would be unable to synthesize proteins.

    (3) Development of abnormal hereditary features would occur in the cell.

    (4) Increased protein absorption would occur through the cell membrane.

                                   14 ____

15. A laboratory setup of a model cell is shown in the diagram.

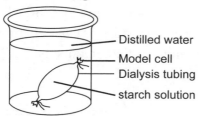

— Distilled water
— Model cell
— Dialysis tubing
— starch solution

    Which observation would most likely be made 24 hours later?

    (1) The contents of the model cell have changed color.

    (2) The diameter of the model cell has increased.

    (3) The model cell has become smaller.

    (4) The amount of distilled water in the beaker has increased.   15 ____

16. A student observes some cells with a compound light microscope as shown in view A.

 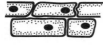

View A   View B

    What did the student most likely do to obtain view B?

    (1) applied a biological stain to the slide

    (2) used electrophoresis

    (3) applied distilled water to the slide

    (4) used a higher magnification   16 ____

17. Molecule X moves across a cell membrane by diffusion. Which row in the chart best indicates the relationship between the relative concentrations of molecule X and the use of ATP for diffusion?

Row	Movement of Molecule X	Use of ATP
(1)	high concentration → low concentration	used
(2)	high concentration → low concentration	not used
(3)	low concentration → high concentration	used
(4)	low concentration → high concentration	not used

                                   17 ____

18. The data table shows the presence or absence of DNA in four different cell organelles.

Data Table

Organelle	DNA
cell membrane	absent
cell wall	absent
mitochondrion	present
nucleus	present

    Information in the table suggests that DNA functions

    (1) within cytoplasm and outside of the cell membrane

    (2) both inside and outside of the nucleus

    (3) only within energy-releasing structures

    (4) within cell vacuoles   18 ____

19. The arrows in the diagram indicate the movement of materials into and out of a single-celled organism.

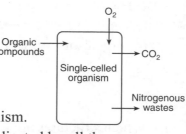

O_2

Organic compounds →

Single-celled organism

→ CO_2

Nitrogenous wastes

    The movements indicated by all the arrows are directly involved in

    (1) the maintenance of homeostasis

    (2) photosynthesis, only

    (3) excretion, only

    (4) the digestion of minerals   19 ____

20. Which row in the chart below contains a cell structure paired with its primary function?

Row	Cell Structure	Function
(1)	ribosome	protein synthesis
(2)	vacuole	production of genetic information
(3)	nucleus	carbohydrate synthesis
(4)	mitochondrion	waste disposal

20 _____

21. The graph below shows the relative concentrations of different ions inside and outside of an animal cell.

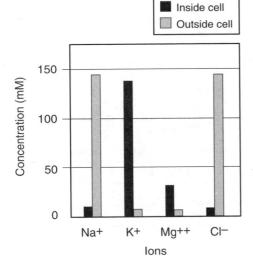

Key
■ Inside cell
▨ Outside cell

Which process is directly responsible for the net movement of K+ and Mg++ into the animal cell?

(1) electrophoresis (3) active transport
(2) diffusion   (4) circulation   21 _____

22. Which sequence represents the levels of biological organization from smallest to largest?

(1) organism → cell → tissue → organelle → organ system → organ
(2) organ system → organ → organism → cell → tissue → organelle
(3) organelle → organ system → cell → organism → tissue → organ
(4) organelle → cell → tissue → organ → organ system → organism   22 _____

23. Some human body cells are shown in the diagrams below.

Cells from skin   Blood cells

Cells from lining of bladder   Cells from lining of trachea

These groups of cells represent different
(1) tissues in which similar cells function together
(2) organs that help to carry out a specific life activity
(3) systems that are responsible for a specific life activity
(4) organelles that carry out different functions   23 _____

24. The diagram represents movement of a large molecule across a membrane.

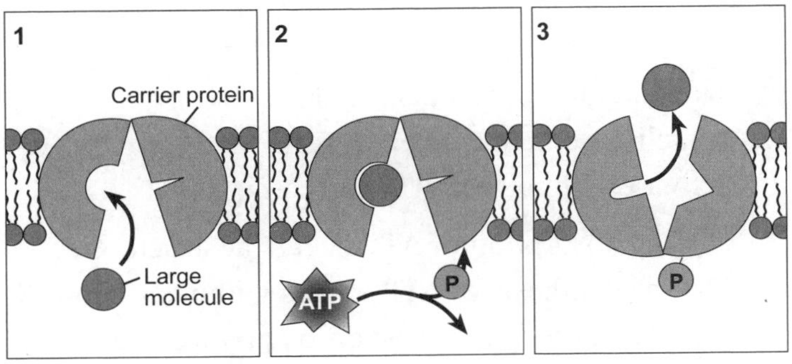

Which process is best represented in this diagram?
(1) active transport   (3) protein building
(2) diffusion   (4) gene manipulation

24 _____

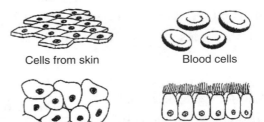

25. A model cell setup is represented in the "Initial State" diagram.

Which diagram below indicates the areas where each of these substances would be located after 20 minutes?

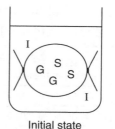

Initial state

Key
S = starch
G = glucose
I = starch indicator

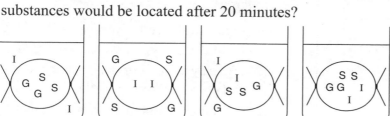

(1)   (2)   (3)   (4)

25_____

26. In living cells, chemical processes, such as synthesis, all require the action of
    (1) specialized antibiotics   (2) hormones   (3) salts   (4) biological catalysts   26_____

27. In a cell, protein synthesis is the primary function of
    (1) ribosomes   (2) mitochondria   (3) chloroplasts   (4) vacuoles   27_____

28. A student prepared four different red blood cell suspensions, as shown in the chart.

Suspension	Contents
A	red blood cells in normal blood serum (0.7% salt solution)
B	red blood cells in 10% salt solution
C	red blood cells in distilled water
D	red blood cells in tap water

a) Which suspension would contain red blood cells that would appear wrinkled and reduced in volume?
    (1) *A*   (2) *B*   (3) *C*   (4) *D*   a_____

b) The change in red blood cell volume is principally due to the movement of
    (1) serum   (2) oxygen   (3) water   (4) salt   b_____

c) Which process is most likely involved in the change in red blood cell volume?
    (1) active transport   (2) evaporation   (3) replication   (4) diffusion   c_____

29. The diagram represents a cell. Which statement concerning ATP and activity within the cell is correct?

(1) The absorption of ATP occurs at structure *A*.
(2) The synthesis of ATP occurs within structure *B*.
(3) ATP is produced most efficiently by structure *C*.
(4) The template for ATP is found in structure *D*.

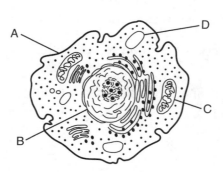

29_____

30. The diagram below represents the distribution of some molecules inside and outside of a cell over time.

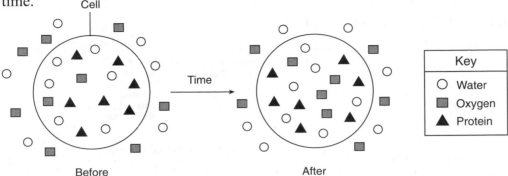

Which factor prevented the protein molecules (▲) from moving out of the cell?

(1) temperature   (2) pH   (3) molecule size   (4) molecule concentration   30 _____

31. The diagram illustrates what happens when a particular solution is added to a wet-mount slide containing red onion cells being observed using a compound light microscope.

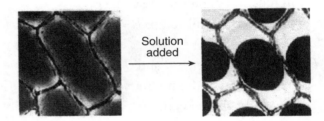

a) Identify a process that caused the change in the cells.

_____

b) What can be done to restore the cell in the right diagram to its original shape?

_____

Base your answers to question 32 on the diagram, which illustrates a transport pathway of CO_2 in the human body.

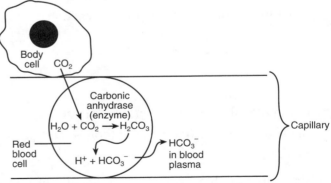

32. *a*) Identify the cellular process that most likely produced the CO_2 in the body cell.

_____

b) Explain why carbon dioxide moves into red blood cells by diffusion rather than by active transport.

_____

c) State the function of a red blood cell within the human body.

_____

33. A model of a cell is prepared and placed in a beaker of fluid as shown in the diagram. The letters *A*, *B*, and *C* represent substances in the initial experimental setup.

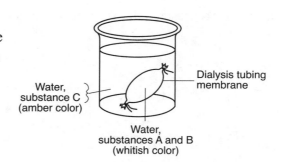

The table summarizes the content and appearance of the cell model and beaker after 20 minutes.

Results After 20 Minutes

	Outside of Cell Model	Inside of Cell Model
Substances	water, A, C	water, A, B, C
Color	amber	blue black

a) Complete the accompanying table to summarize a change in location of substance *C* in the experimental setup.

b) Identify substance *B* and explain why it did not move out of the model cell.

Name of Substance C	Direction of Movement of Substance C	Reason for the Movement of Substance C

Substance *B*: _____

Explanation:_____

34. An experimental setup using a model cell is shown in the diagram. State what cell structure the dialysis tubing represents.

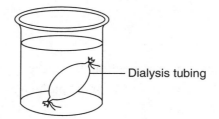

_____

35. Two molecules, *A* and *B*, and their distribution inside and outside of a cell are represented in the diagram.

State one possible reason why molecule *A* could diffuse across the membrane of the cell but molecule *B* could not.

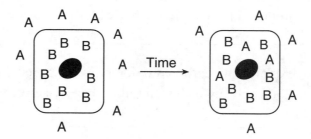

_____

Set 2 – Cells and Cell Processes

36. The accompanying diagram represents a container of water and two different kinds of molecules, *A* and *B*, separated into two chambers by a membrane through which only water and molecule *A* can pass.

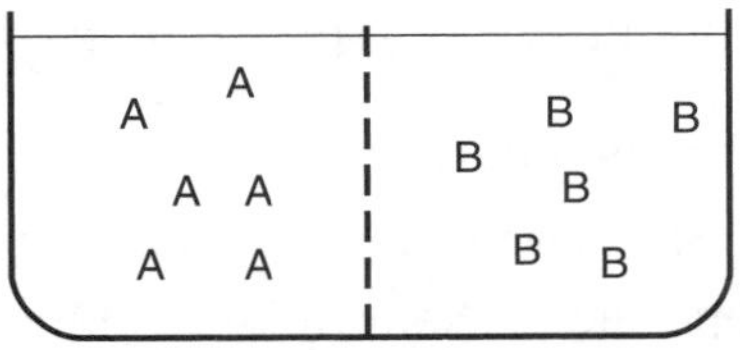

On the diagram of the container to the right, indicate the distribution of molecules *A* and *B* after the net movement of these molecules stops.

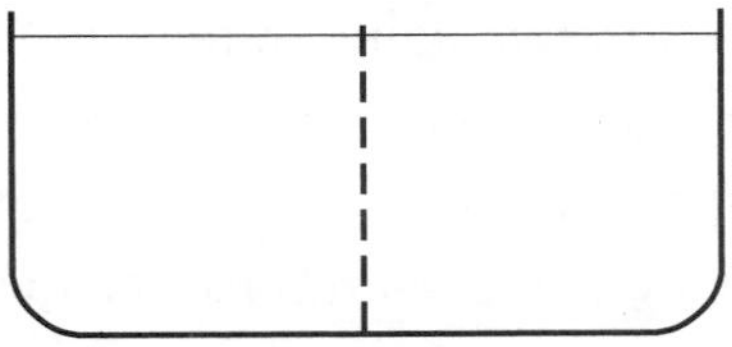

37. Draw an arrow to indicate one part of the plant cell that would not be found in an animal cell. The tip of the arrow must touch the part being identified.

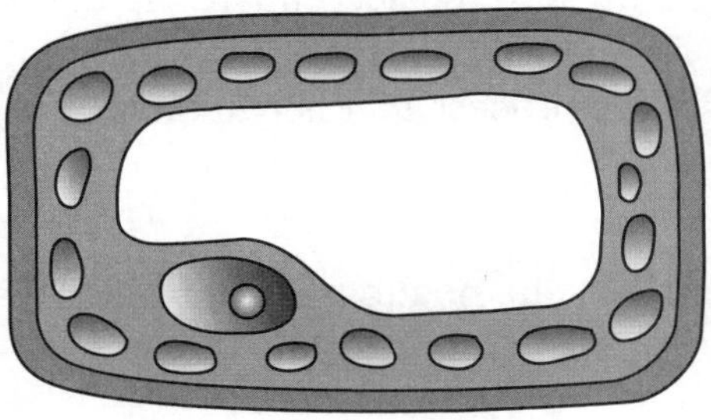

38. The diagram represents what occurred when an onion cell and a red blood cell were placed in distilled water.

Explain why the onion cell does not burst when exposed to distilled water solution.

_____

_____

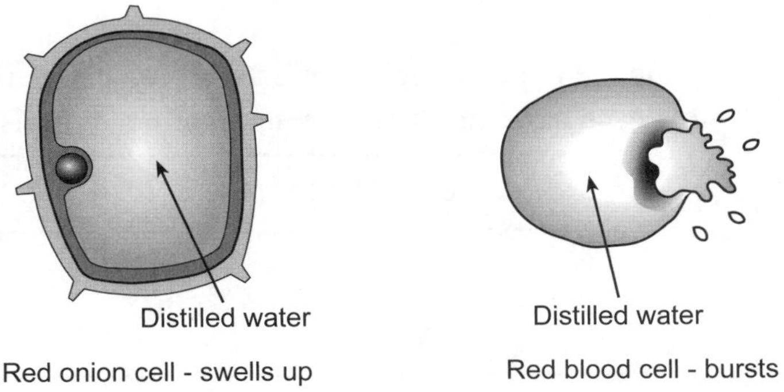

Distilled water
Red onion cell - swells up

Distilled water
Red blood cell - bursts

39. Describe how two of the cell structures listed below interact to help maintain a balanced internal environment in a cell.

     mitochondrion   ribosome   cell membrane   nucleus   vacuole

a) Select *two* of these structures, write their names, and state one function of each.

    1) Structure: _____

       Function: _____

    2) Structure: _____

       Function: _____

b) Describe how each structure you selected contributes to the functioning of the other.

_____

_____

Base your answers to question 40 on the information and data table below.

A student cut three identical slices from a potato. She determined the mass of each slice. She then placed them in labeled beakers and added a different solution to each beaker. After 30 minutes, she removed each potato slice from its solution, removed the excess liquid with a paper towel, and determined the mass of each slice. The change in mass was calculated and the results are shown in the accompanying data table.

Change in Mass of Potato in Different Solutions

Beaker	Solution	Change in Mass
1	distilled water	gained 4.0 grams
2	6% salt solution	lost 0.4 gram
3	16% salt solution	lost 4.7 grams

40. *a*) Identify the process that is responsible for the change in mass of each of the three slices.

_____

b) Explain why the potato slice in beaker 1 increased in mass.

_____

41. Complete the chart below by identifying two cell structures involved in protein synthesis and stating how each structure functions in protein synthesis.

Cell Structure	Function in Protein Synthesis

42. Some of the pain from a sore throat is caused by swelling of moist throat tissue. A common remedy for a sore throat is to gargle (rinse the throat tissue) with salt water. Explain why gargling with salt water would be expected to relieve the pain of a sore throat.

_____

43. State one way in which fresh water algae would likely be affected if scientists try to use them in a salt water environment.

_____

Base your answers to question 44 on the information below.

It has been discovered that plants utilize chemical signals for communication. Some of these chemicals are released from leaves, fruits, and flowers and play various roles in plant development, survival, and gene expression. For example, bean plant leaves infested with spider mites release chemicals that result in an increase in the resistance to spider mites in uninfested leaves on the same plant and the expression of self-defense genes in uninfested bean plants nearby.

Plants can also communicate with insects. For example, corn, cotton, and tobacco under attack by caterpillars release chemical signals that simultaneously attract parasitic wasps to destroy the caterpillars and discourage moths from laying their eggs on the plants.

44. *a*) Identify the specialized structures in the cell membrane that are involved in communication.

_____

b) Explain why chemicals released from one plant species may not cause a response in a different plant species.

_____

_____

45. A laboratory setup for a demonstration is represented in the accompanying diagram. In the setup an indicator can be used to determine if starch diffuses through the membrane into the beaker.

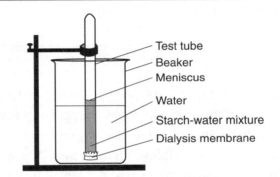

- Test tube
- Beaker
- Meniscus
- Water
- Starch-water mixture
- Dialysis membrane

a) Explain the procedure used.

_____

_____

b) Explain how to interpret the results.

_____

c) Identify another type of organic compound that can be identified with an indicator using this type of laboratory equipment. _____

46. Give the name of an organelle and a name of human body system that have similar functions.

Organelle:_____ Human body system:_____

47. Which cell structure is mainly responsible for releasing energy from food molecules in some single-celled organisms? _____

---

48. A student has a sandwich for lunch. The bread contains starch molecules and various other molecules. After chewing and swallowing some of the sandwich, the starch moves along the digestive system and is digested. The sequence below represents what takes place next.

digested starch → bloodstream → cell → cell structure → ATP

Explain what occurs, beginning with the digestion of starch and ending with ATP production. In your answer, be sure to:

a) identify the molecules that are used to digest the starch _____

b) identify the molecules produced when starch is digested _____

c) explain why starch must be digested before its building block molecules can enter the bloodstream

_____

d) identify the structure in the cell that will produce ATP from the starch building blocks

_____

e) state why ATP is important to cells

_____

49. Termites depend on microbes living in their guts to digest molecules of the large, complex carbohydrate, cellulose. Cellulose is the part of wood termites feed on. The microbes produce a substance called cellulase, which speeds up the breakdown of cellulose into molecules of glucose. Termites cannot make cellulase on their own. Without the help of the microbes, the termites are not able to absorb the nutrients that they need to survive.

Explain why the microbes are necessary in order for the termites to absorb nutrients that they need to survive.

_____

_____

Base your answers to question 50 on the diagram which illustrates a role of hormones.

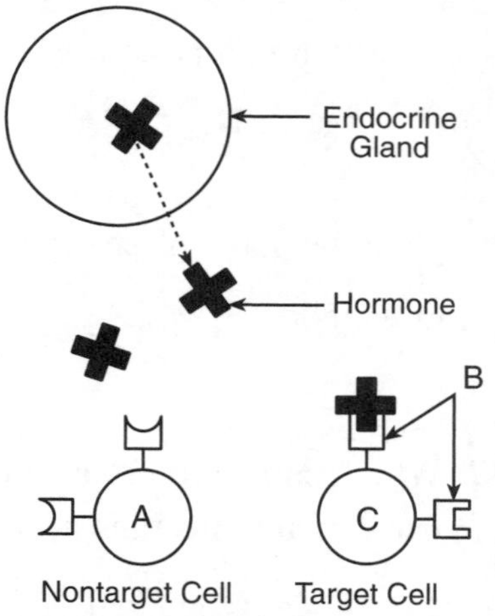

50. a) Identify letter B. _____

b) Explain why cell A is a nontarget cell for the hormone illustrated in the diagram.

_____

_____

Endocrine Gland

Hormone

B

A — Nontarget Cell

C — Target Cell

1. 2   The levels of organization start with the basic unit of life, the cell, and build from that. Tissues are composed of groups of cells, while organs are composed of groups of tissues. Organ systems, such as the digestion system, are made of various organs.

2. 2   Cells, although they are a basic unit of structure, have different functions. The different jobs that cells do within body systems stem from the expression of genetic codes. Certain genes are "turned on" within the DNA, directing the production of specific proteins that provide specific function. Through cell communication, all cells are able to coordinate within a system.

3. 1   Vacuoles are designed to store materials that the cell may require at a later time.

4. 4   Single-celled organisms have various cell parts or organelles that perform essential life processes. These organelles carry out similar functions as those of human organ systems. For example, the organelle lysosome containing enzymes that digest food particles could be compared to the human digestive system.

5. 3   The ribosome provides an organizing role in the assembly of proteins. Amino acids are brought to the ribosome and are sequenced in specific order according to the mRNA code. Growing chains of amino acids become proteins and are released from the ribosome.

6. 3   A cell contains small cell parts called organelles that perform the activities of the cell. These organelles are the functional parts that maintain homeostasis within the cell.

7. 1   The nucleus contains all of the plant's chromosomes which house or contain DNA.

8. 3   Scientists develop theories based on repeated investigations and observations. Theories are widely agreed upon by a large number of scientists.

9. 4   The ribosomes are the site of protein synthesis or production. Information found within the DNA of the nucleus is passed to the ribosome to properly construct particular proteins.

10. 2   The cell membrane contains various proteins that perform specific functions. Transport proteins allow for active transport of molecules across the membrane using the energy molecule, ATP. Another type of membrane protein, is the receptor protein. Receptor proteins have specific shapes that bind with chemical messengers leading to a reaction by the cell. Also, the cell membrane separates the inside contents of the cell from the outside environment, protecting the cell parts.

11. 4   Plants use large amounts of carbon dioxide during the process of photosynthesis. The chloroplast is the site of photosynthesis and requires enzymes for this process to occur. Therefore, the enzyme rubisco would be found in large amounts within the chloroplast.

12. 1 Unicellular organisms are single cells that rely on the activity of their cell organelles for proper function. These cell organelles coordinate and work together to maintain the cell's internal balance or homeostasis. All other choices would mainly be associated with multicellular organisms.

13. 2 Letter *B* represents the semi-permeable cell membrane. The cell membrane functions to move certain materials into or out of both plant and animal cells.

14. 3 Mitochondria are cell organelles that utilize the organic compound glucose and oxygen to create the energy molecule, ATP. This process takes place within the folds and open matrix of the cell structure. Cells have multiple mitochondria to supply the energy needs of the cell and organism.

15. 3 Cellular functions are dependent upon cell organelles and specifically upon the structure of those organelles. For example, the many folds of the mitochondrion provide ample surface area for reactions to take place. The cell membrane's structure provides a means for many molecules to enter or leave the cell.

16. 2 The excretion of most cellular wastes is taken care of by the cell membrane. This occurs either through the process of diffusion of waste molecules from high to low concentrations or by active transport across membranes.

17. 3 Absorption of nutrients and gases in the human body occurs through a thin layer of cells within each organ. In the lungs, oxygen is absorbed through a single cell layer of the alveoli, and in the intestines, nutrients are absorbed through a similar layer in the villi. In single-celled organisms, the cell membrane, a single layer of lipids and proteins, serves to absorb nutrients and gases into the cell.

18. 2 The cell membrane acts as a boundary between the contents of the cell and the outside environment by creating gradients that are necessary for water movement by diffusion. Damage to the cell membrane will have an adverse effect on the cell's function.

19. 3 The direction of diffusion of molecules occurs from an area of higher concentration to an area of lower concentration. In this diagram, there are more molecules of carbon dioxide within the cell than outside the cell, so diffusion will occur moving carbon dioxide out of the cell. All other possible choices represent movement from low concentration to high concentration and would not be considered diffusion.

20. 4 All chemical reactions within cells are collectively known as metabolic processes.

21. 3 Active transport requires the input of energy to move molecules across a membrane. This energy primarily comes from the energy molecule, ATP. Active transport occurs when molecules are too large to move by simple diffusion or the movement is against a gradient.

22. 1 Structure 1 is the nucleus which contains DNA, the genetic material that contains the code for protein synthesis.

23. 3 The active transport of molecule *X* would best be supported by choice 3. Active transport requires energy in the form of ATP and moves molecules and ions from an area of lower to higher concentration (against the gradient).

Cells and Cell Processes

24. 3   Within each cell are structures called organelles. Cells, the basic structural and functional building units of living things, can form various types of tissue. Tissues compose organs and organs, all of similar function, make up a system.

25. 3   Although the cell membrane does provide a boundary around the cell, it is not a barrier. Most cell membranes are semi-permeable allowing materials that are required for proper function to move into and out of the cell. At times, a harmful substance can pass through the membrane and have a toxic effect on the cell.

26. 3   When an onion cell is placed in salt water, water in the cell moves out by osmosis. This occurs because the concentration of water outside of the cell is lower than the concentration inside the cell; therefore, the net movement is out. The plasma or cell membrane will shrivel becoming smaller, but the cell wall will remain the same.

27. 4   Staining specimens allows the microscope viewer to see cell organelles more clearly and details that are not observable in an unstained specimen. For example, a student might stain a cheek cell with methylene blue to make the nucleus more visible.

28. 1   All animal cells have basic organelles that perform specific functions. By examining mouse cells, researchers could apply their mouse cell findings to human cell function and possibly help prevent or cure diseases.

29. 1   Structure A in both Cell X and Cell Y is the cell membrane. The cell membrane serves as a selective exchange site allowing for the movement of nutrients, gases, and waste products. Metabolic wastes would diffuse out of the Cells X and Y through structure A.

30. 2   In the diagram, there are more X's outside of the cell than inside. Moving molecules (X's) out of the cell would require going against the gradient from low to high concentration. In order to move the X molecules out, the energy molecule, ATP, would be required. This is known as active transport.

31. 2   Structure B is a membrane protein. These proteins act as receptors of chemical signals based on the shapes of the protein and the chemical signal molecule. A specifically shaped signal molecule will initiate a cellular response when it binds to a particular protein.

32. a) 1   ATP, the energy molecule, is used in active transport where the movement of molecules goes from a low concentration (few) to a higher concentration (many). In Cell A, the number of molecules within the cell is less than those outside; ATP would be needed in this case. In Cell B, the movement is occurring from a region of many molecules to that of fewer molecules. This would occur naturally through the process of diffusion and would not require ATP.

b)   Answer: mitochondria

Explanation: Mitochondria are cell organelles that carry out cellular respiration, a process that produces the energy molecule, ATP.

33. *a)* 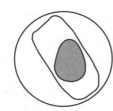 The addition of salt water would create a situation where there was a lower concentration of water molecules outside of the cell than inside the cell. This would lead to osmosis of water out of the cell (net movement from high to low concentration). As a result, the cell membrane would shrivel and pull away from the cell wall. The plant cell wall will remain intact.

b) 4 To return the cell to its original condition, water must move back into the cell. By exposing a shriveled cell to distilled water, osmosis will occur, moving water into the cell because distilled water has a higher concentration of water molecules compared to the water molecules within the cell. In time, the cell membrane would be restored to its original condition.

34. 3 Diagram 3 shows a plant cell that has lost water and has the inner cell membrane pulled in, leaving the cell wall still intact. When a plant cell is placed in a salt solution, water will diffuse out of the cell by osmosis causing the cell membrane to pull in and away from the cell wall. The cell wall still retains its shape and is generally not affected by the salt water.

35. 2 Letter *A* represents digestion, the process where food is broken down into a simpler form that is able to be used at the cellular level. Letter *B* represents diffusion, the process where molecules move through a membrane using a gradient (high to low concentration). In this case, relatively small molecules diffuse from the blood to the cell. Letter *C* represents the process of cellular respiration where energy is produced in the form of ATP molecules within the mitochondria of the cells.

36. 2 The process involved in this diagram is osmosis, the diffusion of water across a membrane. Remember that diffusion is the movement of molecules from a high concentration to lower concentration to reach a dynamic equilibrium (same concentration on both sides of the membrane). When red blood cells are placed in a higher salt solution, they behave like the beaker on the right in the diagram. The red blood cells would lose water and cells would decrease in size.

37. *a)* 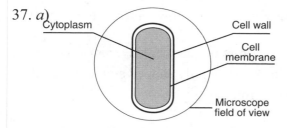 Explanation: In plant cells, the cell wall is the outer wall surrounding the cell. The cell membrane, which regulates movement in and out of the cell, is located directly inside of the cell wall. The cytoplasm is the liquid matrix that fills the inside of the cell and is represented by the shaded gray area.

b) Answer: chloroplast *or* large central vacuole

Explanation: Plant cells are autotrophic and contain these two cell structures, which facilitate the process of photosynthesis.

38. Answer: Least complex   Most complex
           organelle → cell → tissue → organ → organism

Explanation: Organelles are the basic parts of the cells. They allow the cell to carry out life functions. Cells with specific functions can be grouped together to form tissues. Groups of tissues that work together towards a common function are organs. All organs then work together to maintain homeostasis within the organism.

---

39. Acceptable answers include but not limited to:

Structure	Statement
mitochondrion	site of respiration or release of energy
or cell membrane	regulates what enters (or leaves) the cell
or chloroplasts	organelles that carry out the process of photosynthesis or autotrophic nutrition
or nucleus	protein synthesis *or* controls all cellular activities *or* contains DNA

40. Answer:

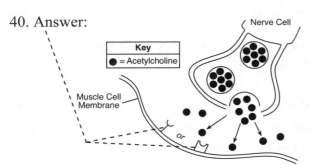

Acceptable responses include a receptor drawn on the muscle cell membrane that has a shape that acetylcholine could fit into.

Explanation: Acetylcholine is a receptor protein, which is shape specific and binds with a specific molecule activating a reaction or process within a cell. For this receptor protein, the receptor must have a round shape.

41. *a)* Answer: Cell 1

Supporting statement: because it contains chloroplast *or* because it has a cell wall

Explanation: Only plant cells contain chloroplasts and a cell wall.

b) Answer: nucleus

Explanation: DNA is found within chromosomes, which are located in the nucleus.

42. Answer: diffusion *or* passive transport

Explanation: Diffusion or passive transport is the movement of molecules from an area of high concentration to an area of low concentration. In the diagram, the solution inside the dialysis tubing contains 10% glucose, making it more concentrated than the water containing 0% glucose. So the net movement of glucose will be from the inside of the artificial cell (10%) to the outside beaker (0%).

43. *a)* Answer: Active transport requires the use of energy by the organism.
   or Diffusion does not require the use of energy by the organism.
   or In active transport, molecules move from a region of lower concentration to a region of higher concentration of those molecules.
   or In diffusion, molecules move from a region of higher concentration to a region of lower concentration of those molecules.

Explanation: Active transport is a means by which material is moved into or out of a cell. Active transport is different from diffusion in that it:
   – requires energy usually in the form of ATP.
   – moves against the concentration gradient, from low to high concentration.

b) Answer: Structure *B* is the cell membrane.

c) Answer: receptor molecules *or* receptor proteins *or* cell receptors *or* receptors

Explanation: Communication between cells is accomplished through the use of proteins located within the cell membrane. The term used to identify these protein molecules could include: receptor proteins, cell receptors, cell recognition proteins or cell markers.

44. *a*) Answer: chloroplasts

Explanation: Chloroplasts, shown as the small darkened ovals, are the cell organelles that carry out the process of photosynthesis or autotrophic nutrition.

b) Answer: ribosome

Explanation: Ribosomes (the small dots) are usually located on the channels of the endoplasmic reticulum that surround the nucleus. Remember that ribosomes are the site of protein synthesis.

c) 3   All cells use energy that is released from ATP. ATP is produced in cell organelles called mitochondria through a process of cellular respiration.

45. *a*)    This experiment is designed to show the process of diffusion. Small starch indicator molecules readily diffuse through the dialysis membrane from a high concentration outside to a low concentration inside. However, the starch molecules are too large to diffuse through the dialysis membrane and will not move. After 1 hour, the expected locations of the molecules will show starch indicator molecules both in and out of the dialysis bag and the starch molecules only inside the bag.

b) Answer: A blue-black color indicates the presence of starch.
or A color change would occur.

Explanation: The starch indicator solution (most likely iodine) would show a color change from amber to blue-black when in the presence of starch. Since the starch indicator diffused into the dialysis bag, a color change would occur in the bag where it contacted starch molecules.

c) Acceptable answers include but are not limited to:
Some molecules are too large to pass.
or Some molecules are insoluble.
or The membrane permeability depends on molecule size.

Explanation: If molecules are large, they may be too big to move readily through the membrane and may be moved through only by phagocytosis or engulfment. Some molecules move through the membrane because they are lipid soluble. If a molecule is insoluble in lipids, it will not be able to pass. Also, the membrane itself is selectively permeable to molecules based on size, shape and solubility. These variables ultimately determine what moves through.

46. *a*) Answer: *B*

Explanation: The cell membrane (letter *B*) allows waste products, especially CO_2, to pass through, eliminating them from the cell. The human excretory system removes waste products from the body.

b) 1   Letter *A* represents the cell organelle known as the mitochondria. The process of cellular respiration, which produces ATP, takes place here.

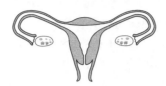
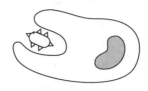
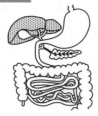

HUMAN PHYSIOLOGY, REPRODUCTION, AND HOMEOSTASIS

Overview:

In multicellular organisms such as humans, the organization of cells into complex structures allows for the maintenance of *homeostasis* – a self-regulating process to maintain the organism's internal conditions. This concept results in a *dynamic equilibrium* of body functions that is maintained by constant feedback and adjustments within the organism. Organisms require systems that coordinate actions and interact with one another. Every system has structures that have a specific function or functions. When homeostasis is disrupted by failure or malfunction within the structure, the organism may experience illness or disease, which could lead to death.

Essential Information:

Organization – The basic organization of function begins with the cell. Specific types of cells have special functions based on their genetic expression. When these cells are grouped together for a common purpose, they are called tissues. Organs contain tissues of varying functions that work towards a common goal. For example, the stomach has several types of tissues, all functioning to aid in digestion. When organs are arranged to interact together, they make up a system, such as the digestive or reproductive system. Each system within the human body plays a role that accomplishes a particular life function by coordinating specific actions within living organisms, and through cell communication and system interaction, homeostasis is maintained throughout the whole organism.

Systems:

Digestive System – The *digestive system* breaks down nutrients into usable form for cells. Large organic compounds, such as carbohydrates and proteins must be broken down into smaller building-block components like simple sugars and amino acids, respectively. Specific organs within this system, like the stomach and small intestine, supply *enzymes* that aid in this digestion. The large intestine functions to absorb water and pass solid waste from the body.

Respiratory System – The *respiratory system* functions to supply the cells with necessary O_2, as well as to remove the waste product CO_2. Specific organs and structures within this system provide necessary conditions for gas exchange. Air is moved in and out of the body through tubes, known as the trachea and bronchi, that lead to the lungs. Within the lungs, tiny air sacs, known as *alveoli*, allow for the diffusion of gases (O_2 and CO_2) across their thin membranes. Alveoli are surrounded by tiny capillaries, which efficiently absorb O_2 for use and release CO_2 for removal. Respiratory pigments, such as *hemoglobin* found on red blood cells, allow gases to be carried to and from the cells. Environmental air pollution as well as personal actions, like smoking, can lead to diseases within the lungs. *Emphysema* can develop where lung function is diminished by the loss of ability to exchange gases. *Asthma* can develop through exposure to allergens or environmental pollutants, which cause bronchi to constrict, limiting airflow.

Circulatory System – The *circulatory system* acts to transport needed nutrients to cells and to remove waste from cells. This system consists of a muscular pump, the heart, which provides the force to circulate blood to all cells then back via various blood vessels. These include *arteries* that carry blood away from the heart, *veins* that return blood to the heart, and thin-walled *capillaries* that allow for molecular exchange at the cellular level. Blood consists of a watery plasma that carries gases, nutrients, and wastes and contains *platelets* that act to clot blood. Specific cells within the blood include *red blood cells* that carry oxygen and the larger *white blood cells* that function in body defense. With an increase in human body activity, the circulatory system responds by increasing the pulse rate (measurement of heart activity). This reflects the circulatory system's role in supplying needed nutrients such as oxygen and glucose to muscle cells.

Excretory System – The *excretory system's* main function is to remove harmful wastes and to maintain water balance. The kidneys act to filter out *urea* – produced in the liver from the breakdown of amino acids. This occurs within the kidney's structural unit known as the *nephron,* which also reabsorbs water to maintain homeostasis. The resulting waste product, urine, is stored in the bladder until it is eliminated from the body through the urethra.

Regulatory Systems – In order to coordinate internal activities with changes from both inside and outside the body, humans rely on both the nervous and the endocrine systems. The *nervous system* responds to external stimuli or changes in the outside environment. Its basic unit of function is the nerve cell or *neuron*. Nerves collect information through the senses and transmit that information by relaying impulses through electronic activity within the nerve cell. At the end of a nerve cell a gap exists called a *synapse* (see diagram 2). Here, chemical messengers, know as *neurotransmitters*, are released from one neuron, traveling over the synapse to the next neuron where it binds to receptor proteins on that cell's membrane, continuing that impulse.

The *endocrine system* uses chemical messengers or *hormones* produced by *glands* to regulate metabolism and internal balance. Hormones are secreted directly into the bloodstream and travel to *target cells* on which the hormone acts. Target cells have specific receptor molecules on their membranes which bind with specific hormones, initiating a cellular response (see diagram 4). Each hormone has a specific function. *Insulin*, produced by the pancreas, allows cells to take in sugar, thus regulating blood sugar levels. *Diabetes* results from a malfunction of the pancreas when not enough insulin or no insulin is produced and cells cannot receive the correct amount of sugar. This causes dangerously high blood sugar levels. The thyroid gland releases thyroxine, responsible for controlling metabolism. The ovary produces *estrogen* and *progesterone* which are involved in female reproductive development and control of the menstrual cycle. Testes produce *testosterone*, responsible for male reproductive development. Levels of hormones are controlled by a mechanism known as *feedback*. Feedback allows for messages to be received by glands which start or stop the production of hormones depending on hormone level. If hormone levels get too high, the gland producing the hormone will reduce or stop releasing the hormone until levels reach a point where more is needed (see diagram 5).

Immune System – The *immune system* aids the body's defense against pathogens. *Pathogens* are disease-causing organisms such as viruses or bacteria. The body reacts to foreign invaders by recognizing foreign proteins or *antigens* they carry. These antigens activate *T cells* which directly attack pathogen-infected cells and activate *B cells* which produce plasma cells that release antibodies. Antibodies have receptor molecules that can bind to antigens or pathogen-infected cells, marking them for

Human Physiology, Reproduction, and Homeostasis

destruction. After an initial immune response, the body also produces *memory cells* that provide immunity for future attacks. *Vaccines* contain small amounts of weakened or heat-killed pathogens and, when administered, will result in an immunity to that particular pathogen. On occasion, the body produces an immune response to a harmless substance, like pollen. This is known as an *allergic reaction*. Individuals who receive a transplant, even if they are a close match, must take medicine to suppress the immune response so that their immune system will not attack the transplanted organ and reject it. *HIV* is a virus that weakens the immune system by destroying T cells leaving its victims with AIDS and unable to fight off other pathogens.

Reproductive System – Sexual reproduction allows for the union of gametes to form a new individual. Specialized structures within the male and female provide the necessary function. In the *testes* of the male, meiosis produces sperm cells (gametes), which mature in the *vas deferens* or sperm duct. Upon release, the sperm are mixed with fluids from glands that provide nutrients and a medium for movement and exit the male's body through the urethra in the penis. In females, the *menstrual cycle* regulates the process of reproduction based on release of hormones. Estrogen and progesterone released from the ovary prepare and maintain the uterine lining for pregnancy. Meiosis occurs in the ovaries producing an egg cell in cyclic fashion, once a month. The egg cells mature and are released from the ovary, then travel down the *fallopian tube* or oviduct towards the *uterus*, where depending on fertilization, they will be implanted in the uterine wall or released through the vagina. *Fertilization* takes place within the fallopian tube where the sperm enters the egg and forms a *zygote*. The genetic information from the sperm and egg fuse together providing a complete set of genetic instructions (having full number of chromosomes). After fertilization, the zygote begins a series of rapid cell divisions or mitosis until it forms a ball of cells. At this point, *differentiation* begins to occur. All cells resulting from cell divisions have the same DNA, but certain cells use specific genes that reflect a specific function. For example, liver cells and muscle cells have the same DNA, but certain genes used in liver cells are not used in muscle cells, so their function will be different. The developing *embryo* (up to 8 weeks) moves to the uterus and implants in the uterine wall where a placenta and umbilical cord will develop. The *placenta* provides a means of exchange for nutrients, wastes, and gases between the developing fetus and mother. The blood of the baby and mother will not mix; the exchange takes place by diffusion. The *umbilical cord* connects the baby to the placenta and acts to transport nutrients, gases, and waste. The *fetus* (after 8 weeks) will develop within the uterus until the time of birth. The health of the baby can be directly impacted by the action of the mother. Pregnant mothers should refrain from smoking and using drugs or alcohol and should maintain a healthy diet to ensure proper organ development of the embryo and fetus.

Additional Information:

- When the pancreas fails to produce adequate amounts of insulin, a condition known as diabetes can occur. The body cells will fail to receive adequate amounts of sugar for metabolism. Individuals with this type of diabetes may require insulin to be introduced via injection to help maintain homeostasis. Other types of diabetes are brought on by unhealthy lifestyles, such as obesity and lack of exercise.

- Poor diet choices and lack of exercise can lead to conditions that are harmful to the circulatory system. Cholesterol and fats can build up in blood vessels leading to high blood pressure, as well as heart attacks.

- Smoking can lead to a lower birth weight baby, drugs can lead to developmental problems within the nervous system of the fetus and alcohol can lead to fetal alcohol syndrome (FAS).

Diagrams:

1. **Respiratory and Excretory System** – This diagram represents two of the systems found within the human body, the respiratory and the excretory systems. In the respiratory system, lungs (structure *A*) allow for gas exchange through small air sacs known as alveoli. The excretory system is represented by the kidneys (structure *B*), which filter out harmful wastes and maintain water balance, and the urinary bladder (structure *C*), which stores urine.

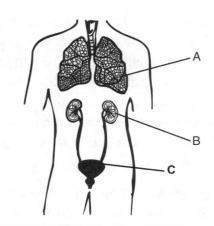

2. **The Nervous System** – The nervous system is made up of many nerves that transmit electrical impulses. Between nerve cells are gaps known as synapses as shown in the lower diagram. Chemical messengers known as neurotransmitters travel from nerve cell *A* to nerve cell *B* and connect with receptor molecules labeled within area 1. When the receptor receives the message, it initiates an impulse to continue through the next nerve cell.

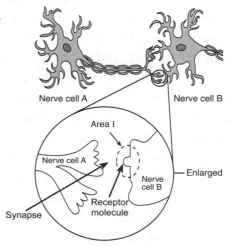

3. **Hormones in the Endocrine System** – The endocrine system is composed of glands that secrete chemical messengers known as hormones. In this diagram, the pituitary gland secretes hormones that target three glands, the thyroid, adrenal, and pancreas, which also secrete chemicals that maintain homeostasis within the human body.

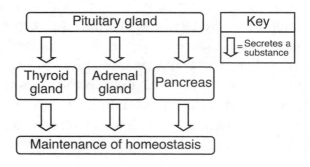

4. **Chemical Messengers and Receptors** – This diagram shows how chemical messengers work on specific cells by binding to special receptors on the cell's membrane. A secreting cell releases hormones or chemical messages into the bloodstream that flow to specific target cells that contain receptors. The shape of the receptor matches the shape of the chemical messenger, initiating a reaction within the target cell.

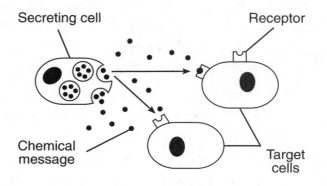

Human Physiology, Reproduction, and Homeostasis

5. **Feedback and Dynamic Equilibrium** – This diagram provides a visual representation of the process of feedback. Feedback is a mechanism where processes within the human body are regulated based on levels of activity. When levels are too high, the activity shuts down, and when levels are too low, activity increases. In the diagram, glands secrete chemicals which move to organs and cause a change in activity. Depending on the level of activity, the change will affect the amount of chemical produced by the gland. Dynamic equilibrium results when all systems are properly functioning.

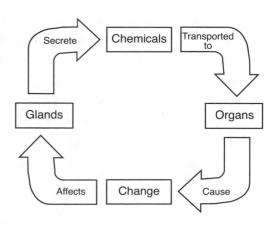

6. **Importance of Cell Receptors in The Immune System** – The diagram to the right represents a component of the immune response, the body's defense against pathogens and foreign invaders. Antibodies, produced by specialized white blood cells called *B* cells, have specific receptors that bind to antigens or foreign proteins on infected cells or on pathogens. The shape of the antibody receptor fits with a particular antigen, identifying it as foreign. When the antibodies bind to these cells, the cells are then marked for destruction by other white blood cells.

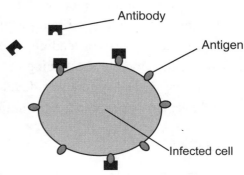

7. **Immune Response** – The diagram represents an immune response that can occur in the human body. Antibodies are proteins produced by the immune system that attach themselves to an antigen using specific receptor molecules. The antigen, a foreign protein or pathogen, is then marked for destruction. White blood cells will engulf the antigen, eliminating the foreign intruder.

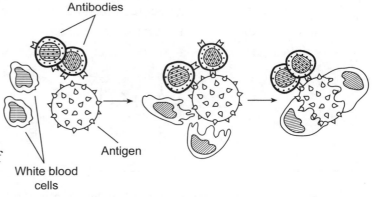

8. **Female Reproduction System** – This diagram represents the female reproductive system. This system contains several structures, each with a specific function. Structure *A* is the ovary where egg or gamete production takes place by meiosis. Structure *B* is the fallopian tube which carries eggs from the ovary to the uterus. Fertilization takes place here. Structure *C* is the uterus, which serves to hold a developing fetus. Structure *D*, the placenta, is where the exchange of nutrients, wastes, and gases occur.

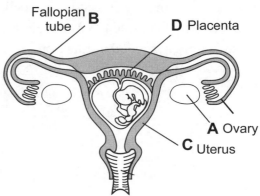

9. **Male Reproduction System** – This diagram represents the male reproductive system. Structure *A* is the testes where sperm production takes place and testosterone is produced. Structure *B* is the sperm duct or vas deferens which stores sperm until ready for use. Structure *C* is the urethra, which serves as a conduit for the sperm to exit the male's body. Structure *D* is the penis that will act to deliver the sperm into the female's body.

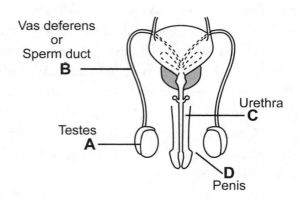

10. **Reproduction and Development** – The processes of reproduction and development are represented in this diagram. The male contributes a sperm (*A*) and a female contributes an egg (*B*) leading to fertilization (*C*) producing a zygote, containing the full set of genetic instructions. The zygote will develop into an embryo (*D*) and eventually become a fetus until birth.

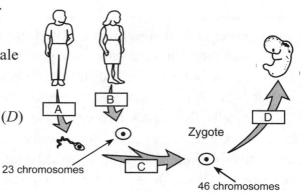

11. **Cell Division after Fertilization** – The process of development and differentiation is represented in the diagram below. After a zygote is formed at *A*, it begins a series of rapid mitotic cell divisions, producing a ball like structure as shown in steps *B* to *D*. In steps *F* and *G*, the embryo begins to carry out differentiation, a process where cells take on specific functions.

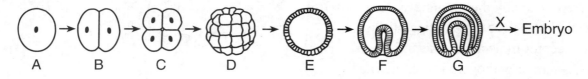

12. **Differentiation** – In the process of differentiation, a fertilized cell will differentiate into specific types of cells (Skin, muscle, and nerve cells, etc.) that carry out specific functions. Each of these cells, containing the same DNA, develops specific functions because certain genes in each cell are used or turned on to direct that function.

Human Physiology, Reproduction, and Homeostasis

Vocabulary Refresher

Group A *Directions* - Match the correct definition for the following terms:

1. _____Dynamic equilibrium

2. _____Digestive system

3. _____Cell Communication

4. _____Enzymes

5. _____Respiratory system

6. _____Hemoglobin

7. _____Emphysema

8. _____Asthma

9. _____Circulatory system

10. _____Capillaries

11. _____Arteries

12. _____Veins

13. _____Platelets

14. _____Diabetes

A. The system of organs involved in the intake and exchange of oxygen and carbon dioxide.

B. A respiratory disease in which lungs have a diminished ability to absorb oxygen.

C. A condition in which the bronchi tubes become restricted due to a reaction to allergens or environmental air pollutants.

D. Muscular blood vessels that transport blood away from the heart.

E. Blood vessels that transport blood back to the heart.

F. The use of chemical signals that transfer information from one cell to another.

G. The smallest of all blood vessels that allow for exchanges to occur at the cellular level.

H. Acts to transport nutrients and oxygen to cells and to remove waste products from cells.

I. A set of conditions that are constantly changing within an organism, in order to maintain a stable environment for the organism.

J. A group of organs that all work towards breaking down nutrients into a smaller, usable form for cell use.

K. A disorder that occurs when the body fails to utilize insulin to process sugars.

L. Blood cell fragments used to clot blood.

M. A respiratory pigment, located on red blood cells, mainly responsible for transporting oxygen.

N. Protein molecules that act as biological catalysts, which speed up chemical reactions.

Group B *Directions* - Match the correct definition for the following terms:

1. _____Excretory system

2. _____Hormones

3. _____Nervous system

4. _____Fertilization

5. _____Antigen

6. _____Red blood cells

7. _____White blood cells

8. _____Glands

9. _____Urea

10. _____Nephron

11. _____Homeostasis

12. _____Pathogen

13. _____Neurotransmitters

14. _____Estrogen and Progesterone

A. Disc shaped cells used to carry oxygen and carbon dioxide within the blood.

B. Cells which act to defend the human body against pathogens and foreign invaders.

C. A filtering structural unit located in the kidney that removes waste matter from the blood.

D. Maintaining a stable environment within an organism.

E. A water-soluble by-product of metabolism that is filtered out by the kidneys and excreted as urine.

F. Made up of millions of nerve cells that respond to external stimuli or changes from the outside environment.

G. Chemical substances that transmit nerve impulses across a synapse.

H. An agent that causes disease, especially a living microorganism such as bacteria and virus.

I. A substance (foreign protein) that when introduced into the body stimulates the production of an antibody; these substances are found in toxins, bacteria, cells of transplanted organs, etc.

J. Chemical messengers that are produced and secreted by glands into the bloodstream where they travel to target cells to illicit a response.

K. Hormones produced by the ovary that are responsible for maintaining the uterus.

L. The union of male and female gametes to form a zygote. This occurs in the fallopian tube (oviduct).

M. Groups of tissues that secrete specific hormones.

N. A system of organs involved in the removal of harmful waste as well as to maintain water balance.

Human Physiology, Reproduction, and Homeostasis

Group C   *Directions* - Match the correct definition for the following terms:

1. _____Vaccines

2. _____Feedback

3. _____B cells

4. _____Receptor proteins

5. _____Synapse

6. _____Endocrine system

7. _____Memory cells

8. _____Insulin

9. _____Target cells

10. _____Testosterone

11. _____Differentiation

12. _____T cells

13. _____Immune system

14. _____Ovary

A. Membrane proteins that bind with specific molecules to produce a cellular response.

B. The bodily system that consists of glands and the hormones that they secrete.

C. Cells that contain specific receptors that will bind with specific hormones to produce a specific reaction.

D. A hormone produced by the pancreas that allows cells to take in sugar, thus regulating blood sugar levels.

E. The organ that produces the hormones, estrogen and progesterone, which are involved in female reproductive development as well as promotes gamete (egg) formation.

F. A mechanism that allows for the regulation of hormones or body temperature levels by increasing or decreasing activity within that system.

G. A hormone that is produced primarily in the testes and is responsible for the development of male sex characteristics.

H. A system that is involved in the defense of the human body through action of white blood cells.

I. Type of white blood cells that produce plasma cells which release antibodies.

J. Type of white blood cells that directly attack pathogen-infected cells and serve to activate other white blood cells.

K. Contain weakened pathogens that create an immunity to that particular pathogen.

L. T and B cells that have receptors to recognize previous pathogens and readily begin an immune response.

M. The junction or gap at which a nerve impulse passes across from one nerve to another.

N. A process that occurs after rapid cell division of the zygote where cells begin to develop different functions based on gene expression.

Group D *Directions* - Match the correct definition for the following terms:

1. _____ Umbilical cord

2. _____ Fetus

3. _____ Uterus

4. _____ Allergic reaction

5. _____ HIV

6. _____ Menstrual cycle

7. _____ Antibodies

8. _____ Fallopian tubes

9. _____ Embryo

10. _____ Zygote

11. _____ AIDS

12. _____ Testes

13. _____ Vas deferens

14. _____ Placenta

A. An condition in which the body produces an immune response to a normally harmless substance, like pollen.

B. Secreted in response to antigens, they have receptor molecules that can bind to antigens or infected cells marking them for destruction.

C. A virus that weakens the immune system by destroying T cells.

D. A severe immunological disorder caused by the HIV virus where the human immune system is weakened and compromised.

E. A pair of slender ducts through which the egg passes from the ovaries to the uterus in the female reproductive system.

F. A flexible cord-like structure that connects the fetus to the placenta; it transports nourishment, gases, and waste products via the arteries and veins found within.

G. Where sperm cells mature and are stored.

H. Formed when the sperm and egg unite – has a full set of chromosomes.

I. A membranous organ that provides a means of exchange for nutrients, wastes, and gases between the developing fetus and mother.

J. A developing baby after 8 weeks.

K. This recurring monthly occurrence in women regulates reproduction by releasing an egg produced in the process known as ovulation.

L. A developing baby up to 8 weeks of life.

M. A muscular organ located in the pelvic cavity of females in which the fertilized egg implants and develops.

N. Male organs where the process of sperm production takes place through the process of meiosis.

Human Physiology, Reproduction, and Homeostasis

1. Which situation indicates that a disruption of homeostasis has taken place?

   (1) the presence of hormones that keep the blood sugar level steady
   (2) the maintenance of a constant body temperature
   (3) cell division that is involved in normal growth
   (4) a rapid rise in the number of red blood cells   1 _____

2. A human liver cell is very different in structure and function from a nerve cell in the same person. This is best explained by the fact that

   (1) different genes function in each type of cell
   (2) liver cells can reproduce while the nerve cells cannot
   (3) liver cells contain fewer chromosomes than nerve cells
   (4) different DNA is present in each type of cell   2 _____

3. Which substances may form in the human body due to invaders entering the blood?

   (1) nutrients   (3) antibodies
   (2) vaccines   (4) red blood cells   3 _____

4. A protein on the surface of HIV can attach to proteins on the surface of healthy human cells. These attachment sites on the surface of the cells are known as

   (1) receptor molecules
   (2) genetic codes
   (3) molecular bases
   (4) inorganic catalysts   4 _____

5. To communicate between cells, many multicellular animals use

   (1) nerve signals and respiratory gases
   (2) respiratory gases and hormones
   (3) bones and muscles
   (4) nerve signals and hormones   5 _____

6. Cellular communication is illustrated in the diagram below.

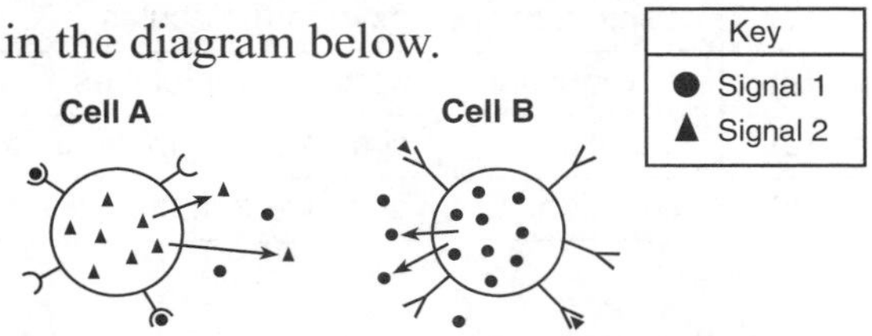

Key
● Signal 1
▲ Signal 2

   Cell A   **Cell B**

   Information can be sent from

   (1) cell A to cell B because cell B is able to recognize signal 1
   (2) cell A to cell B because cell A is able to recognize signal 2
   (3) cell B to cell A because cell A is able to recognize signal 1
   (4) cell B to cell A because cell B is able to recognize signal 2   6 _____

7. Which activity would stimulate the human immune system to provide protection against an invasion by a microbe?

   (1) receiving antibiotic injections after surgery
   (2) choosing a well-balanced diet and following it throughout life
   (3) being vaccinated against chicken pox
   (4) receiving hormones contained in mother's milk while nursing   7 _____

8. Which developmental process is represented by the diagram below?

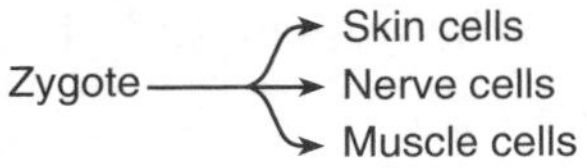

   Zygote ——→ Skin cells
          ——→ Nerve cells
          ——→ Muscle cells

   (1) fertilization   (3) evolution
   (2) differentiation   (4) mutation   8 _____

9. The diagram below represents one metabolic activity of a human.

Metabolic Activity A

[   ] ⟶ B B B B
Protein

Letters *A* and *B* are best represented by which row in the chart?

Row	Metabolic Activity A	B
(1)	respiration	oxygen molecules
(2)	reproduction	hormone molecules
(3)	excretion	simple sugar molecules
(4)	digestion	amino acid molecules

9 _____

10. Contractile vacuoles maintain water balance by pumping excess water out of some single-celled pond organisms. In humans, the kidney is chiefly involved in maintaining water balance. These facts best illustrate that

(1) tissues, organs, and organ systems work together to maintain homeostasis in all living things
(2) interference with nerve signals disrupts cellular communication and homeostasis within organisms
(3) a disruption in a body system may disrupt the homeostasis of a single-celled organism
(4) structures found in single-celled organisms can act in a manner similar to tissues and organs in multicellular organisms   10 _____

11. Certain microbes, foreign tissues, and some cancerous cells can cause immune responses in the human body because all three contain

(1) antigens   (3) fats
(2) enzymes   (4) cytoplasm   11 _____

12. Which statement best describes how a vaccination can help protect the body against disease?

(1) Vaccines directly kill the pathogen that causes the disease.
(2) Vaccines act as a medicine that cures the disease.
(3) Vaccines cause the production of specific molecules that will react with and destroy certain microbes.
(4) Vaccines contain white blood cells that engulf harmful germs and prevent them from spreading throughout the body.   12 _____

13. An important method of communication between cells in an organism is shown in the diagram.

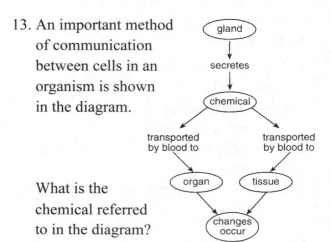

What is the chemical referred to in the diagram?

(1) a hormone important in maintaining homeostasis
(2) an enzyme detected a cell membrane receptor
(3) DNA necessary regulating cell functions
(4) a food molecule taken in by an organism   13 _____

14. The human reproductive system is regulated by
(1) restriction enzymes
(2) antigens
(3) complex carbohydrates
(4) hormones   14 _____

Set 1 – Human Physiology, Reproduction, and Homeostasis

15. Which statement describes a feedback mechanism involving the human pancreas?

(1) The production of estrogen stimulates the formation of gametes for sexual reproduction.
(2) The level of oxygen in the blood is related to heart rate.
(3) The level of sugar in the blood is affected by the amount of insulin in the blood.
(4) The production of urine allows for excretion of cell waste.   15 _____

16. In the human pancreas, acinar cells produce digestive enzymes and beta cells produce insulin. The best explanation for this is that

(1) a mutation occurs in the beta cells to produce insulin when the sugar level increases in the blood
(2) different parts of an individual's DNA are used to direct the synthesis of different proteins in different types of cells
(3) lowered sugar levels cause the production of insulin in acinar cells to help maintain homeostasis
(4) the genes in acinar cells came from one parent while the genes in beta cells came from the other parent   16 _____

17. Which process normally occurs at the placenta?

(1) Oxygen diffuses from fetal blood to maternal blood.
(2) Materials are exchanged between fetal and maternal blood.
(3) Maternal blood is converted into fetal blood.
(4) Digestive enzymes pass from maternal blood to fetal blood.   17 _____

18. Structures in a human female are represented in the diagram. A heavy dose of radiation would have the greatest impact on genetic information in future offspring if it reached gametes developing within structure

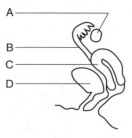

(1) A   (3) C
(2) B   (4) D   18 _____

19. Some body structures of a human male are represented in the diagram. An obstruction in the structures labeled **X** would directly interfere with the

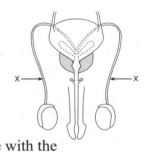

(1) transfer of sperm to a female
(2) production of sperm
(3) production of urine
(4) transfer of urine to the external environment   19 _____

20. The diagram below represents human reproductive systems.

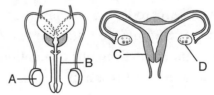

Which statement best describes part of the human reproductive process?

(1) Testosterone produced in *A* is transferred to *D*, where it influences embryonic development.
(2) Testosterone produced in *D* influences formation of sperm within *B*.
(3) Estrogen and progesterone influence the activity of *C*.
(4) Progesterone stimulates the division of the egg within *C*.   20 _____

21. Which structures in diagram I and diagram II carry out a similar life function?

I   II

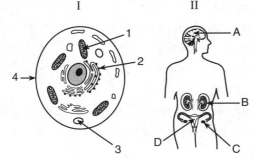

(1) 1 and *C*   (3) 3 and *A*
(2) 2 and *D*   (4) 4 and *B*   21 _____

22. To increase chances for a successful organ transplant, the person receiving the organ should be given special medications. The purpose of these medications is to

(1) increase the immune response in the person receiving the transplant
(2) decrease the immune response in the person receiving the transplant
(3) decrease mutations in the person receiving the transplant
(4) increase mutations in the person receiving the transplant   22 _____

23. In sexually reproducing species, the number of chromosomes in each body cell remains the same from one generation to the next as a direct result of

(1) meiosis and fertilization
(2) mitosis and mutation
(3) differentiation and aging
(4) homeostasis and dynamic equilibrium   23 _____

24. Which organ system in humans is most directly involved in the transport of oxygen?

(1) digestive   (3) excretory
(2) nervous   (4) circulatory   24 _____

25. The diagram represents an event that occurs in the blood.

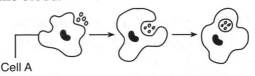

Cell A

Which statement best describes this event?

(1) Cell *A* is a white blood cell releasing antigens to destroy bacteria.
(2) Cell *A* is a cancer cell produced by the immune system and it is helping to prevent disease.
(3) Cell *A* is a white blood cell engulfing disease-causing organisms.
(4) Cell *A* is protecting bacteria so they can reproduce without being destroyed by predators.   25 _____

26. The diagram below represents an interaction between parts of an organism.

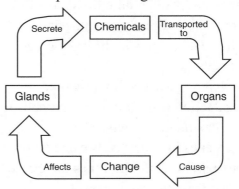

The term chemicals in this diagram represents

(1) starch molecules
(2) DNA molecules
(3) hormone molecules
(4) receptor molecules   26 _____

27. Which hormone does not directly regulate human reproductive cycles?

(1) testosterone (3) insulin
(2) estrogen   (4) progesterone   27 _____

28. A large number of sperm cells are produced by males every day. This large number of sperm cells increases the chance that

(1) at least one sperm cell will be reached when the eggs swim toward the sperm cells in the ovary
(2) several sperm cells will unite with an egg so the fertilized egg will develop properly
(3) some of the sperm cells will survive to reach the egg
(4) enough sperm cells will be present to transport the egg from where it is produced to where it develops into a fetus

28 _____

29. Some organs of the human body are represented in the accompanying diagram.

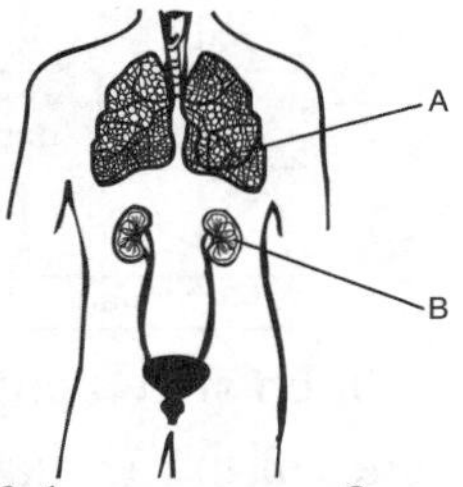

Which statement best describes the functions of these organs?

(1) B pumps blood to A for gas exchange.
(2) A and B both produce carbon dioxide, which provides nutrients for other body parts.
(3) A releases antibodies in response to an infection in B.
(4) The removal of wastes from both A and B involves the use of energy from ATP.

29 _____

30. Kangaroos are mammals that lack a placenta. Therefore, they must have an alternate way of supplying the developing embryo with

(1) nutrients
(2) carbon dioxide
(3) enzymes
(4) genetic information

30 _____

31. Which cell process occurs only in organisms that reproduce sexually?

(1) mutation   (3) meiosis
(2) replication   (4) mitosis   31 _____

Base your answers to question 32 the diagram below.

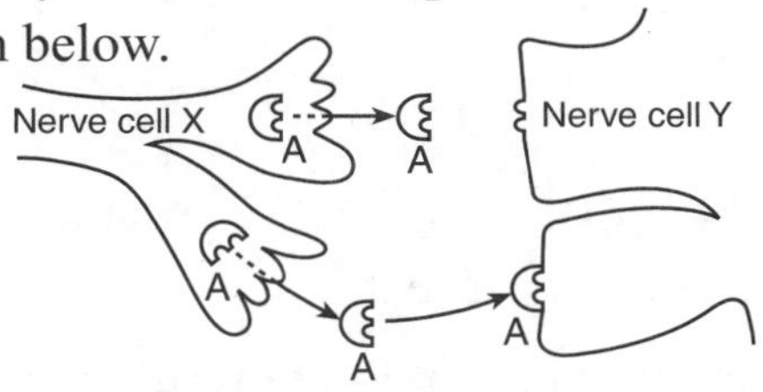

Nerve cell X   A   A   Nerve cell Y
A   A

32. a) The process represented in the diagram best illustrates

(1) cellular communication
(2) muscle contraction
(3) extraction of energy from nutrients
(4) waste disposal   a _____

b) Which statement best describes the diagram?

(1) Nerve cell X is releasing receptor molecules.
(2) Nerve cell Y is signaling nerve cell X.
(3) Nerve cell X is attaching to nerve cell Y.
(4) Nerve cell Y contains receptor molecules for substance A.   b _____

c) A drug is developed that, due to its molecular shape, blocks the action of substance A. Which shape would the drug molecule most likely resemble?

(1)   (2)   (3)   (4)   c _____

33. Which two systems are most directly involved in providing molecules needed for the synthesis of fats in human cells?

(1) digestive and circulatory
(2) excretory and digestive
(3) immune and muscular
(4) reproductive and circulatory   33 _____

34. The most immediate response to a high level of blood sugar in a human is an increase in the

(1) muscle activity in the arms
(2) blood flow to the digestive tract
(3) activity of all cell organelles
(4) release of insulin   34 ____

35. The virus that causes AIDS is damaging to the body because it

(1) targets cells that fight invading microbes
(2) attacks specific red blood cells
(3) causes an abnormally high insulin level
(4) prevents the normal transmission of nerve impulses   35 ____

36. Some stages in the development of an individual are listed below.

(A) differentiation of cells into tissues
(B) fertilization of egg by sperm
(C) organ development
(D) mitotic cell division of zygote

Which sequence represents the correct order of these stages?

(1) A–B–C–D   (3) D–B–C–A
(2) B–C–A–D   (4) B–D–A–C   36 ____

37. A function of white blood cells is to

(1) transport oxygen to body cells
(2) produce hormones that regulate cell communication
(3) carry glucose to body cells
(4) protect the body against pathogens   37 ____

38. The diagram below illustrates some functions of the pituitary gland. The pituitary gland secretes substances that, in turn, cause other glands to secrete different substances.

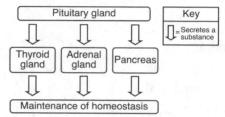

Which statement best describes events shown in the diagram?

(1) Secretions provide the energy needed for metabolism.
(2) The raw materials for the synthesis of secretions come from nitrogen.
(3) The secretions of all glands speed blood circulation in the body.
(4) Secretions help the body to respond to changes from the normal state   38 ____

39. Which phrase best describes a process represented in the diagram below?

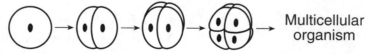

Fertilized egg

(1) a zygote dividing by mitosis   (3) a gamete dividing by mitosis
(2) a zygote dividing by meiosis   (4) a gamete dividing by meiosis   39 ____

Set 1 – Human Physiology, Reproduction, and Homeostasis

40. The diagram shows the interaction between blood sugar levels and pancreatic activity. This process is an example of

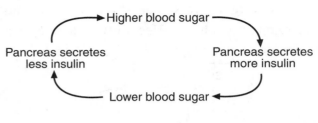

(1) a feedback mechanism maintaining homeostasis
(2) an immune system responding to prevent disease
(3) the digestion of sugar by insulin
(4) the hormonal regulation of gamete production

40_____

41. The sequence of diagrams below represents some events in a reproductive process.

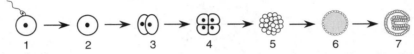

To regulate similar events in human reproduction, what adaptations are required?

(1) the presence of genes and chemicals in each cell in stages 1 to 7
(2) an increase in the number of genes in each cell in stages 3 to 5
(3) the removal of all enzymes from the cells in stage 7
(4) the elimination of mutations from cells after stage 5

41_____

42. The diagram represents what can happen when homeostasis in an organism is threatened. Which statement provides a possible explanation for these events?

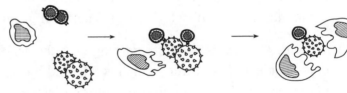

(1) Antibiotics break down harmful substances by the process of digestion.
(2) Some specialized cells mark and other cells engulf microbes during immune reactions.
(3) Embryonic development of essential organs occurs during pregnancy.
(4) Cloning removes abnormal cells produced during differentiation.

42_____

43. The data in the graph below show evidence of disease in the human body.

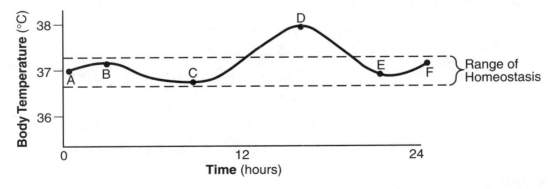

A disruption in dynamic equilibrium is indicated by the temperature change between points

(1) *A* and *B*   (2) *B* and *C*   (3) *C* and *D*   (4) *E* and *F*

43_____

Base your answers to question 44 on the diagram below and on your knowledge of biology. The diagram represents the effect of two chemical substances, *A* and *B*, in maintaining the level of glucose in the blood in humans.

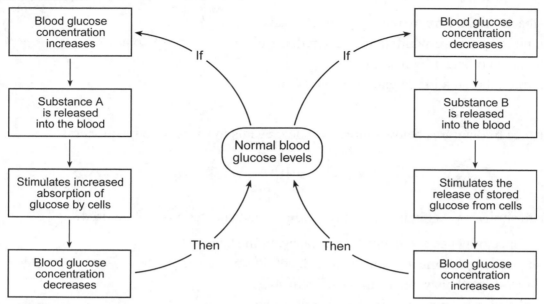

44. *a*) The interaction of substances *A* and *B* is an example of
(1) a genetic mutation
(3) an immune response
(2) homeostatic feedback
(4) active transport

a_____

b) Which statement is correct regarding the substances involved in these interactions?
(1) Substance *A* is insulin, which is released by cells in the pancreas.
(2) Substance *B* is a chemical receptor molecule produced by blood cells.
(3) Both substances *A* and *B* are classified as biological catalysts.
(4) Substance *A* is a chemical that is produced by specialized blood cells.

b_____

The diagrams below represent organs of two individuals. The diagrams are followed by a list of sentences. For each phrase in question 45, select the sentence from the list below that best applies to that phrase. Then record its number in the space provided.

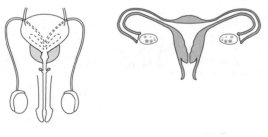

Individual A   Individual B

1. The phrase is correct for both Individual *A* and Individual *B*.

2. The phrase is not correct for either Individual *A* or Individual *B*.

3. The phrase is correct for Individual *A*, only.

4. The phrase is correct for Individual *B*, only

45. *a*) Contains organs that produce gametes _____

b) Contains organs involved in internal fertilization _____

c) Contains a structure in which a zygote divides by mitosis _____

Base your answers to question 46 on the structures in the diagram of human blood that help to maintain homeostasis in humans.

46. *a*) Identify the cell labeled **X**. _____

   b) State one way a cell such as cell **X** helps to maintain homeostasis.

   _____

   _____

47. Using appropriate information, fill in spaces *A* and *B* in the chart. In space *A* identify an organ in the human body where molecules diffuse into the blood. In space *B* identify a specific molecule that diffuses into the blood at this organ. Rows 1 and 2 must have different answers.

	An organ in the human body where molecules diffuse into the blood	A specific molecule that diffuses into the blood at this organ
1	A	B
2	A	B

48. What term or phrase does letter **X** most likely represent?

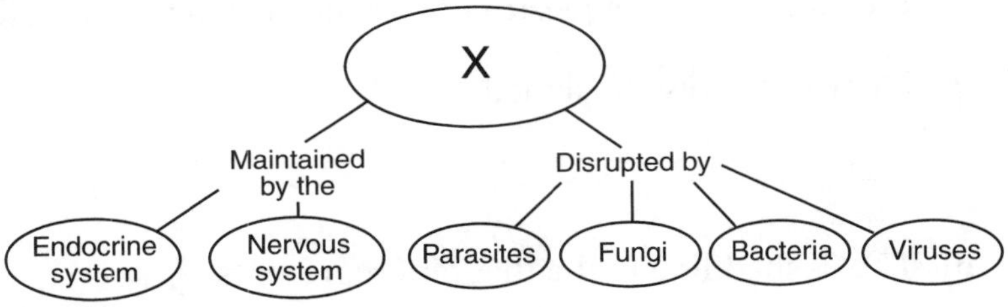

   _____

49. The types of human cells shown are different from one another, even though they all originated from the same fertilized egg and contain the same genetic information. Explain why these genetically identical cells can differ in structure and function.

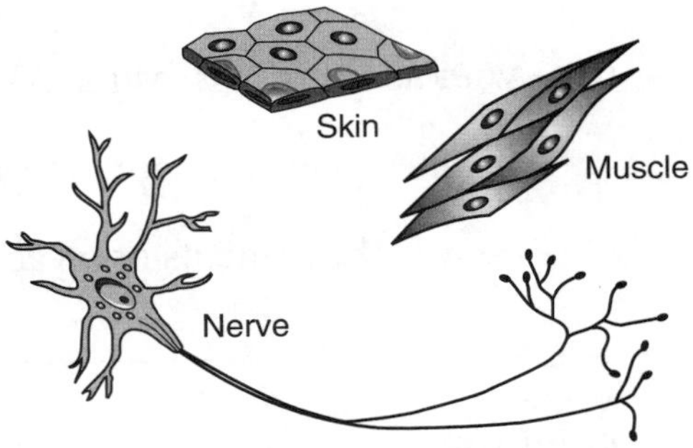

   _____

   _____

   _____

50. Estrogen is one of the hormones produced by human females. Identify *one* organ that produces estrogen and state *one* specific function of estrogen in a human female.

   Organ: _____

   Function: _____

Base your answers to questions 51 on the statement and diagram.

Women are advised to avoid consuming alcoholic beverages during pregnancy.

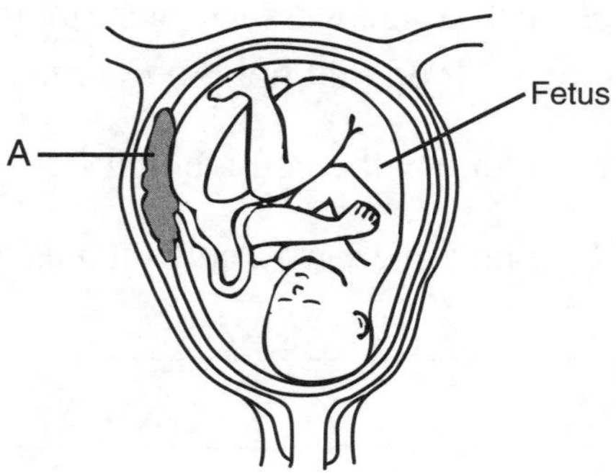

51. a) Identify the structure labeled *A* and explain how the functioning of structure *A* is essential for the normal development of the fetus.

Structure *A*: _____

Function: _____

_____

b) Explain why consumption of alcoholic beverages by a pregnant woman is likely to be more harmful to her fetus than to herself.

_____

_____

c) What structure is the fetus being developed in? _____

Base your answers to question 52 on the accompanying diagram.

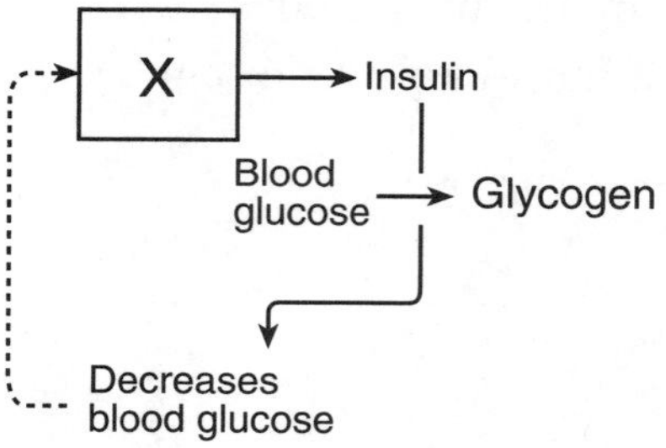

52. a) Identify the organ labeled **X**.

_____

b) The dashed line in the diagram represents

_____

Base your answers to question 53 on the information below.

Vaccines play an important role in the ability of the body to resist certain diseases.

53. a) Describe the contents of a vaccine.

_____

b) Identify the system in the body that is most directly affected by a vaccination.

_____

c) Explain how a vaccination results in the long-term ability of the body to resist disease.

_____

_____

1. What usually results when an organism fails to maintain homeostasis?

   (1) Growth rates within organs become equal.
   (2) The organism becomes ill or may die.
   (3) A constant sugar supply for the cells is produced.
   (4) The water balance in the tissues of the organism stabilizes. 1 _____

2. Which statement accurately compares cells in the human circulatory system to cells in the human nervous system?

   (1) Cells in the circulatory system carry out the same life function for the organism as cells in the nervous system.
   (2) Cells in the circulatory system are identical in structure to cells in the nervous system.
   (3) Cells in the nervous system are different in structure from cells in the circulatory system, and they carry out different specialized functions.
   (4) Cells in the nervous system act independently, but cells in the circulatory system function together. 2 _____

3. Feedback interactions in the human body are important because they

   (1) determine the diversity necessary for evolution to occur
   (2) direct the synthesis of altered genes that are passed on to every cell in the body
   (3) regulate the shape of molecules involved in cellular communication
   (4) keep the internal body environment within its normal range 3 _____

4. Hormones and secretions of the nervous system are chemical messengers that

   (1) store genetic information
   (2) carry out the circulation of materials
   (3) extract energy from nutrients
   (4) coordinate system interactions 4 _____

5. The diagram represents cells and hormones present in the human body.

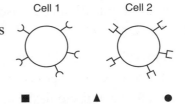

   Which statement correctly describes an interaction between the hormones and the cells?
   (1) Hormone *A* is synthesized by cell 2 and targets cell 1.
   (2) Hormone *B* bonds with both cell 1 and cell 2.
   (3) Specific reactions carried out by cell 1 are regulated by hormone *C*.
   (4) The specialized receptor molecules on cell 1 secrete hormone *B*. 5 _____

6. In the body of a human, the types of chemical activities occurring within cells are most dependent on the

   (1) biological catalysts present
   (2) size of the cell
   (3) number of chromosomes in the cell
   (4) kind of sugar found on each chromosome 6 _____

7. Drugs to reduce the risk of rejection are given to organ transplant patients because the donated organ contains

   (1) foreign antigens
   (2) foreign antibodies
   (3) DNA molecules
   (4) pathogenic microbes 7 _____

8. Communication between cells is affected
   if there is decreased ability to produce

   (1) digestive enzymes and gametes
   (2) antibodies and chloroplasts
   (3) hormones and nerve impulses
   (4) antibiotics and guard cells   8 _____

9. People with AIDS are unable to fight
   multiple infections because the virus
   that causes AIDS

   (1) weakens their immune systems
   (2) produces antibodies in their blood
   (3) attacks muscle tissue
   (4) kills pathogens   9 _____

10. The main function of the human
    digestive system is to

    (1) rid the body of cellular waste materials
    (2) process organic molecules so they
        can enter cells
    (3) break down glucose in order to
        release energy
    (4) change amino acids into proteins
        and carbohydrates   10 _____

11. The immune system of humans may
    respond to chemicals on the surface
    of an invading organism by

    (1) releasing hormones that break
        down these chemicals
    (2) synthesizing antibodies that mark
        these organisms to be destroyed
    (3) secreting antibiotics that attach to
        these organisms
    (4) altering a DNA sequence in
        these organisms   11 _____

12. Many vaccinations stimulate the
    immune system by exposing it to

    (1) antibodies   (3) mutated genes
    (2) enzymes   (4) weakened microbes
                                           12 _____

13. The diagram below represents a process that
    occurs during normal human development.

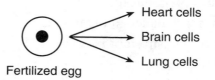

Fertilized egg

    Which statement is correct regarding the
    cells and DNA?

    (1) All the cells have identical DNA.
    (2) The DNA of the fertilized egg differs
        from the DNA of all the other cells.
    (3) The DNA of the fertilized egg differs
        from some, but not all, of the other cells.
    (4) Only the fertilized egg contains DNA.
                                           13 _____

14. A single cell and a multicellular organism
    are represented below.

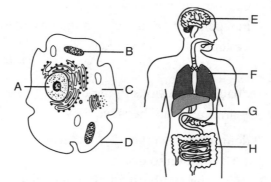

    Which structures are correctly paired with
    their primary function?

    (1) A and G—transmission of nerve impulses
    (2) B and E—photosynthesis
    (3) C and H—digestion of food
    (4) D and F—gas exchange   14 _____

15. Many viruses infect only a certain type of cell because they bind to certain

(1) other viruses on the surface of the cell
(2) mitochondria in the cell
(3) hormones in the cell
(4) receptor sites on the surface of the cell   15 _____

16. The interaction of which two systems provides the molecules needed for the metabolic activity that takes place at ribosomes?

(1) digestive and circulatory
(2) reproductive and excretory
(3) immune and nervous
(4) respiratory and muscular   16 _____

17. Some human white blood cells help destroy pathogenic bacteria by

(1) causing mutations in the bacteria
(2) engulfing and digesting the bacteria
(3) producing toxins that compete with bacterial toxins
(4) inserting part of their DNA into the bacterial cells   17 _____

18. What will most likely happen to wastes containing nitrogen produced as a result of the breakdown of amino acids within liver cells of a mammal?

(1) They will be digested by enzymes in the stomach.
(2) They will be removed by the excretory system.
(3) They will be destroyed by specialized blood cells.
(4) They will be absorbed by mitochondria in nearby cells.   18 _____

19. In some individuals, the immune system attacks substances such as grass pollen that are usually harmless, resulting in

(1) an allergic reaction
(2) a form of cancer
(3) an insulin imbalance
(4) a mutation   19 _____

20. As a human red blood cell matures, it loses its nucleus. As a result of this loss, a mature red blood cell lacks the ability to

(1) take in material from the blood
(2) release hormones to the blood
(3) pass through artery walls
(4) carry out cell division   20 _____

21. Which transplant method would prevent the rejection of tissue after an organ transplant?

(1) using organs cloned from the cells of the patient
(2) using organs produced by genetic engineering to get rid of all proteins in the donated organs
(3) using organs only from pigs or monkeys
(4) using an organ donated by a close relative because the proteins will always be identical to those of the recipient   21 _____

22. Which system is correctly paired with its function?

(1) immune system—intake and distribution of oxygen to cells of the body
(2) excretory system—remove potentially dangerous materials from the body
(3) digestive system—transport energy-rich molecules to cells
(4) circulatory system—produce building blocks of complex compounds   22 _____

23. In the diagram of a single-celled organism shown below, the arrows indicate various activities taking place.

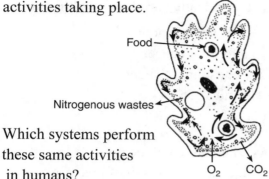

Which systems perform these same activities in humans?

(1) digestive, circulatory, and immune
(2) excretory, respiratory, and reproductive
(3) respiratory, excretory, and digestive
(4) respiratory, nervous, and endocrine   23 _____

Base your answers to question 24 on the diagram below of a cell associated with coordination.

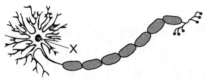

24. a) Structure **X** would be involved in the

(1) storage of digestive enzymes
(2) absorption of energy from the Sun
(3) development of pathogens
(4) synthesis of proteins   a _____

b) Which statement best describes a function of the entire structure shown in the diagram?

(1) It unites with an egg cell during fertilization.
(2) It synthesizes a hormone involved in the control of blood sugar level.
(3) It releases chemicals involved in cellular communication.
(4) It controls the replication of genetic material.   b _____

25. Which statement correctly describes the genetic makeup of the sperm cells produced by a human male?

(1) Each cell has pairs of chromosomes and the cells are usually genetically identical.
(2) Each cell has pairs of chromosomes and the cells are usually genetically different.
(3) Each cell has half the normal number of chromosomes and the cells are usually genetically identical.
(4) Each cell has half the normal number of chromosomes and the cells are usually genetically different.   25 _____

26. An activity that occurs in the human body is shown below.

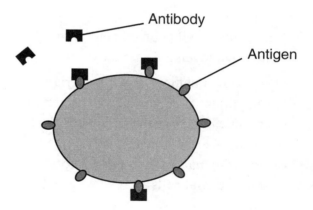

This activity helps to

(1) provide protection against pathogens
(2) produce antibiotics to control disease
(3) eliminate harmful gene alterations
(4) regulate production of ATP by the cell   26 _____

27. Human egg cells are most similar to human sperm cells in their

(1) degree of motility
(2) amount of stored food
(3) chromosome number
(4) shape and size   27 _____

28. The diagram below represents three human body systems.

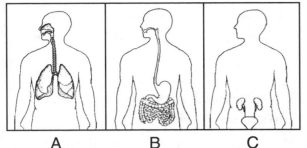

A   B   C

Which row in the chart below correctly shows what systems *A*, *B*, and *C* provide for the human body?

Row	System A	System B	System C
(1)	blood cells	glucose	hormones
(2)	oxygen	absorption	gametes
(3)	gas exchange	nutrients	waste removal
(4)	immunity	coordination	carbon dioxide

28 _____

29. Regulation of sexual reproductive cycles of human males is related most directly to the presence of the hormone

(1) estrogen   (3) testosterone
(2) progesterone   (4) insulin   29 _____

Base your answers to question 30 on the diagram below, which represents the human female reproductive system.

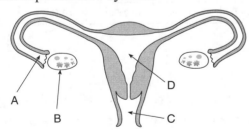

30. New inherited characteristics may appear in offspring as a result of new combinations of existing genes or may result from mutations in genes contained in cells produced by structure

(1) *A*   (2) *B*   (3) *C*   (4) *D*   30 _____

31. The diagram represents the reproductive system of a mammal.

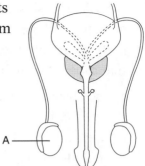

The hormone produced in structure *A* most directly brings about a change in

(1) the ability to carry out respiration
(2) physical characteristics
(3) the rate of digestion
(4) blood sugar concentration   31 _____

32. Estrogen has a direct effect on the

(1) formation of a zygote
(2) changes within the uterus
(3) movement of an egg toward the sperm
(4) development of a placenta within the ovary   32 _____

33. Sexual reproduction involves the processes listed below.

Processes

A. Differentiation   C. Gamete production
B. Fertilization   D. Mitosis

Which sequence represents the order in which these processes occur?

(1) $A \rightarrow B \rightarrow C \rightarrow D$
(2) $B \rightarrow A \rightarrow C \rightarrow D$
(3) $C \rightarrow B \rightarrow D \rightarrow A$
(4) $D \rightarrow B \rightarrow C \rightarrow A$ 33 _____

34. For a human zygote to become an embryo, it must undergo

(1) fertilization   (3) meiotic divisions
(2) recombination   (4) mitotic divisions

34 _____

35. German measles is a disease that can harm an embryo if the mother is infected in the early stages of pregnancy because the virus that causes German measles is able to

(1) be absorbed by the embryo from the mother's milk
(2) be transported to the embryo in red blood cells
(3) pass across the placenta
(4) infect the eggs   35 _____

36. The reproductive system of the human male produces gametes and

(1) transfers gametes to the female for internal fertilization
(2) produces enzymes that prevent fertilization
(3) releases hormones involved in external fertilization
(4) provides an area for fertilization   36_____

37. A diagram of human female reproductive structures is shown below.

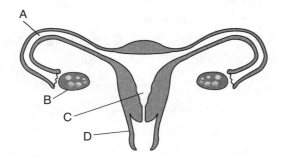

Which structure is correctly paired with its function?

(1) A — releases estrogen and progesterone
(2) B — produces and releases the egg
(3) C — provides the usual site for fertilization
(4) D — nourishes a developing embryo   37 _____

38. The structure that makes nutrients most directly available to a human embryo is the

(1) gamete   (3) stomach
(2) ovary   (4) placenta   38 _____

39. Which reproductive structure is correctly paired with its function?

(1) uterus—usual site of fertilization
(2) testis—usual location for egg development
(3) ovary—delivers nutrients to the embryo
(4) sperm—transports genetic material
                                            39 _____

40. As women age, their reproductive cycles stop due to decreased

(1) digestive enzyme production
(2) production of ATP
(3) levels of specific hormones
(4) heart rate   40 _____

41. Which row in the chart below indicates the correct process for each event indicated?

Row	Formation of Egg	Formation of Sperm	Growth of Embryo
(1)	mitosis	mitosis	meiosis
(2)	mitosis	meiosis	mitosis
(3)	meiosis	mitosis	meiosis
(4)	meiosis	meiosis	mitosis

                                            41 _____

42. Abnormalities present in the cells that line the uterus may prevent the production of offspring by directly interfering with the

(1) development of the embryo
(2) differentiation of gametes into zygotes
(3) secretion of estrogen by the ovary
(4) production and release of egg cells
                                            42 _____

Set 2 – Human Physiology, Reproduction, and Homeostasis

43. The diagram below represents events involved as energy is ultimately released from food.

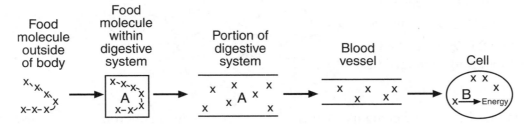

Which row in the accompanying table best represents the chain of **X**s and letters *A* and *B* in the diagram?

X-X-X-X-X-X-X	A and B
(1) nutrient	antibodies
(2) nutrient	enzymes
(3) hemoglobin	wastes
(4) hemoglobin	hormones

43_____

44. Part of embryonic development in a species is illustrated in the accompanying diagram. Which set of factors plays the most direct role in controlling the events shown in the diagram?

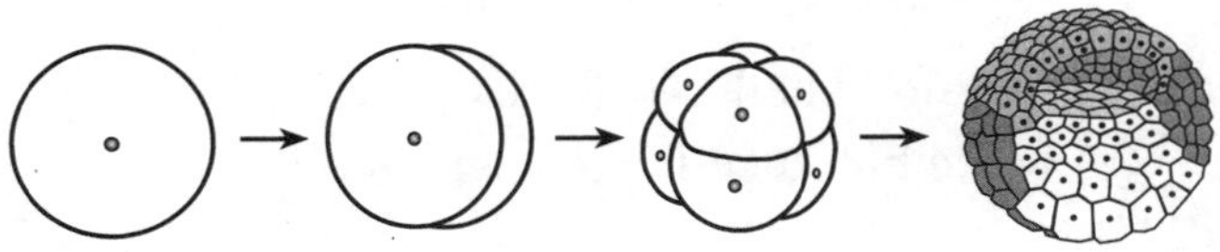

(1) genes, hormones, and cell location
(2) antibodies, insulin, and starch
(3) ATP, amino acids, and inorganic compounds
(4) abiotic resources, homeostasis, and selective breeding

Fertilized egg   **Embryo**

44_____

45. The data in the table indicate the presence of specific reproductive hormones in blood samples taken from three individuals. An **X** in the hormone column indicates a positive lab test for the appropriate levels necessary for normal reproductive functioning in that individual.

Data Table

Individuals	Hormones Present		
	Testosterone	Progesterone	Estrogen
1		X	X
2			X
3	X		

Which processes could occur in individual 3?

(1) production of sperm, only
(2) production of sperm and production of eggs
(3) production of eggs and embryonic development
(4) production of eggs, only

45_____

46. Which activity most directly involves the process represented in the diagram below?

(1) a gamete reproducing sexually
(2) a white blood cell engulfing bacteria
(3) a zygote being produced in an ovary
(4) an animal repairing damaged tissue

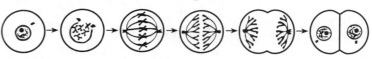

46_____

47. Which row in the chart below contains an event that is paired with an appropriate response in the human body?

Row	Event	Response
(1)	a virus enters the bloodstream	increased production of antibodies
(2)	fertilization of an egg	increased levels of testosterone
(3)	dehydration due to increased sweating	increased urine output
(4)	a drop in the rate of digestion	increased respiration rate

47_____

48. The diagram shows a cell in the human body engulfing a bacterial cell. The cell labeled **X** is most likely a

(1) red blood cell
(2) white blood cell
(3) liver cell
(4) nerve cell

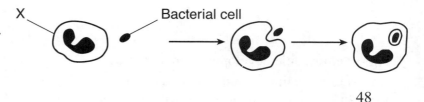

48_____

49. The graph shows the levels of glucose and insulin in the blood of a human over a period of time. This graph represents

(1) an allergic reaction
(2) an antigen-antibody reaction
(3) maintenance of homeostasis
(4) autotrophic nutrition

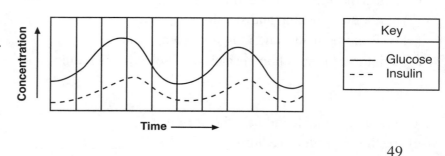

49_____

50. Humans require multiple systems for various life functions. Two vital systems are the circulatory system and the respiratory system. Select one of these systems, write its name in the chart below, then identify two structures that are part of that system, and state how each structure you identified functions as part of the system.

System:	
Structure	Function
(1)	
(2)	

51. Cell communication involves a cell detecting and responding to signals from other cells. Receptor molecules play an important role in these reactions. Human cells have insulin receptors that are needed for the movement of glucose out of the blood.

   a) State one way that the shape of the insulin receptor is related to its role in cell communication.

   _____

   _____

   b) A typical human liver cell can have over 90,000 insulin receptors. If a genetic error occurred, resulting in each liver cell in a person having only 1,000 insulin receptors, what specific effect would this have on the liver cells?

   _____

   _____

Base your answers to question 52 on the diagram of activities in the human body.

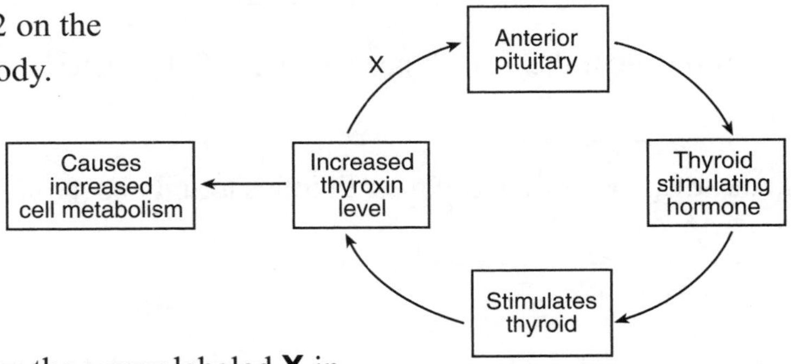

52. *a*) This diagram illustrates part of
   (1) a feedback mechanism
   (2) an enzyme pathway
   (3) a digestive mechanism
   (4) a pattern of learned behavior

   b) Describe the action represented by the arrow labeled **X** in the diagram and state one reason that this action is important.

   Action of **X** : _____

   Reason : _____

   c) Identify one hormone involved in another biological relationship and an organ that is directly affected by the hormone you identified.

   Hormone: _____   Organ affected: _____

53. State one way white blood cells protect the body from foreign microbes.

   _____

54. Acetylcholine is a chemical secreted at the ends of nerve cells. This chemical helps to send nerve signals across synapses (spaces between nerve cells). After the signal passes across a synapse, an enzyme breaks down the acetylcholine. LSD is a drug that blocks the action of this enzyme. Describe one possible effect of LSD on the action of acetylcholine.

   _____

   _____

Base your answer to question 55 on the information below.

Immunization protects the human body from disease. The success of vaccinations can be seen in the fact that smallpox has been eliminated worldwide from the list of common infectious diseases. The only remaining smallpox viruses on Earth are thought to be those kept in certain research laboratories. The United States is now committed to the goal of immunizing all children against common childhood diseases. However, many parents are choosing not to immunize their children against childhood diseases such as diphtheria, whooping cough, and polio. For example, the mother of a newborn baby is concerned about having her child receive the DPT (diphtheria, whooping cough, and tetanus) vaccine. Since these diseases are caused by bacteria, she believes antibiotic therapy is a safe alternative to vaccination.

55. Discuss the use of antibiotics and vaccines in the treatment and prevention of bacterial diseases. In your answer be sure to include:

a) what is in a vaccine _____

b) how a vaccine promotes immunity _____

c) one advantage of the use of vaccinations to fight bacterial diseases

_____

d) one disadvantage of the use of antibiotics to fight bacterial diseases

_____

56. Consuming large volumes of soft drinks containing sugar during the day can disrupt homeostasis. Describe how the human body responds to restore sugar balance. In your answer, be sure to:

a) identify the hormone responsible for restoring homeostasis _____

b) identify the organ that releases this hormone _____

c) state one possible reason why sugar levels may remain high even though this hormone has been released _____

57. Explain how the change in heart rate helps to maintain homeostasis during exercise.

_____

58. Identify the relationship that exists between a virus and a human when the virus infects the human.

_____

59. Identify the organ that produces insulin. _____

Set 2 – Human Physiology, Reproduction, and Homeostasis

Base your answer to question 60 on the information below and on your knowledge of biology.

The Critical Role of the Placenta

The proper functioning of the placenta is critical to the growth and development of a healthy fetus. For example, the placenta appears to act as a nutrient sensor. It regulates the amounts and types of nutrients that are transported from the mother to the fetus.

Improper functioning of the placenta can alter the structure and function of specific cells and organ systems in the developing fetus, putting it at risk for health problems as an adult. For example, in some pregnancies, the placenta develops a resistance to blood flow. This resistance appears to force the heart of the fetus to work harder. This could result in an increased chance of the individual developing heart disease as an adult. A group of hormones known as glucocorticoids affects the development of all the tissues and organ systems. One of the things this group of hormones does is to alter cell function by changing the structure of cell membrane receptors.

60. Discuss the importance of the placenta in the development of a healthy fetus. In your answer, be sure to:

a) identify *two* factors that could influence the nutrients that can pass from the mother to the fetus

_____ and _____

b) identify the group of hormones that alter cell membrane receptors and explain how this alteration can affect cell function   Hormone: _____

Explanation: _____

c) state the role of the uterus in the development of the fetus and the placenta

_____

61. Nutrients in a diet, such as proteins, carbohydrates, and minerals, play an important role in homeostasis within the human body. Lack of these nutrients can lead to malfunctions that disrupt this internal balance. Explain how diet can influence homeostasis. In your answer, be sure to:

a) select a nutrient from the passage and write it on the line. Nutrient: _____

b) state one role this nutrient plays in the body

_____

c) describe, using one specific example, how a decrease in this nutrient can alter homeostasis

_____

62. Organ systems of the human body interact to maintain a balanced internal environment. As blood flows through certain organs of the body, the composition of the blood changes because of interactions with those organs. State one change in the composition of the blood as it flows through the respiratory system.

_____

63. State one reason that most foods must be digested before they can enter a cell.

_____

Base your answers to question 64 on the information below.

Human reproduction is influenced by many different factors.

64. *a)* Identify one reproductive hormone and state the role it plays in reproduction.

Hormone: _____

Role: _____

b) Identify the structure in the uterus where the exchange of material between the mother and the

developing fetus takes place. _____

c) Identify one harmful substance that can pass through this structure and describe the negative effect it can have on the fetus.

Substance: _____

Negative effect: _____

Base your answers to question 65 on the passage below.

When humans perspire, water, urea, and salts containing sodium are removed from the blood. Drinking water during extended periods of physical exercise replenishes the water but not the sodium. This increase in water dilutes the blood and may result in the concentration of sodium dropping low enough to cause a condition known as hyponatremia. Symptoms of hyponatremia include headache, nausea, and lack of coordination. Left untreated, it can lead to coma and even death. The body has a variety of feedback mechanisms that assist in regulating water and sodium concentrations in the blood. The kidneys play a major role in these mechanisms, as they filter the blood and produce urine.

65. *a)* Many runners pour water on their bodies during a race. Explain how this action helps to maintain homeostasis.

_____

b) How would running in a marathon on a warm day most likely affect urine production? Support your answer.

Urine production: _____

Supporting statement: _____

c) Many people today drink sport drinks containing large amounts of sodium. Describe one possible effect this might have on a person who is not very active.

_____

66. All organisms need to reproduce for the continuation of their species. Discuss the process of reproduction in humans. In your answer, be sure to:

a) identify one hormone present in a female that is involved in regulating the reproductive cycle

_____

b) state one way the nucleus of a sex cell is different from the nucleus of a body cell

_____

c) state how the normal chromosome number for humans is maintained from one generation to the next. _____

_____

d) identify one action by the mother that can influence the development of the embryo and state a result of that influence.

Action: _____

Result: _____

67. The immune system protects against foreign substances and even some cancers. Explain how the immune system functions. In your answer, be sure to:

a) identify one way the immune system fights pathogens

_____

b) identify the substance in a vaccine that stimulates the immune system

_____

c) describe the response of the immune system to the vaccine

_____

d) identify one disease that damages the immune system and state how it affects this system

Disease:_____

Affects:_____

e) Most people who get vaccinated develop immunity to the disease. Explain why the contents of the vaccine usually do not cause people to get sick.

_____

68. Suggest one way that doctors or patients can help to reduce the chances of bacteria becoming resistant to an antibiotic. _____

_____

69. State the relationship between intensity of physical activity and pulse rate.

_____

1. 4   Homeostasis is the maintenance of balance within a living organism. A rapid rise in the number of red blood cells would create a disruption in the circulatory system. The increase in red blood cells would disrupt that balance and thus homeostasis.

2. 1   Cell structure and function are the result of the expression (function) of genes within that cell. The type of cell (liver vs. nerve) and each cell's job is determined by which genes have been "turned on" within that cell.

3. 3   Antibodies are produced by the immune system when it detects harmful antigens. Each type of antibody is unique and defends the body against one specific type of antigen.

4. 1   Proteins found on the surface of cells and on the surface of viruses (HIV) that allow for attachment based on shape are known as receptors. Receptor molecules play an important role in the immune system.

5. 4   Nerves collect information through the senses and transmit that information via impulses. Impulses are transmitted from nerve cell to nerve cell relaying a message for a particular response. The endocrine system uses chemical messengers or hormones produced by glands to regulate metabolism and internal balance. Hormones are secreted directly into the bloodstream and travel to target cells on which the hormone acts.

6. 3   Information can be sent from Cell *B* (with round signals) to Cell *A* (with round receptors) due to there matching shape. Communication between cells involves chemical signals and membrane receptors. In order for the "message" to be received, the receiving cell must have the correctly shaped receptor to match the shape of the signal.

7. 3   The human immune system responds to an invasion by microbes by carrying out an immune response. This involves white blood cells, specifically T cells and B cells. These cells attack the microbes, or produce antibodies, as well as producing memory cells. Memory cells will ensure a swift response to any subsequent attacks by the same microbe. Vaccines carry a weakened or dead form of the microbe. T cells and B cells will carry out the immune response against this vaccine and provide memory cells for future protection.

8. 2   Differentiation is the process where developing embryonic cells are genetically programmed into a type of cell with a certain function. For example, certain cells will be programmed to become skin cells, while other cells are programed to become nerve cells.

9. 4   The metabolic process best represented by the diagram would be digestion – the breaking down of materials into smaller useful forms. As diagrammed, the organic protein is broken down into its building block components – amino acids (*B*).

10. 4   Both contractile vacuoles and kidneys have a similar function – maintaining water balance. Although found in different organisms, both structures function to maintain homeostasis (in this case, water balance) within that organism.

11. 1   Foreign materials or foreign proteins that enter or grow within the human body are known as antigens. These antigens will cause a immune response because white blood cells will recognize these antigens as foreign to the human body and attack them.

12. 3   Vaccines contain weakened or heat-killed microbes that, when injected into the human body initiate an immune response. An immune response will activate white blood cells to attack infected cells using specific molecules and to mark microbes for destruction using antibodies.

13. 1   Glands secrete hormones directly into the bloodstream and travel to target cells on which the hormone acts. Levels of hormones are controlled by a mechanism known as feedback. Feedback allows for messages to be received by glands, which start or stop the production of hormones depending on hormone level.

14. 4   Regulation of the human reproductive system is controlled by hormones. Hormones from the pituitary gland stimulate development of the ovaries and testes, and hormones from pituitary gland and the ovaries regulate the menstrual cycle.

15. 3   Insulin, produced by the pancreas, allows cells to take in sugar, thus regulating blood sugar levels. This constantly changing situation requires a feedback mechanism to maintain the correct hormone balance.

16. 2   The pancreas has two different regions – digestion and blood sugar maintenance. Each with a specific function. The cells in these two regions use different areas of their DNA to direct the production of different proteins within the cell. Digestive enzymes are produced in the digestive section of the pancreas, whereas hormones are produced in the endocrine or sugar-maintenance area of the pancreas.

17. 2   The placenta is the site of exchange between the blood of the mother (maternal) and that of the baby (fetal). Materials such as nutrients, wastes, and gases are exchanged. Even harmful substances such as alcohol and drugs can be passed from mother to baby at the placenta.

18. 1   The diagram represents the female reproductive system. Structure *A* represents the ovary where female gametes, eggs, are developed. Radiation can cause mutations within the eggs and these mutations can be passed onto future generations.

19. 1   Structure **X** is the vas deferens or sperm duct. Its function is the storage and path of mature sperm to the urethra where it will be sent out of the male and transferred to the female body.

20. 3   Estrogen and progesterone are female hormones that influence the menstrual cycle. They are responsible for maintaining the lining of the uterus (letter *C*). Both estrogen and progesterone are produced in the ovary of the female.

21. 4   Structure 4 is the cell membrane. Its function includes regulating the movement of materials into and out of the cell. Structure *B* is the kidney, its function is regulation by filtering harmful wastes out of the body and re-absorbing useful materials back into the blood.

22. 2   Persons receiving an organ transplant must take medication that reduces their immune response to prevent their body from attacking and rejecting the foreign proteins in that organ. Remember, the immune system attacks any foreign protein or antigen that enters the body.

23. 1   Meiosis is the process which allows for the production of sperm and egg. This process reduces the chromosome number to half that of the original body cell amount. When the genetic information found in the chromosomes of the sperm and the egg unite during fertilization, the original chromosome number is restored in the next generation.

24. 4   Oxygen transport is carried out by the circulatory system. Red blood cells, containing hemoglobin, transport oxygen throughout the body. The heart pumps the blood containing oxygen to the cellular level.

25. 3   White blood cells are large cells with distinct nuclei that are capable of engulfing pathogens. In the diagram, Cell *A* represents a white blood cell that is engulfing smaller particles which may represent disease-causing organisms.

26. 3   Hormones are chemical messengers secreted by glands that are transported to specific target organs by the bloodstream. These hormones produce changes and through feedback mechanisms can affect the activity of the gland.

27. 3   Insulin, produced in the pancreas, is a hormone that regulates blood sugar levels. All other listed hormones play a role in reproduction.

28. 3   It takes only one sperm cell to fertilize the egg, but many die during the journey to the egg. To ensure that fertilization does occur, many sperm cells are produced and released for this process to be successful.

29. 4   Structures *A* (lungs) and *B* (kidneys) are both organs of excretion, responsible for the removal of metabolic wastes. Each organ requires an input of energy (ATP) to accomplish this process. The lungs excrete the waste product carbon dioxide and the kidneys excrete urea, salt, and water.

30. 1   The placenta is the site for exchange of nutrients, wastes, and gases between the mother and developing embryo. Mammals without a placenta must use alternative means to supply the nutrients to their embryo/fetus. Kangaroos have a pouch where nutrients are provided for the developing embryo/fetus.

31. 3   The process of meiosis reduces the chromosome number to half that of the original body cell amount. Meiosis is the process allowing for the production of sperm and egg in organisms that reproduce sexually.

32. *a*) 1   The diagram represents the "communication" of an impulse between two nerve cells at the synapse. Substance *A*, a neurotransmitter, transfers the impulse from one cell to the other, thus allowing a nerve impulse to travel along a pathway.

   b) 4   Receptor molecules are located on the dendrites of nerve cells (cell Y) that match up with the shape of structure *A*, a neurotransmitter being released from nerve cell X.

   c) 2   Substance *A*, a neurotransmitter, has a specific shape. This shape allows it to bind to nerve cell Y's membrane in a lock and key fashion. Choice 2 best fits that lock and key shape with substance *A*.

33. 1   At the cellular level, all materials (nutrients) required for the synthesis process (of fats, protein, etc.) must be brought to the cell. The digestive system breaks down needed nutrients into usable form, and the circulatory system transports these nutrients to the cell.

34. 4   The regulation of blood sugar is accomplished through the endocrine response of the pancreas. The hormone insulin is released in response to a high blood sugar level.

35. 1   The AIDS virus, HIV, attacks or targets white blood cells that are directly responsible for fighting invading microbes or pathogens. The HIV virus weakens the human immune system and renders that person unable to fight against viruses or bacteria.

36. 4   Once fertilization occurs, new cells immediately develop by the process of mitotic cell division producing a zygote. Then differentiation occurs, where cells are genetically programmed (certain genes are expressed) to perform certain functions or have particular structures. These eventually develop into organs.

37. 4   Immune systems or defense systems of some organisms use white blood cells to protect against foreign invaders or pathogens. White blood cells either attack pathogens directly, mark pathogens for destruction, or engulf and digest pathogens, thus protecting the individual.

38. 4   The maintenance of homeostasis allows the body to regulate or keep an internal balance. Secretions from glands allow the body to respond to any change that occurs and adjust to that change so that balance is restored. In this case, the pituitary, thyroid, adrenal, and the pancreas glands all produce secretions to help maintain homeostasis.

39. 1   A newly fertilized egg is known as a zygote. In the zygote, mitosis is occurring. Mitosis is a form of cell division where two daughter cells are produced from a parent cell that are genetically identical to the parent cell, having the full amount of chromosomes.

40. 1   Homeostasis is the maintenance of a stable internal environment. In this diagrammed interaction, the pancreas, a part of the endocrine system, plays a role in the regulation of blood sugar. This process is known as a feedback mechanism.

41. 1   In the sequence of stages shown, stage 1 shows fertilization where sperm enters the egg setting off a series of rapid cell divisions. These divisions, stages 3 to 5, lead to the initial differentiation of cells. All of these processes require genetic information from the genes as well as chemicals, usually enzymes, to proceed.

42. 2   The diagram represents cells within an immune response. The introduction of microbes (antigens, the round "spiked" particles) will cause this response. Part of the immune response may involve antibodies (the dark small particles) acting as markers on the antigen to signal white blood cells, which will then engulf the foreign invader.

43. 3   Between position *C* and *D*, the graph shows that the body temperature was outside the range of homeostasis. At this high body temperature, the internal body environment is not within its normal range, and dynamic equilibrium is disrupted.

44. *a*) 2   To regulate blood glucose levels in humans, chemical messengers are produced to increase or decrease those sugar levels. Homeostatic feedback allows for those levels to be decreased or increased with substance *A* or *B* respectively, maintaining a normal blood glucose level.

   b) 1   Insulin is a chemical messenger produced in the pancreas, which allows cells to take in glucose from the blood, thus reducing blood glucose levels. According to the diagram, substance *A* does that.

45. *a*) 1   Diagram *A* represents the male reproductive system containing the testes, and diagram *B* represents the female reproductive system containing the ovaries. Each of these glands is responsible for the formation of gametes (sperm and eggs, respectively).

   b) 1   The male (*A*) has a penis to direct sperm into the female body. The female (*B*) has a vagina which serves to receive and funnel sperm into uterus and oviducts so that internal fertilization can occur. Remember, fertilization takes place within the oviduct of the human female.

   c) 4   A zygote forms after fertilization has taken place. The zygote divides mitotically as it grows within the oviduct and uterus of the female.

Human Physiology, Reproduction, and Homeostasis

46. *a)* Answer: white blood cell

Explanation: Structure *X* represents a white blood cell. In blood, white blood cells are somewhat larger than red blood cells and have lobed nuclei.

b) Answer: destroys foreign antigens

Explanation: White blood cells are involved in the body's immune response. They perform several functions, they attack antigens or foreign proteins and may engulf foreign proteins.

47.

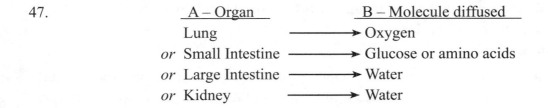

Explanation: Diffusion is a process where a molecule moves from an area of high concentration to low concentration or along a concentration gradient. In each case, the molecule that diffuses (B), moves across the cell membrane and passes through a capillary wall into the blood. This process allows organisms to maintain homeostasis.

48. Answer: Letter **X** can represent any of the following terms: regulation *or* homeostasis *or* dynamic equilibrium *or* coordination *or* human body *or* organism

Explanation: The diagram defines the process of regulation within an organism in its environment. Every living thing must maintain a constant internal balance, yet is subject to disruption by foreign invaders and pathogens, such as: parasites, fungi, bacteria and viruses. Letter *X* represents the processes by which an organism tries to maintain this balance – homeostasis.

49. Answer: Different parts of genetic information are used in different cells.
or Different cells are influenced by their environments in the body.

Explanation: During the process of differentiation, cells are genetically programmed (certain genes are expressed) to perform certain functions or have particular structures. They become specialized for one type of job. For example, skin cells provide a barrier, muscle cells allow for movement, and nerve cells transmit impulses.

50. Organ: ovary/adrenal gland

Function: regulate the reproductive system
or Estrogen affects the development of the sex organs/sex cells.
or Estrogen plays a role in the menstrual cycle.

Explanation: Estrogen, produced by the ovary, is a hormone that regulates the uterus lining during the female menstrual cycle.

51. *a*) Answer: Structure *A* is the placenta.

Function: The placenta is essential for development because it serves as the exchange surface (site) for nutrients, wastes, and gases between mother and fetus. The placenta is a tissue rich in blood vessels found in the uterus. It supplies needed nutrients by diffusion to the umbilical cord, which transports these nutrients to the baby's circulatory system. Remember that the blood of the mother does not come into contact with that of the baby.

b) Acceptable responses include, but are not limited to:
When the alcohol from the mother's bloodstream enters the fetus, the relative amount is much greater due to the smaller size of the fetus.
or The fetus is still developing.

Explanation: Alcohol will enter the baby's system through exchange at the placenta. The amount of alcohol in relationship to the size of the fetus is much greater than it is to the size of the mother and could lead to poisoning or developmental problems of the fetus. Because the fetus is developing organs and a nervous system, addition of alcohol could affect that development. This condition is known as Fetal Alcohol Syndrome (FAS).

c) Answer: uterus

Explanation: The uterus is the organ where the fetus develops in.

52. *a*) Answer: Letter **X** is the pancreas.

Explanation: The pancreas produces the hormone, insulin, which regulates blood sugar.

b) Answer: a feedback mechanism

Explanation: A feedback mechanism regulates the production of a hormone. The dashed line represents feedback information to the pancreas (**X**), which would reduce or increase the production of insulin as needed.

53. Answers:
a) A vaccine contains dead or weakened pathogens or their products.

b) the immune system

c) White blood cells produce antibodies for a particular pathogen.
or White blood cells are prepared to recognize a particular pathogen in the future.
or causes the immune system to produce antibodies
or stimulates an immune response

Explanation: Vaccines contain small amounts of weakened pathogens, and when administered, will result in an immunity to that particular pathogen. White blood cells in the body, like T cells and B cells, react to foreign invaders by recognizing foreign proteins or antigens they carry. These antigens activate T cells, which directly attack pathogen-infected cells, and activate B cells, which produce plasma cells that release antibodies.

Human Physiology, Reproduction, and Homeostasis

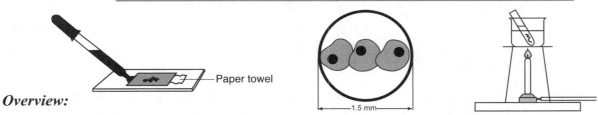

—Paper towel

—1.5 mm—

Overview:

Scientists and researchers rely on information gained from experimentation and laboratory activities to make informed decisions about the living environment. Proper equipment, procedures, and safety all play a vital role in providing accurate data for both scientific investigation and ethical determinations. Information is shared with other colleagues for revision and approval. New laboratory discoveries provide for advances in medicine, biotechnology, and understanding our natural environment.

Essential Information:

The Microscope – Scientists rely on lab equipment to carry out experiments and investigate hypotheses. The microscope is a valuable tool that provides a window into the microscopic world. *Compound microscopes* have two types of magnifying lenses, an eyepiece of specific magnification and several *objective lenses* which range from a lower to higher magnification. To initially focus the microscope, a coarse adjustment knob is used under low power. The coarse adjustment should never be used with high power because there is a danger of damaging the lens or the slide. Under high power, the fine adjustment is used to finalize the focus to achieve greater detail and resolution. The field of view is the area that is visible through the eyepiece. Under low power, a larger portion of the specimen is viewed with more light availability, compared to viewing under high power. When an objective lens is switched from low to high power, the field of view decreases. To ensure proper viewing of the specimen, it should be centered in the middle of the field before switching to high power. The action of the lens changes the actual view of an object making it appear upside down and backwards. For example the letter "e" would appear "ə". To view a specimen, a *wet mount slide* is made by placing the specimen in a drop of water on the slide and lowering a cover slip over the specimen at an angle. This prevents the formation of bubbles that could interfere with accurate viewing. Specimens can also be stained to enhance views. By placing an eyedropper with *stain* on one side of the cover slip of a wet mount slide and a paper towel on the opposite side, stain can be drawn under the cover slip, reaching the specimen and thus highlighting features. *Electron microscopes* rely on electron beams to provide great magnification and detail. They are typically located in research facilities.

Indicators and Chromatography – In the laboratory, *indicators* are used to check for the presence of a substance. Indicators change color to signal that a substance is present or provide a pH value for that substance. Some common substances that can be checked for with an indicator include simple sugars, like glucose and starch. The use of a pH indicator will show a specific color that indicates a pH range within the solution. Occasionally it becomes necessary to separate and identify substances in a mixture. The process of chromatography allows for this separation through the movement of different substances based on their chemical properties. Paper chromatography, the most common type used in high school laboratories, uses a special paper partially immersed in a solvent. Based on the attraction to the paper, the chemical properties of the substances, and the interaction with the solvent, substances travel with the solvent at different rates up the paper, creating patterns and measurable distances for reference and identification purposes.

Laboratory Safety – Laboratory safety is critical to the success of experiments and the health of scientists. One important rule in all experiments is to always follow directions. When working with chemicals or heating materials, one should always wear protective goggles, gloves, and an apron. When heating materials in glassware, always point the opening of the glassware away from the face and eyes to avoid injury from accidental splashes by overheating.

Experimental Design – Good experiments begin with the identification of a problem. Careful observations lead scientists to the development of hypotheses or tentative explanations. To test a *hypothesis*, scientists and researchers set up *controlled experiments* where data from a manipulated variable is compared to a control. The *control* is the part of the experiment which remains unchanged and usually is the normal condition or does not receive treatment. All other conditions within an experiment should be kept the same so that only one variable is being tested at a time. Important to all good experiments is the accurate collection of data. Any measurement of data should be precise and include units. The data collected should be organized into charts and tables, and if possible graphed to be analyzed. *Inferences*, or conclusions made from the results, can be drawn from the data and used to either accept or reject (refute) the hypothesis. *Valid experiments* are those that are tested many times or tested on many subjects (large #'s) concluding with the same result each time. These results are also peer reviewed by other colleagues and are able to withstand scrutiny. When hypotheses have been repeatedly tested through scientific methods and inquiry, and the same conclusion or result is reached, those hypotheses may become a *theory* – a statement or principal that is used as the basis for future predictions.

At times, certain experiments raise ethical questions that must be evaluated as right (ethical) or wrong (unethical). There is a great deal of debate about the ethical guidelines for research and the possible potential benefit to society an experiment might bring. Two such highly debated ongoing experiments are cloning and stem cell research.

Organization of Data – Data may be organized in various forms. The *data table* is a simple yet efficient method of organization. Each table should have a title, and every column should be labeled with terms or phrases of data collected along with appropriate units. Data should be organized with the independent or manipulated values either increasing or decreasing in number as one moves down the column. The associated dependent values should match up accordingly. Graphs can be useful tools to help visualize and organize data. Each graph should have a title that reflects the information portrayed. The horizontal axis represents values for the *independent variable*, the variable which has been manipulated; and the vertical axis represents values for the *dependent variable*, that which has been influenced by manipulation of the independent variable. Each axis should be labeled with an appropriate term or phrase as well as units (for example g/mL). The scale for each axis must be based on the values determined by the experiment. Values should be spread out along each axis with each increment representing an equal value for that axis. In Living Environment line-graphs, breaks are not acceptable for scale values. Scales should start at zero. Careful plotting of all values are expected on a *line graph*, with points usually surrounded with a shape, like a circle, to help define that value. In line graphs, points may be connected with a line point-to-point or by a best-fit line. Graph lines should not extend to zero if there are no values at that point. *Bar graphs* can also be used where information is presented with shaded-in areas reflecting certain values on the dependent axis. Bar graphs are commonly used when comparing data collected from different ranges of values, such as the number of individuals and their average pulse rate range after exercising or how much pollutant was emitted into the atmosphere by different human activities.

Dichotomous Key – A *dichotomous key* is a tool that helps to identify an organism or object. The key consists of a series of steps which usually contain two different sets of physical characteristics and direct the user to more detailed information or to the identification of the object or organism.

For example: 1a. Organism has 6 legs .... go to step 2
1b. Organism has 8 legs .... Arachnid (spider)
2a. Organism has wings .... go to step 3
2b. Organism does not have wings .... go to step 16

When using the key, it is helpful to have appropriate pictures for reference. For every organism, the user should always start at the first step of the dichotomous key. When making a key, it is important to choose physical features that separate one organism from another.

Additional Information:

- Conversions:

Distance	Volume	Mass
1 m = 100 cm	1 L = 1000 mL	1 kg = 1000 g
1 m = 1000 mm		1 g = 1000 mg
1 cm = 10 mm		

- A meniscus is the curved surface at the top of a column of a liquid. When reading a volume of water within a graduated cylinder, at eye level, read the lowest part of the meniscus.

- Researchers in labs also may use a centrifuge, which spins test tubes or vials very fast to separate substances in liquid mixtures (i.e. suspensions). The densest materials will be pushed to the bottom of the tubes, and the least dense substance to the top.

- The pH measures the strength of acidity or alkalinity of a substance. The scale ranges from 0 to 14, with 0 being the strongest acid, 7 being neutral, and 14 being the strongest base. The pH scale is used to measure acidity of rain and digestive enzymes environments.

Diagrams:

1. **Compound Light Microscope** – The microscope has several important parts that function to provide a magnified view of the specimen. Letter *A* represents the eyepiece which contains a lens that provides magnification. Letter *C* represents the objective lenses, which collect light and also magnify the specimen. Each objective lens has a magnification value, usually referred to as low and high power. Letter *B* is the coarse adjustment, which is used to focus under low power. Letter *E* is the fine adjustment, which produces a small amount of focus under high power for added detail. Letter *D* represents the light source, which either could be a lamp (light bulb) or a mirror. Letter *F* is the diaphragm, which allows the user to regulate the amount of light entering the microscope.

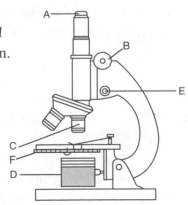

2. **Field of View** – In these diagrams, the fields of view under a microscope for both a low power objective (10x) and a high power objective (40x) are shown. Although both organisms appear to be the same relative size, the specimen under the low power objective is actually larger than the organism under the high power objective in real life. This is because under high power the organism is magnified 40 times (40x), while the organism under low power is only magnified 10 times (10x).

Organism A viewed with 10× objective

Organism B viewed with 40× objective

Low Power

High Power

3. **Wet Mount Slide** – The technique of making a wet mount slide is shown here. A specimen is placed on a slide with a drop of water. The cover slip is carefully lowered over the specimen at an angle to prevent any bubbles from forming. Bubbles could interfere with proper viewing of the specimen.

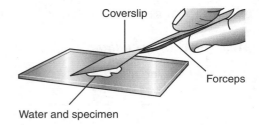

Coverslip

Forceps

Water and specimen

4. **Staining** – When stains are applied to microscope slides, they allow the viewer to have an enhanced view of the specimen revealing more detail. View *A* is a before view of a cell, and View *B* shows the cell after it has been stained, providing much more detail within the cell. Staining can be done by positioning a dropper with stain on one side of the cover slip, and gently adding stain under the slide. Placing a paper towel on the opposite side of the cover slip will draw the stain through so it reaches the specimen.

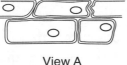

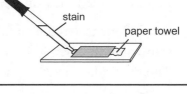

View A

View B

stain

paper towel

5. **Lab Safety** – The student in the diagram is following proper laboratory safety by wearing protective eye-wear (goggles) and an apron. The student also has placed glassware so that the tops are not pointing at the student's face. In the laboratory, following directions is an important safety rule to prevent injury and accidents.

6. **Measurements** – Accurate measurements are important to collecting valid information for experiments. The metric ruler is being used to determine the length of the organism. The organism would be measured from the tip of its tail, located at the 1.0 cm mark, to its head at the 3.5 cm mark and would measure 2.5 cm or 25 mm.

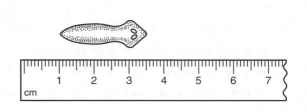

Laboratory and Science Skills

7. **Data Table** – As shown in this diagram, a data table should contain a title to identify the experiment (what it is about), labels for each column (Group, Temperature, and *D* – the gas), as well as appropriate units (°C and mL). The values for the independent variable (in this case temperature) are arranged in increasing order from 5°C to 80°C, and the values for the dependent variable, *D* (the gas), are matched up accordingly.

**Average Amount of Gas Produced (D)
After 30 Minutes at Various Temperatures**

Group	Temperature (°C)	D (mL)
1	5	0
2	20	5
3	40	12
4	60	6
5	80	3

8. **Line Graph vs. Bar Graph** – Graphs provide a visual representation of the collected data giving a clearer picture of the data and results. Relationships are revealed and conclusions can be drawn from graphs.

   These diagrams show the differences between a line graph and a bar graph. The line graph represents a series of plotted points that are connected by a line. The line only reflects data collected and, in this case, does not extend to zero or beyond 43 weeks. The bar graph shows data represented by shaded-in areas that reach certain values for various ranges of pulse rates. Each graph has a title, and the axes are labeled with terms and units.

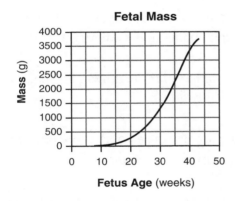

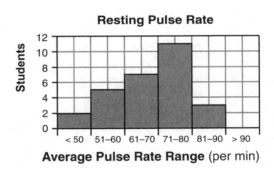

9. **Chromatography** – Chromatography is a technique that allows for the separation of substances within a mixture. The mixture is placed on the paper in the position marked "original spot" and then placed into a solvent that will carry the mixture up the paper. Depending on the chemical properties of the substances in the mixture, each will travel at different rates and distances. The different color bands represent the different substances that were in the original mixture, separated out along the paper.

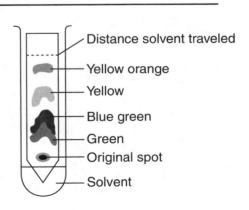

Vocabulary Refresher

Group A   *Directions* - Match the correct definition for the following terms:

1. _____ Compound light microscope

2. _____ Objective lens

3. _____ Fine adjustment

4. _____ Wet mount slide

5. _____ Stain

6. _____ Electron microscope

7. _____ Coarse adjustment

8. _____ Indicator

9. _____ Chromatography

10. _____ Hypothesis

11. _____ Valid experiment

12. _____ Field of view

A. Light collecting lenses, located near the sample being viewed; there is usually a high and low magnification range.

B. A procedure in which a specimen is suspended in a drop of water contained between the slide and a coverslip.

C. An experiment that can be preformed by other researchers utilizing the same conditions, while achieving the same results within an acceptable range.

D. A chemical substance that changes color to signify the presence of a specific substance.

E. Great magnification is achieved with this instrument by utilizing an electron beam that illuminates a specimen.

F. A laboratory technique used for the separation of mixtures usually with special paper and a solvent.

G. A substance used to highlight features of a specimen for viewing with a microscope.

H. This focusing apparatus is used under low power to initially get the specimen in viewing range.

I. Used to finalize the focus of an object under high power magnification.

J. An instrument that uses multiple lenses to magnify an object.

K. An educated guess that is supported or refuted based on the outcome of an experiment.

L. The area that is visible through the eye-piece.

Laboratory and Science Skills

Group B *Directions* - Match the correct definition for the following terms:

1. _____Theory

2. _____Data table

3. _____Independent variable

4. _____Dependent variable

5. _____Line graph

6. _____Bar graph

7. _____Dichotomous key

8. _____Inference

9. _____Research plan

10. _____Measurement

11. _____Meniscus

A. This tool allows the user to work through a series of steps to arrive at the identification of some object or organism, like a wildflower or reptile.

B. The variable that is changed or manipulated within the experiment.

C. A visual display of information or data that is usually shaded-in to reflect certain values on the dependent axis.

D. The curve in the upper part of a liquid is caused by the attraction of the liquid to the container. For water, measure the lowest part of the water curve.

E. A concept that has been repeatedly tested, and is widely accepted as the explanation to a scientific occurrence.

F. The variable that is measured in an experiment. It is influenced by the independent variable.

G. A comparison of a physical property to a set standard to arrive at an accurate answer.

H. An assumption based on observations.

I. An organized series of steps to implement a scientific experiment.

J. An organization chart for listing measurements, numbers or other types of information used or obtained in an experiment.

K. A type of chart that displays results/information as a series of data points connected by line segments.

1. A student observes that an organism is green. A valid conclusion that can be drawn from this observation is that

   (1) the organism must be a plant
   (2) the organism cannot be single celled
   (3) the organism must be an animal
   (4) not enough information is given to determine whether the organism is a plant or an animal   1 _____

2. The current knowledge concerning cells is the result of the investigations and observations of many scientists. The work of these scientists forms a well-accepted body of knowledge about cells. This body of knowledge is an example of a

   (1) hypothesis
   (2) controlled experiment
   (3) theory
   (4) research plan   2 _____

3. An experimental design included references from prior experiments, materials and equipment, and step-by-step procedures. What else should be included before the experiment can be started?

   (1) a set of data
   (2) a conclusion based on data
   (3) safety precautions to be used
   (4) an inference based on results   3 _____

4. Researchers performing a well-designed experiment should base their conclusions on

   (1) the hypothesis of the experiment
   (2) data from repeated trials of the experiment
   (3) a small sample size to ensure a reliable outcome of the experiment
   (4) results predicted before performing the experiment   4 _____

5. Why do scientists consider any hypothesis valuable?

   (1) A hypothesis requires no further investigation.
   (2) A hypothesis may lead to further investigation even if it is disproved by the experiment.
   (3) A hypothesis requires no further investigation if it is proved by the experiment.
   (4) A hypothesis can be used to explain a conclusion even if it is disproved by the experiment   5 _____

6. In his theory, Lamarck suggested that organisms will develop and pass on to offspring variations that they need in order to survive in a particular environment. In a later theory, Darwin proposed that changing environmental conditions favor certain variations that promote the survival of organisms. Which statement is best illustrated by this information?

   (1) Scientific theories that have been changed are the only ones supported by scientists.
   (2) All scientific theories are subject to change and improvement.
   (3) Most scientific theories are the outcome of a single hypothesis.
   (4) Scientific theories are not subject to change.   6 _____

7. Diagrams, tables, and graphs are used by scientists mainly to

   (1) design a research plan for an experiment
   (2) test a hypothesis
   (3) organize data
   (4) predict the independent variable   7 _____

8. A great deal of information can now be obtained about the future health of people by examining the genetic makeup of their cells. There are concerns that this information could be used to deny an individual health insurance or employment. These concerns best illustrate that

(1) scientific explanations depend upon evidence collected from a single source
(2) scientific inquiry involves the collection of information from a large number of sources
(3) acquiring too much knowledge in human genetics will discourage future research in that area
(4) while science provides knowledge, values are essential to making ethical decisions using this knowledge   8 _____

9. Students were asked to determine if they could squeeze a clothespin more times in a minute after resting than after exercising. An experiment that accurately tests this question should include all of the following except

(1) a hypothesis on which to base the design of the experiment
(2) a large number of students
(3) two sets of clothespins, one that is easy to open and one that is more difficult to open
(4) a control group and an experimental group with equal numbers of students of approximately the same age   9 _____

10. Paper chromatography is a laboratory technique that is used to

(1) separate different molecules from one another
(2) stain cell organelles
(3) indicate the pH of a substance
(4) compare relative cell sizes   10 _____

11. Which statement best describes the term theory as used in the gene-chromosome theory?

(1) A theory is never revised as new scientific evidence is presented.
(2) A theory is an assumption made by scientists and implies a lack of certainty.
(3) A theory refers to a scientific explanation that is strongly supported by a variety of experimental data.
(4) A theory is a hypothesis that has been supported by one experiment performed by two or more scientists.   11 _____

12. Students in a class recorded their resting pulse rates and their pulse rates immediately after strenuous activity. The data obtained are shown in the histograms below.

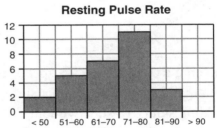

Resting Pulse Rate

Average Pulse Rate Range (per min)

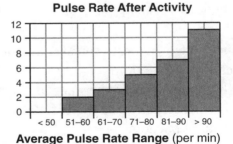

Pulse Rate After Activity

Average Pulse Rate Range (per min)

An appropriate label for the y-axis in each histogram would be
(1) Number of Students
(2) Average Number of Heartbeats
(3) Time (min)
(4) Amount of Exercise   12 _____

13. A biologist formulates a hypothesis, performs experiments to test his hypothesis, makes careful observations, and keeps accurate records of his findings. In order to complete this process, the biologist should

(1) adjust the data to support the hypothesis
(2) eliminate data that do not support the hypothesis
(3) write a research paper explaining his theories before performing his experiments, in order to gain funding sources
(4) evaluate the findings and, if necessary, alter the hypothesis based on his findings, and test the new hypothesis   13 _____

14. Which laboratory procedure is represented in the diagram?

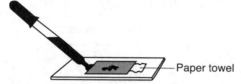
Paper towel

(1) placing a coverslip over a specimen
(2) removing a coverslip from a slide
(3) adding stain to a slide without removing the coverslip
(4) reducing the size of air bubbles under a coverslip   14 _____

15. Which statement best expresses a basic scientific assumption?
(1) Interpretation of experimental results has provided explanations for all natural phenomena.
(2) If a conclusion is valid, similar investigations by other scientists should result in the same conclusion.
(3) For any conclusion to be valid, the design of the experiment requires that only two groups be compared.
(4) After a scientist formulates a conclusion based on an experiment, no further investigation is necessary   15 _____

16. The development of an experimental research plan should not include a

(1) list of safety precautions for the experiment
(2) list of equipment needed for conducting the experiment
(3) procedure for the use of technologies needed for the experiment
(4) conclusion based on data expected to be collected in the experiment
        16 _____

17. During a laboratory activity, a group of students obtained the data shown below.

Pulse Rate Before and After Exercise

Student Tested	Pulse Rate at Rest (beats/min)	Pulse Rate After Exercise (beats/min)
A	70	97
B	74	106
C	83	120
D	60	91
E	78	122
Group Average		107

Which procedure would increase the validity of the conclusions drawn from the results of this experiment?

(1) increasing the number of times the activity is repeated
(2) changing the temperature in the room
(3) decreasing the number of students participating in the activity
(4) eliminating the rest period before the resting pulse rate is taken   17 _____

18. When using a compound light microscope, the most common reason for staining a specimen being observed is to

(1) keep the organism from moving around
(2) make the view more colorful
(3) determine the effects of chemicals on the organism
(4) reveal details that are otherwise not easily seen   18 _____

19. A clear plastic ruler is placed across the middle of the field of view of a compound light microscope. A row of cells can be seen under low-power magnification (100×).

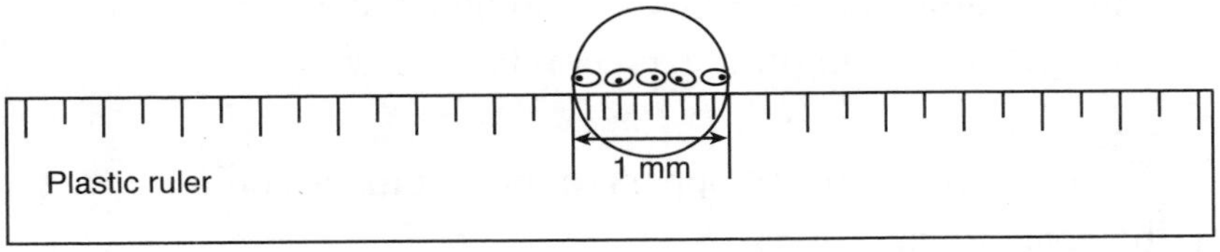

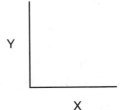

Plastic ruler   1 mm

What is the average length of a single cell in millimeters (mm)?

(1) 1.0 mm   (2) .10 mm   (3) .20 mm   (4) .5 mm   19_____

20. Information concerning the diet of crocodiles of different sizes is contained in the table.

Percentage of Crocodiles of Different Lengths and Their Food Sources

Food Source	Group A 0.3–0.5 Meter	Group B 2.5–3.9 Meters	Group C 4.5–5.0 Meters
mammals	0	18	65
reptiles	0	17	48
fish	0	62	38
birds	0	17	0
snails	0	25	0
shellfish	0	5	0
spiders	20	0	0
frogs	35	0	0
insects	100	2	0

Which statement is not a valid conclusion based on the data?

(1) Overharvesting of fish could have a negative impact on group *C*.

(2) The smaller the crocodile is, the larger the prey.

(3) Group *B* has no preference between reptiles and birds.

(4) Spraying insecticides would have the most direct impact on group *A*.   20_____

21. Research indicates that many plants prevent the growth of other plants in their habitat by releasing natural herbicides (chemicals that kill plants). These substances are known as allelochemicals. Experiments have confirmed that chemicals in the bark and roots of black walnut trees are toxic, and when released into the soil they limit the growth of crop plants such as tomatoes, potatoes, and apples. Studies on allelochemical effects help explain the observation that almost nothing grows under a black walnut tree even though light and moisture levels are adequate for growth.

When using the set of axis shown to the right, to show the effect of black walnut allelochemicals on the number of plants, which labels would be appropriate for axis *X* and axis *Y*?

Y

X

(1) *X* — Number of Plants
     Y — Distance from Walnut Tree Trunk (meters)

(2) *X* — Distance from Walnut Tree Trunk (meters)
     Y — Number of Plants

(3) *X* — Number of Plants
     Y — Time (days)

(4) *X* — Time (days)
     Y — Number of Plants   21_____

22. The diagram shows a student heating some test tubes with chemicals in them during a laboratory activity.

Explain why putting stoppers in the test tubes could be dangerous.

_____

_____

Base your answers to question 23 on the diagram below. The diagram represents six insect species.

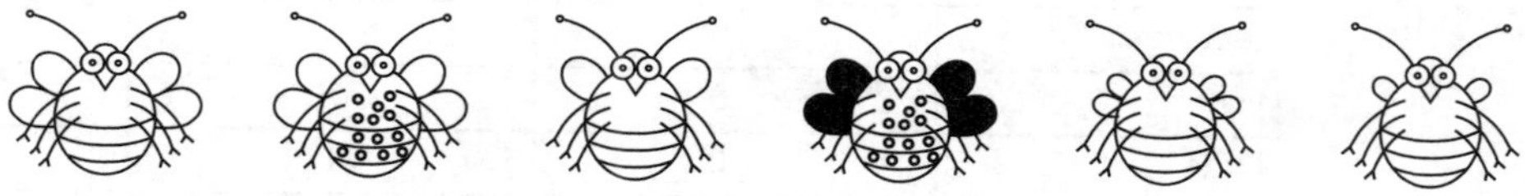

Species E   Species F

23. *a)* A dichotomous key to these six species is shown below. Complete the missing information for sections 5.a. and 5.b. so that the key is complete for all six species.

Dichotomous Key

1. a. has small wings .... go to 2
   b. has large wings..................................... go to 3

2. a. has a single pair of wings .... Species A
   b. has a double pair of wings .... Species B

3. a. has a double pair of wings .... go to 4
   b. has a single pair of wings..................... Species C

4. a. has spots ....go to 5
   b. does not have spots............................... Species D

5. a. _____ .... Species E

   b. _____ .... Species F

b) Use the key to identify the drawings of species *A*, *B*, *C*, and *D*. Place the letter of each species on the line located below the drawing of the species.

Species ___   Species E   Species ___   Species F   Species ___   Species ___

Set 1 – Laboratory and Science Skills

24. Fill in all of the blanks in parts 2 and 3 of the dichotomous key below, so that it contains information that could be used to identify the four animals shown below.

I   II   III   IV

1. a. Legs present.. Go to 2
   b. Legs not present... Go to 3

Characteristic   Organism

2. a. _____ .... _____

   b. _____ .... _____

3. a. _____ .... _____

   b. _____ .... _____

25. An experiment was carried out to determine how competition for living space affects plant height. Different numbers of plants were grown in three pots, *A*, *B*, and *C*. All three pots were the same size. The data collected are shown in the table below.

	Average Daily Plant Height (mm)						
	Day 1	Day 2	Day 3	Day 4	Day 5	Day 6	Day 7
Pot A—5 plants	2	4	6	8	10	14	16
Pot B—10 plants	2	4	6	8	10	12	12
Pot C—20 plants	2	2	2	6	6	8	8

Analyze the experiment that produced the data shown in the table. In your answer be sure to:

a) state a hypothesis for the experiment _____

_____

b) identify one factor, other than pot size, that should have been kept the same in each experimental group

_____

c) identify the dependent variable _____

d) state whether the data supports or fails to support your hypothesis and justify your answer

_____

_____

Base your answers to question 26 on the information and data table.

The effect of temperature on the action of pepsin, a protein-digesting enzyme present in stomach fluid, was tested. In this investigation, 20 milliliters of stomach fluid and 10 grams of protein were placed in each of five test tubes. The tubes were then kept at different temperatures. After 24 hours, the contents of each tube were tested to determine the amount of protein that had been digested. The results are shown in the table.

Protein Digestion at Different Temperatures

Tube #	Temperature (°C)	Amount of Protein Digested (grams)
1	5	0.5
2	10	1.0
3	20	4.0
4	37	9.5
5	85	0.0

26. *a*) The dependent variable in this investigation is the

(1) size of the test tube
(2) time of digestion
(3) amount of stomach fluid
(4) amount of protein digested

a_____

Using the information in the above data table, construct a line graph on the grid, following the directions below.

b) Mark an appropriate scale on each axis.

c) Plot the data on the grid. Surround each point with a small circle and connect the points.

Example:

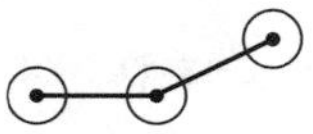

d) Give an explanation on why the enzyme failed to digest any protein in tube #5.

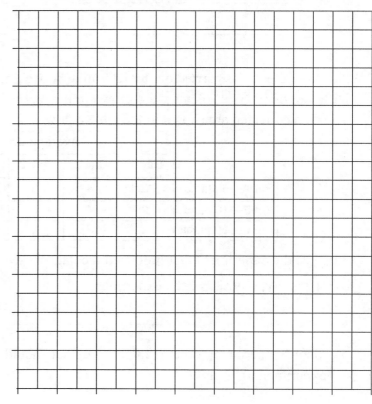

Protein Digestion at Different Temperatures

Amount of Protein Digested (grams)

Temperature (°C)

_____

_____

e) If a sixth test tube identical to the other tubes was kept at a temperature of 30°C for 24 hours, the amount of protein digested would most likely be

(1) less than 1.0 gram
(2) between 1.0 and 4.0 grams
(3) between 4.0 and 9.0 grams
(4) more than 9.0 grams

e_____

27. A chromatography setup is shown.

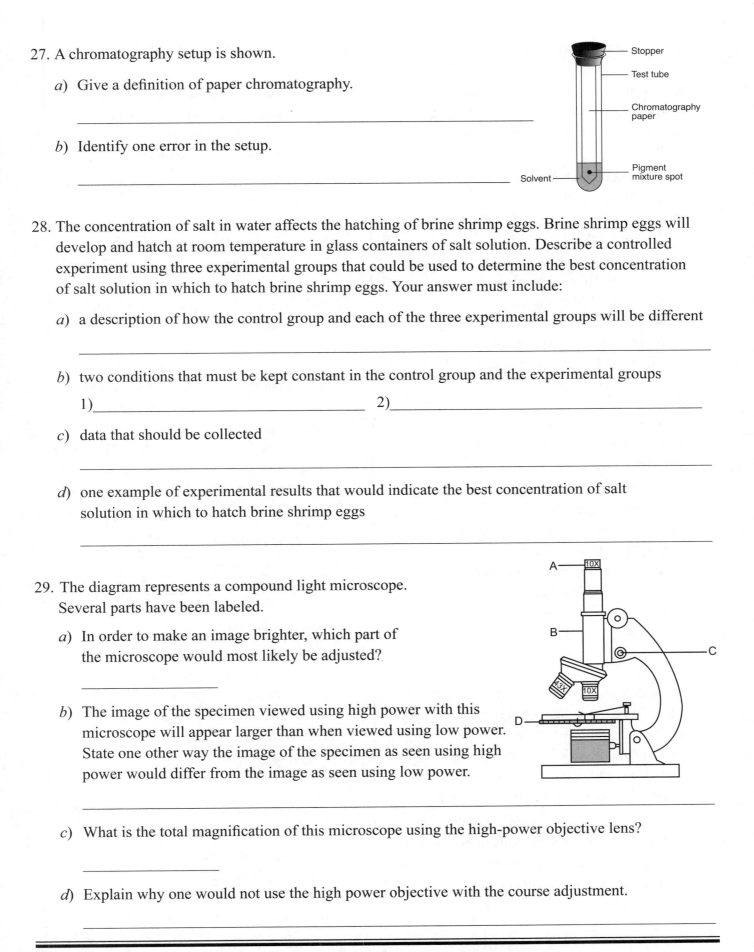

a) Give a definition of paper chromatography.

_____

b) Identify one error in the setup.

_____

28. The concentration of salt in water affects the hatching of brine shrimp eggs. Brine shrimp eggs will develop and hatch at room temperature in glass containers of salt solution. Describe a controlled experiment using three experimental groups that could be used to determine the best concentration of salt solution in which to hatch brine shrimp eggs. Your answer must include:

a) a description of how the control group and each of the three experimental groups will be different

_____

b) two conditions that must be kept constant in the control group and the experimental groups

1)_____ 2)_____

c) data that should be collected

_____

d) one example of experimental results that would indicate the best concentration of salt solution in which to hatch brine shrimp eggs

_____

29. The diagram represents a compound light microscope. Several parts have been labeled.

a) In order to make an image brighter, which part of the microscope would most likely be adjusted?

_____

b) The image of the specimen viewed using high power with this microscope will appear larger than when viewed using low power. State one other way the image of the specimen as seen using high power would differ from the image as seen using low power.

_____

c) What is the total magnification of this microscope using the high-power objective lens?

_____

d) Explain why one would not use the high power objective with the course adjustment.

_____

1. Which statement describes the best procedure to determine if a vaccine for a disease in a certain bird species is effective?

   (1) Vaccinate 100 birds and expose all 100 to the disease.
   (2) Vaccinate 100 birds and expose only 50 of them to the disease.
   (3) Vaccinate 50 birds, do not vaccinate 50 other birds, and expose all 100 to the disease.
   (4) Vaccinate 50 birds, do not vaccinate 50 other birds, and expose only the vaccinated birds to the disease.   1 _____

2. Scientists have cloned sheep but have not yet cloned a human. The best explanation for this situation is that

   (1) the technology to clone humans has not been explored
   (2) human reproduction is very different from that of other mammals
   (3) there are many ethical problems involved in cloning humans
   (4) cloning humans would take too long   2 _____

3. A student formulated a hypothesis that cotton will grow larger bolls (pods) if magnesium is added to the soil. The student has two experimental fields of cotton, one with magnesium and one without. Which data should be collected to support this hypothesis?

   (1) height of the cotton plants in both fields
   (2) diameter of the cotton bolls in both fields
   (3) length of the growing season in both fields
   (4) color of the cotton bolls in both fields   3 _____

4. Which source would provide the most reliable information for use in a research project investigating the effects of antibiotics on disease causing bacteria?

   (1) the local news section of a newspaper from 1993
   (2) a news program on national television about antigens produced by various plants
   (3) a current professional science journal article on the control of pathogens
   (4) an article in a weekly news magazine about reproduction in pathogens   4 _____

5. A student hypothesized that lettuce seeds would not sprout (germinate) unless they were exposed to darkness. The student planted 10 lettuce seeds under a layer of soil and scattered 10 lettuce seeds on top of the soil. The data collected are shown in the table.

   Data Table

Seed Treatment	Number of Seeds Germinated
Planted under soil	9
Scattered on top of soil	8

   One way to improve the validity of these results would be to

   (1) conclude that darkness is necessary for lettuce seed germination
   (2) conclude that light is necessary for lettuce seed germination
   (3) revise the hypothesis
   (4) repeat the experiment   5 _____

6. In an appropriately designed experiment, a scientist is able to test the effect of

   (1) a single variable
   (2) multiple variables
   (3) the hypothesis
   (4) scientific observations   6 _____

7. A scientist is planning to carry out an experiment on the effect of heat on the function of a certain enzyme. Which would not be an appropriate first step?

(1) doing research in a library
(2) having discussions with other scientists
(3) completing a data table of expected results
(4) using what is already known about the enzyme   7_____

8. Which statement best describes a scientific theory?

(1) It is a collection of data designed to provide support for a prediction.
(2) It is an educated guess that can be tested by experimentation.
(3) It is a scientific fact that no longer requires any evidence to support it.
(4) It is a general statement that is supported by many scientific observations.   8_____

9. Tomato plants in a garden are not growing well. The gardener hypothesizes that the soil is too acidic. To test this hypothesis accurately, the gardener could

(1) plant seeds of a different kind of plant
(2) move the tomato plants to an area with less sunlight
(3) change the pH of the soil
(4) reduce the amount of water available to the plant   9_____

10. A coverslip should be used for preparing a

(1) frog for dissection
(2) solution of iodine for food testing
(3) wet mount of elodea (a simple plant)
(4) test to determine the pH of a solution   10_____

11. In Texas, researchers gave a cholesterol-reducing drug to 2,335 people and an inactive substitute (placebo) to 2,081. Most of the volunteers were men who had normal cholesterol levels and no history of heart disease. After 5 years, 97 people getting the placebo had suffered heart attacks compared to only 57 people who had received the actual drug. The researchers are recommending that to help prevent heart attacks, all people (even those without high cholesterol) take these cholesterol-reducing drugs. In addition to the information above, what is another piece of information that the researchers must have before support for the recommendation can be justified?

(1) Were the eating habits of the two groups similar?
(2) How does a heart attack affect cholesterol levels?
(3) Did the heart attacks result in deaths?
(4) What chemical is in the placebo?   11_____

12. Scientific studies have indicated that there is a higher percentage of allergies in babies fed formula containing cow's milk than in breast-fed babies. Which statement represents a valid inference made from these studies?

(1) Milk from cows causes allergic reactions in all infants.
(2) Breast feeding prevents all allergies from occurring.
(3) There is no relationship between drinking cow's milk and having allergies.
(4) Breast milk most likely contains fewer substances that trigger allergies.   12_____

13. The analysis of data gathered during a particular experiment is necessary in order to

(1) formulate a hypothesis for that experiment
(2) develop a research plan for that experiment
(3) design a control for that experiment
(4) draw a valid conclusion for that experiment   13_____

14. Which statement about the use of independent variables in controlled experiments is correct?

(1) A different independent variable must be used each time an experiment is repeated.
(2) The independent variables must involve time.
(3) Only one independent variable is used for each experiment.
(4) The independent variables state the problem being tested.   14_____

15. Which statement most accurately describes scientific inquiry?

(1) It ignores information from other sources.
(2) It does not allow scientists to judge the reliability of their sources.
(3) It should never involve ethical decisions about the application of scientific knowledge.
(4) It may lead to explanations that combine data with what people already know about their surroundings.   15_____

16. While viewing a specimen under high power of a compound light microscope, a student noticed that the specimen was out of focus. Which part of the microscope should the student turn to obtain a clearer image under high power?

(1) eyepiece   (3) fine adjustment
(2) coarse adjustment (4) nosepiece
                                              16_____

17. A biologist used the Internet to contact scientists around the world to obtain information about declining amphibian populations. He was able to gather data on 936 populations of amphibians, consisting of 157 species from 37 countries. Results showed that the overall numbers of amphibians dropped 15% a year from 1960 to 1966 and continued to decline about 2% a year through 1997.

What is the importance of collecting an extensive amount of data such as this?

(1) Researchers will now be certain that the decline in the amphibian populations is due to pesticides.
(2) The data collected will prove that all animal populations around the world are threatened.
(3) Results from all parts of the world will be found to be identical.
(4) The quantity of data will lead to a better understanding of the extent of the problem.   17_____

18. A student used the low-power objective of a compound light microscope and observed a single-celled organism as shown in the diagram below.

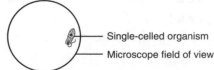

When he switched to high power, the organism was no longer visible. This most likely happened because switching to high power made the

(1) field too bright to see the organism
(2) image too small to be seen
(3) area of the slide being viewed smaller
(4) fine-adjustment knob no longer functional   18_____

19. Conclusions based on an experiment are most likely to be accepted when

(1) they are consistent with experimental data and observations
(2) they are derived from investigations having many experimental variables
(3) scientists agree that only one hypothesis has been tested
(4) hypotheses are based on one experimental design   19 _____

20. A microscope slide viewed with high power can most likely be damaged by

(1) adding distilled water
(2) rotating the coarse adjustment knob
(3) adding salt water
(4) rotating the fine adjustment knob
                                                              20 _____

21. A slide of human blood cells was observed in focus under the low-power objective of a compound light microscope that had clean lenses. When the microscope was switched to high power, the image was dark and fuzzy. Which parts of the microscope should be used to correct this situation?

(1) nosepiece and coarse adjustment
(2) diaphragm and ocular
(3) objective and fine adjustment
(4) diaphragm and fine adjustment   21_____

22. The diagrams below show four different onecelled organisms (shaded) in the field of view of the same microscope using different magnifications. Which illustration shows the largest onecelled organism?

| 100x | 400x | 100x | 400x |
| (1) | (2) | (3) | (4) |
22_____

23. Paper chromatography is a method used in

(1) comparing the shapes of plant leaves
(2) separating mixtures of plant pigments
(3) comparing habitats of different plants
(4) separating individual DNA fragments of plants   23 _____

24. How much water should be removed from the graduated cylinder shown to leave 5 milliliters of water in the cylinder?

(1) 6 mL   (3) 11 mL
(2) 7 mL   (4) 12 mL

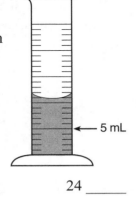
← 5 mL

24 _____

25. A peppered moth and part of a metric ruler are represented in the diagram below.

 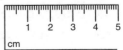
Wingspan

Which row in the chart below best represents the ratio of body length to wingspan of the peppered moth?

Row	Body Length:Wingspan
(1)	1:1
(2)	2:1
(3)	1:2
(4)	2:2

25_____

26. The diagram shows how a coverslip should be lowered onto some single-celled organisms during the preparation of a wet mount. Why is this a preferred procedure?

(1) The coverslip will prevent the slide from breaking.
(2) The organisms will be more evenly distributed.
(3) The possibility of breaking the coverslip is reduced.
(4) The possibility of trapping air bubbles is reduced.   26 _____

27. Students were asked to design a lab that investigated the relationship between exercise and heart rate. Heart rate was determined by recording the pulse rate in beats per minute. The students hypothesized that increased exercise results in an increased heart rate. The class results for the experiment are shown in the graph below.

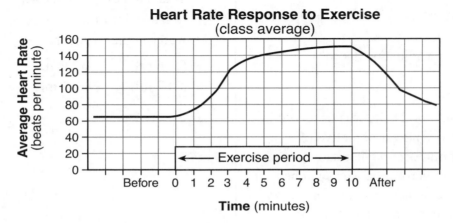

a) Which statement is best supported by the graph?
   (1) Before exercising, the average pulse rate was 65; four minutes after exercising, the average pulse rate was 65.
   (2) After four minutes of exercising, the average pulse rate was 120; two minutes after exercising, the average pulse rate was 120.
   (3) While exercising, the highest average pulse rate was 150; before exercising, the average pulse rate was 65.
   (4) Two minutes before exercising, the average pulse rate was 80; after two minutes of exercise, the average pulse rate was 140.   a _____

b) Students in a different science class carried out the same experiment. The data they obtained did not support the hypothesis that increased exercise results in increased heart rate. The most scientifically sound way to deal with this situation is to
   (1) write a new hypothesis
   (2) read about pulse rate in a biology textbook
   (3) have the students in both classes vote to decide which hypothesis is correct
   (4) ask students in a third class to do the experiment and see if their results support the hypothesis   b _____

28. A student hypothesizes that the pulse rate of a person and background music that is playing are related. The student designs an experiment to test this hypothesis. What would be an appropriate control for this experiment? _____

_____

29. A student performed an experiment to determine if treating 500 tomato plants with an auxin (a plant growth hormone) will make them grow faster. The results are shown in the table.

Explain why the student can not draw a valid conclusion from these results.

_____

_____

Days	Average Stem Height (cm)
1	10
5	13
10	19
15	26
20	32
25	40

30. Two students collected data on their pulse rates while performing different activities. Their average results are shown in the data table.

State one way that this investigation could be improved.

Data Table

Activity	Average Pulse Rate (beats/min)
sitting quietly	70
walking	98
running	120

_____

_____

31. You have been assigned to design an experiment to determine the effects of light on the growth of tomato plants. In your experimental design be sure to:

a) state one hypothesis to be tested

_____

b) identify the independent variable in the experiment _____

c) describe the type of data to be collected

_____

_____

32. What is the approximate length of the earthworm shown in the diagram below?

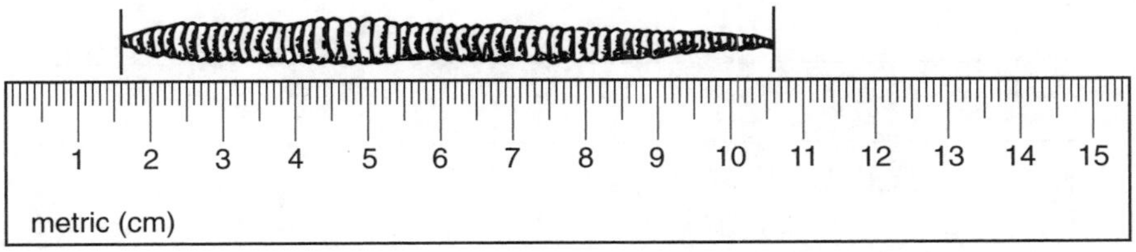

_____ cm

33. A certain plant has white flower petals and it usually grows in soil that is slightly basic. Sometimes the plant produces flowers with red petals. A company that sells the plant wants to know if soil pH affects the color of the petals in this plant. Design a controlled experiment to determine if soil pH affects petal color. In your experimental design be sure to:

a) state the hypothesis to be tested in the experiment

_____

b) state one way the control group will be treated differently from the experimental group

_____

c) identify two factors that must be kept the same in both the control group and the experimental group

1. _____   2. _____

d) identify the dependent variable in the experiment_____

e) state one result of the experiment that would support the hypothesis

_____

_____

Base your answers to question on the information below.

In an investigation, 34 students in a class determined their pulse rates after performing each of three different activities. Each activity was performed three times during equal time intervals. The average results are shown in the accompanying graph.

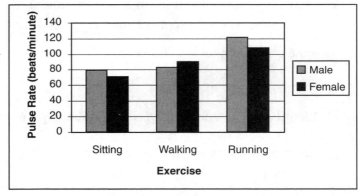

34. *a*) Before constructing the graph it would have been most helpful to organize the results of the investigation in

(1) a research plan   (2) an equation   (3) a data table   (4) a generalization   a_____

b) Some students concluded that males always have a higher pulse rate than females. Does the graph support this conclusion? _____

Justify your answer. _____

_____

35. The drugs usually used to treat high blood pressure do not affect blood vessels in the lungs. Bosentan is a new drug being studied as a treatment for high blood pressure in the lungs. In an experiment, patients treated with bosentan showed an improvement in the distance they could walk without fatigue within 12 weeks.

Design an experiment to test the effectiveness of bosentan as a drug to treat high blood pressure in the lungs. In your answer be sure to:

a) state the hypothesis your experiment will test

_____

b) state how the control group will be treated differently from the experimental group

_____

c) state two factors that must be kept the same in both the experimental and control groups

1. _____   2. _____

d) state the type of data that should be collected to determine if the hypothesis is supported

_____

Base your answers to question 36 on the information below.

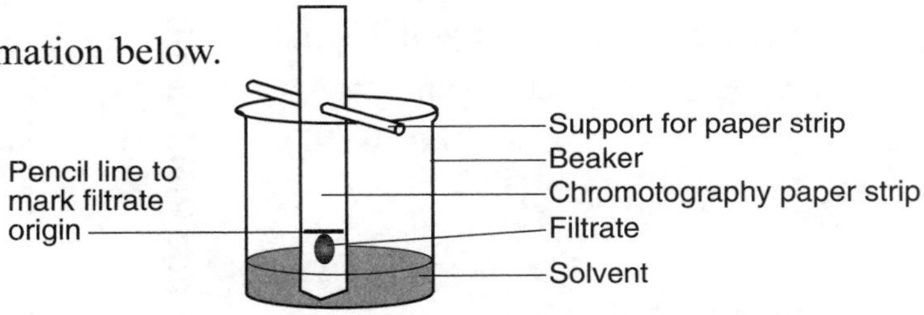

Paper chromatography can be used to investigate evolutionary relationships.

Leaves from a plant were ground and mixed with a solvent. The mixture of ground leaves and solvent was then filtered. Using a toothpick, twenty drops of the filtrate (material that passed through the filter) were placed at one spot on a strip of chromatography paper.

This procedure was repeated using leaves from three other species of plants. A separate strip of chromatography paper was prepared for each plant species. Each of the four strips of chromatography paper was placed in a different beaker containing the same solvent for the same amount of time. One of the laboratory setups is shown above.

Pencil line to mark filtrate origin

Support for paper strip
Beaker
Chromotography paper strip
Filtrate
Solvent

36. a)   State one reason for using a new toothpick for the filtrate from each plant.

_____

b) State one way the four strips would most likely be different from each other after being removed from the beakers.

_____

_____

Base your answers to question 37 on the information and data table below.

A number of bean seeds planted at the same time produced plants that were later divided into two groups, *A* and *B*. Each plant in group *A* was treated with the same concentration of gibberellic acid (a plant hormone). The plants in group *B* were not treated with gibberellic acid. All other growth conditions were kept constant. The height of each plant was measured on 5 consecutive days, and the average height of each group was recorded in the data table below.

Data Table

	Average Plant Height (cm)				
	Day 1	**Day 2**	**Day 3**	**Day 4**	**Day 5**
Group A	5	7	10	13	15
Group B	5	6	6.5	7	7.5

Directions for question 37: Using the information in the data table, construct a line graph on the grid, following the directions below.

37. *a*) Mark an appropriate scale on the axis labeled "Average Plant Height (cm)."

b) Plot the data for the average height of the plants in group *A*. Surround each point with a small circle and connect the points.

Example:

c) Plot the data for the average height of the plants in group *B*. Surround each point with a small triangle and connect the points.

Example:

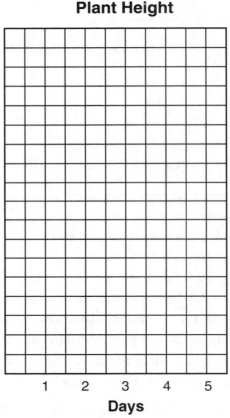

Plant Height

Key
⊙ Group A
△ Group B

d) Identify the independent variable. _____

e) State a valid conclusion that can be drawn concerning the effect of gibberellic acid on bean plant growth.

_____

38. A dichotomous key is shown below.

Dichotomous Key

1. a. tail fins are horizontal.................go to 2
    b. tail fins are vertical....................go to 3

2. a. has teeth or tusk.......................go to 4
    b. has no teeth...........................Balaena mysticetus

3. a. has gill slits behind mouth............go to 5
    b. has no gill slits........................Lepidosiren paradoxa

4. a. black with white underside...........Orcinus orca
    b. tusk, gray with dark spots............Monodon monoceros

5. a. head is hammer shaped...............Sphyrna mokarran
    b. tail fins are half the body length......Alopias vulpinus

Use the dichotomous key to identify the scientific
name of the organism represented to the right.

_____

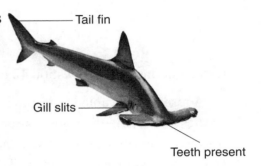

Tail fin

Gill slits

Teeth present

Base your answers to question 39 on the diagram
of a microscope.

39. *a*) Information about which two lettered parts is needed in
order to determine the total magnification of an object
viewed with the microscope in the position shown?

_____ and _____

b) Which lettered part should be used to
focus the image while using high power? _____

c) State two ways the image seen through the microscope
differs from the actual specimen being observed.

1)_____

2)_____

d) Show how the letter (e) would appear when vied under a compound microscope. _____

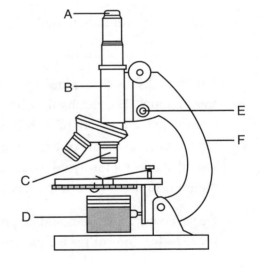

40. State one advantage of using a stain to study frog skin cells with a microscope.

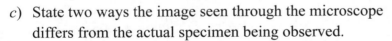

Set 2 – Laboratory and Science Skills   **Page 219**

41. A student squeezed a clothespin as many times as possible in a 30-second time period. The student repeated this procedure nine more times in quick succession. The data obtained are in the accompanying chart. State one hypothesis that this data would support concerning the relationship between number of trials and number of squeezes in 30 seconds.

Trial	Number of Squeezes in 30 Seconds
1	32
2	29
3	28
4	27
5	26
6	25
7	23
8	21
9	19
10	17

_____

_____

Base your answers to question 42 on the information below.

A researcher wanted to test the effectiveness of a new antibiotic on *Streptococcus pyrogenes*, the species of bacteria that causes strep throat. Bacteria were added to dish 1, dish 2, and dish 3. A disk soaked in the new antibiotic was then placed in dish 2. Dish 3 was set up as the control. The dishes are shown in the diagram.

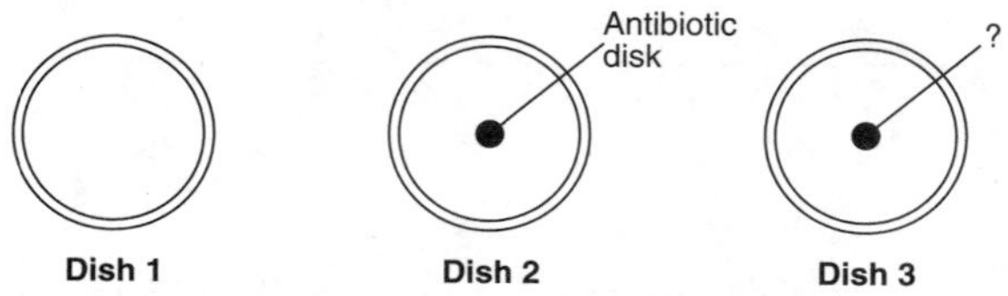

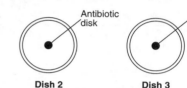

42. *a)* State one appropriate hypothesis for this experiment.

_____

b) All three dishes were placed in an incubator at 37°C for 24 hours. The results for dish 1 are shown. Complete the diagram of dish 2 shown below to represent an example of experimental results that would support your hypothesis. Explain how your diagram supports your hypothesis.

c) Describe how dish 3 should be prepared so it can serve as the control for the experiment.

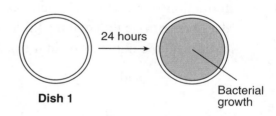

Dish 2 after 24 hours

_____

_____

43. The image of a specimen viewed using high power with a microscope will appear larger than when viewed using low power. State one other way the image of the specimen as seen using high power would differ from the image as seen using low power.

_____

Base your answers to question 44 on the information below.

Each year, a New York State power agency provides its customers with information about some of the fuel sources used in generating electricity. The table applies to the period of 2002–2003.

Using the information given, construct a bar graph on the grid below.

Fuel Sources Used

Fuel Source	Percentage of Electricity Generated
hydro (water)	86
coal	5
nuclear	4
oil	1
solar	0

44. *a*) Mark an appropriate scale on the axis labeled "Percentage of Electricity Generated."

   b) Construct vertical bars to represent the data. Shade in each bar.

   c) Identify one fuel source in the table that is considered a fossil fuel.

   _____

   d) Identify one fuel source in the table that is classified as a renewable resource.

   _____

   e) From the Fuel Source list, identify one fuel that is known to release CO_2 as a by-product of combustion.

   _____

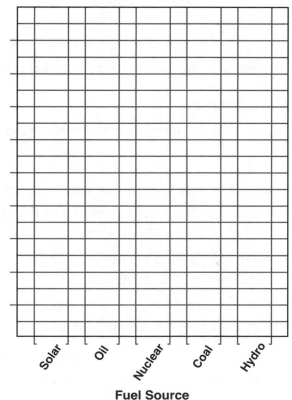

Fuel Sources Used

Percentage of Electricity Generated

Solar   Oil   Nuclear   Coal   Hydro

Fuel Source

45. A laboratory procedure involving a microscope slide is represented in the diagram.

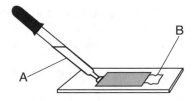

   a) State *one* purpose for this procedure.

   _____

   b) Identify *one* specific substance represented by the liquid in *A*.

   _____

   c) State the purpose of the paper towel labeled *B*.

   _____

46. Scientists have been experimenting with different forms of alternate energy to help reduce the amount of fossil fuels that are burned. They studied yeast, which convert plant materials into ethanol, a form of alcohol that can be used in automobiles. These experiments were carried out at room temperature. The scientists wondered whether more ethanol would be produced at different temperatures.

Design an experiment to determine the effect of temperature on ethanol production by yeast. In your answer, be sure to:

a) state *one* hypothesis the experiment would test _____

b) state how the control group would be treated differently from the experimental group

_____

_____

c) identify *two* factors that must be kept the same in both the experimental and control groups

_____ and _____

d) identify the independent variable in the experiment_____

47. Some poinsettia plants have green leaves that turn red. A garden club decided to study the color change of poinsettia plants. Knowing that poinsettias change color during the short daylight periods of winter, they decided to investigate the effect of different daylight lengths on color change.

Design a controlled experiment using three experimental groups that could be used to determine if the number of hours of daylight has an effect on the color change of poinsettias. In your experimental design, be sure to:

a) state *one* hypothesis the experiment would test

_____

b) state *one* way the three experimental groups would differ

_____

c) identify *two* factors that must be kept the same in all three groups

_____ and _____

d) identify the independent variable in the experiment_____

e) describe experimental results that would support your hypothesis

_____

48. Describe how a student could use a microscope to compare the size of frog skin cells to the size of human skin cells.

_____

49. The diagram below represents a setup used in an experiment to determine the effect of temperature on fermentation. Fermentation is a type of respiration in yeast that produces alcohol and a gas. Five setups were used. Each was kept at a different temperature. The number of gas bubbles released in each tube was counted and recorded in the data table below.

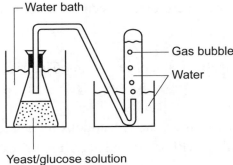

Water bath

Gas bubble

Water

Yeast/glucose solution

Temperature (°C)	Rate of Fermentation (gas bubbles per minute)
15	10
20	40
25	70
30	100
35	130

Respiration in Yeast

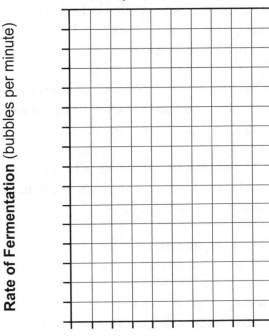

Rate of Fermentation (bubbles per minute)

Temperature (°C)

a) Mark an appropriate scale, without any breaks, on each labeled axis.

b) Plot the data, connect the points, and surround each point with a small circle.

Example:

c) Approximately how many bubbles produced at 27°C. _____

d) Identify the dependent variable.

_____

e) State the relationship between the rate of fermentation and temperature.

_____

50. Before deciding whether a conclusion was valid or invalid, students looked at the results of the entire class. Explain why the results of the entire class were analyzed, rather than just the results of one individual student.

_____

_____

51. A student hypothesized that drinking tea would cause an increase in pulse rate. He measured his pulse 20 minutes after drinking a glass of tea. It was 86 beats per minute. State one error in the experiment.

_____

1. 4   The color green does not define just one group of organisms. There are green protist, such as Euglena, and green animals, such as lizards and snakes. Therefore, a green color could not be used to conclusively identify a group.

2. 3   Scientists develop theories based on repeated investigations and observations. Theories are widely agreed upon by a large number of scientists.

3. 3   In designing experiments, before the experiment is performed, the precautions for a safe experiment must be considered. All other given choices will be arrived at during the experiment or after it is performed.

4. 2   After evaluating data collected from an experiment, scientists can determine if their hypothesis was valid and thus come up with a conclusion. This conclusion should be based on many trials to ensure a valid experiment.

5. 2   A hypothesis provides a basis for performing an experiment or test. The hypothesis suggests a conclusion, whether valid or not, can be used to gain additional information that may help answer scientific questions.

6. 2   Over time, as new information becomes available through experimentation, observations, or with technological advances, theories are modified to accommodate or reflect the new scientific data.

7. 3   During an experiment, much data is collected. This information needs to be placed in an organized system. This is usually some type of data table from which the information can be graphed to better analyze the data and draw a valid conclusion.

8. 4   The decision to undergo genetic testing for an inherited disease is an intensely personal choice. In some cases a mutation is discovered that may express itself, leading to an untreatable disease, such as Huntington's disease. Ethical questions and human values become important when considering consequences of any action that may be taken regarding one's personal health information.

9. 3   An accurate experiment should have only one testable variable. The addition of another clothespin, being difficult to open, creates two variables: exercise vs. resting and easy vs. difficult clothespins. One could not determine if it is the exercise or the clothespin type that affects the number of squeezes. All other answers are parts of a valid experimental setup.

10. 1   Paper chromatography is a process whereby substances within a solvent are separated by traveling up the paper. The molecular weight and solubility of the different substances will determine how far up the paper the molecules travel. The resulting specific patterns on the paper help to determine the identity of these substances.

11. 3   A theory attempts to provide a scientific explanation to a posed event or process. Theories are formulated as a result of many different investigations and the accumulation of information or data. As new scientific evidence is presented, a theory maybe revised or changed.

12. 1   The *x*-axis is shown to be the Average Pulse Rate Range (per min). This represents choices 2 and 3. The *y*-axis range is from 0 to 12 and would represent the Number of Students being involved.

13. 4   As part of a solid scientific method, scientists always evaluate data and develop conclusions based on that data. The data will either support or refute the original hypothesis. If the evaluation refutes the original hypothesis, the scientist formulates a new hypothesis and carries out further experiments.

14. 3   The lab procedure represented in the diagram involves the introduction of stain to a wet mount slide. The stain is carefully added by the eye dropper to one side of the coverslip, while a paper towel on the other side absorbs water. This absorption process pulls the stain across the slide under the coverslip without disturbing the coverslip.

15. 2   In experiments, valid conclusions must be repeatable. Other scientists should be able to carry out an identical investigation and arrive at the same conclusion to deem it valid

16. 4   Conclusions are never made based on the data expected to be collected. Rather, conclusions are determined by the supporting data actually collected from an experiment.

17. 1   By increasing the number of times an activity is repeated, the amount of data available to base a conclusion on increases. This leads to an increase in the validity of the conclusion.

18. 4   Staining specimens allows the microscope viewer to see details clearer or reveal details that are not observable in an unstained specimen. For example, a student might stain a cheek cell with methylene blue to make the nucleus more visible.

19. 3   Using the information provided in the diagram, there are 5 cells within the 1 mm field of view. Divide 1 mm by 5 cells, gives the answer of 0.20 mm per cell.

20. 2   According to the chart, the smaller the crocodile, such as Group *A*, the smaller their prey. As the crocodile size increases from Groups *A* to *C*, so does the size of the prey.

21. 2   The *x*-axis in this research is the independent variable being Distance from the Walnut Tree Trunk. The Number of Plants will be the dependent variable that is placed on the *y*-axis. The relationship reflected in this graph is that the number of plants will depend on the distance from the walnut tree and the effects of allelochemicals.

22. Acceptable answers include, but are not limited to:

The stoppers would pop out of heated test tubes and possibly injure someone.

or The test tubes may explode.

Explanation: If the test tube with a stopper is heated, the stopper would pop out or the test tube or may explode due to increased pressure. Both of these situations present danger to the student and could lead to a serious injury from flying glass or heated liquid.

23. *a)* Answer:

5.a. has light *or* white *or* clear wings

5.b. has dark *or* black *or* shaded wings

Explanation: In a dichotomous key used to identify organisms, each section or step will have two choices that describe a difference between organisms. In the case of 5a and 5b of Species *E* and *F* respectively, the only visible difference is that of their wings. The missing information is provided in the answer section above.

b)

Species _D_ Species _E_ Species _C_ Species _F_ Species _B_ Species _A_

Explanation: For this question, you must use the dichotomous key to identify all the unknown insects. Always start each unknown identification at step 1. For example, for the first bug on the left, starting at step 1, we have two choices: small wings or large wings. This bug has large wings so follow the dots to the right where it directs you to go to 3. At step 3, our choice involves the number of wings (single or double). This insect has double wings so following the dots to the right, it directs us to go to 4. This insect at step 4 does not have spots so following dots to the right we see that it is species *D*. Repeat this procedure for all unknown species, starting at step 1.

24. Answer:

2.a. Four legs ....   IV (Dog)

2.b. Eight legs......   II (Spider)

3.a. Fins present......   III (Fish)

3.b. Fins not present or segments present........   I (Earthworm)

Explanation: A dichotomous key is a tool used to identify organisms. At each step, two choices are offered that distinguish a difference between organisms. For example, from step 1a, Legs present, we must look at the animals with legs (Dog and Spider). The task then is to find differences, such as the number of legs. At step 2 we identify these differences 2a – 4 legs and 2b – 8 legs, which is the identification of the animal. Continue the same process to arrive at all answers.

25. *a)* Hypothesis: Competition decreases plant height.   *or*   Competition increases plant height.

    or   Competition has no effect on plant height.

b) Same factor: same soil type or amount

    or   same environmental conditions such as sunlight, water, temperature

    or   same type of plants

c) Dependent variable: height *or* size of plant

d) Data statement:

The data supports my hypothesis because plants in the pot with the greatest number of plants are the shortest.

or The data does not support hypothesis because plants in Pot *C* (20 plants) are shorter than plants in Pot *A* (5 plants).

or Data did not support my hypothesis because the number of plants in the pot did affect the height or size of the plants.

Explanation: Most experiments are carried out to test hypotheses. A hypothesis is a suggested explanation to a problem; in this case, how competition affects plant height. In a valid experiment, there should be only one variable, all other factors must be kept the same to provide valid data. The dependent variable is the factor that is changed based on the manipulation of another factor (variable). In this experiment, the height or size of the plant (dependent variable) depends on the number of plants in each pot (independent variable). The data collected clearly shows that competition does affect plant height or size. The pot with the most plants (Pot *C*) had the shortest plants and Pot *A* with the fewest plants and less competition had the tallest plants.

26. *a*) 4 The amount of protein digested is dependent upon the temperature, the independent variable.

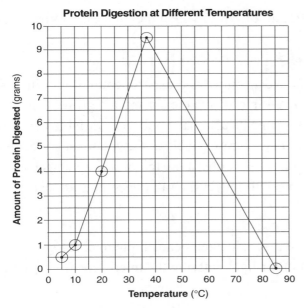

Protein Digestion at Different Temperatures

Y-axis: Amount of Protein Digested (grams), X-axis: Temperature (°C)

b) The *x*-axis (Temperature) interval should be 2 lines for every 10 degrees. The intervals for the *y*-axis (Amount of Protein Digested) should be 2 lines for every gram. Remember, always spread the scale along the axis for a better representative view of the graphed relationship.

c) Explanation: Accurately plot each point on the graph. Be sure to circle each point and connect each point with a line.

d) All enzymes have an optimum temperature range. As the temperature range increases from this optimum range the enzyme activity decreases or stops working due to a change in its shape.

e) 3 By interpreting the data graphed, at temperature 30°C, follow that line upward until it intersects your graphed line. This should correspond to approximately 7.5 grams of protein digested. This number fits into the range of 4.0 to 9.0 grams.

27. *a)* Paper chromatography is a laboratory technique that involves the use of a solvent to separate different molecules from one another.

b) Pigment spot is below surface of the solvent. *or* Level of the solvent is too high.

Explanation: If the pigment spot on the chromatography paper is below the solvent surface, the pigment will dissolve into the solvent and not move up the paper with the solvent. By placing the pigment spot above the solvent, a separation of pigments will occur as the solvent moves up the paper, carrying the pigment's molecules with it.

28. *a)* *Control vs. Experimental groups*: The control group will be in a 0% salt solution, while the experimental groups will be in varying salt concentrations, such as 2%, 4%, and 6%.
or The control group will be in normal seawater, while the experimental groups will have different salt concentrations.

b) *Constant conditions:* (Two conditions must be given.)
the number of brine *or* the temperature *or* shrimp eggs in each group
or the amount of liquid in each container *or* species of brine shrimp
or the size of each container *or* the number of days observed *or* the type of container

c) *Data collected:* The total number of brine shrimp eggs hatched after a given time in each of the different salt concentrations.

d) *Example of experimental results:* the concentration of salt in which the greatest number of shrimp eggs hatched in a given time frame
or The concentration in which brine shrimp eggs hatch faster is best.

Explanation: In a valid experiment, you must have a control and experimental group. In this case, the variable will be different concentrations of salt into which the shrimp are grown. The control could be normal salt water or no salt. Valid experiments also have only one variable that is tested, so all other factors must be kept constant. In order to draw conclusions, you must collect data and analyze data. In this experiment, the data should reflect either how many shrimp eggs hatch or how soon they hatch. The most or fastest hatches will reflect the salt concentration that is the best concentration.

29. *a)* D   Explanation: The diaphragm is a structure that is located beneath the microscope stage that allows the user to regulate the amount for light entering the microscope. This will make the image brighter if desired.

b) Acceptable responses include, but are not limited to: More detail will be seen.
or You might not see the entire specimen in the field of view. *or* The image might appear darker.

Explanation: The image viewed under high power will be darker. Because the field of view of the image is smaller with high power, there is less light available to view that image.

c) 430   Explanation: To determine the total magnification of a compound microscope, one multiplies the magnification of the eyepiece lens (10x) times that of the high power objective lens (43x). Therefore, the total magnification is $10x \times 43x = 430x$ total magnification.

d) There is a danger of damaging the lens or slide.
